BASIC
WRITING SKILLS
WITH
READINGS

BASIC
WRITING SKILLS
WITH
READINGS

R. KENT SMITH
UNIVERSITY OF MAINE

JOHN LANGAN
ATLANTIC COMMUNITY COLLEGE

CAROLE MOHR

TOWNSEND PRESS   Marlton, NJ 08053

Books in the Townsend Press Writing Series:

BASIC ENGLISH BRUSHUP
BASIC ENGLISH BRUSHUP, SHORT VERSION
ENGLISH BRUSHUP
BASIC WRITING SKILLS WITH READINGS
WRITING SKILLS WITH READINGS
A BASIC READER FOR COLLEGE WRITERS
THE TOWNSEND THEMATIC READER

Send book orders and requests for desk copies or supplements to:

Townsend Press
1038 Industrial Drive
Berlin, New Jersey 08009

For even faster service, call us at our toll-free number:

1-800-772-6410

Or FAX your request to:

1-609-753-0649

ISBN 0-944210-70-8

Acknowledgments

Carson, Ben, M.D., with Cecil Murphey. "Do It Better!" From *Think Big*, copyright © 1992 by Benjamin Carson, M.D.
Reprinted by permission of Zondervan Publishing House.

Coleman, Jean. "Learning Survival Strategies." Reprinted by permission.

Peck, M. Scott. "Responsibility." Copyright © 1978 by M. Scott Peck, M.D. Reprinted by permission of Simon & Schuster, Inc.

Petricic, Anna-Maria. "Knowledge Is Power." Reprinted by permission.

Piassa, Bernadete. "Half a Pound of Ham." Reprinted by permission.

Russell, Daisy. "A Journey Into Light." Reprinted by permission.

Contents

PART THREE

Readings for Writing   303

Preface to the Instructor

Basic Writing Skills with Readings will help students learn the basics of effective writing. It is an all-in-one text that includes a basic rhetoric, a convenient handbook, and high-interest readings.

The book is organized into three easy-to-use parts. Part One is a guide to the goals of effective writing followed by a series of activities to help students practice and master those goals. Part Two is a handbook of grammar, punctuation, and usage that includes exercises and tests as well. Part Three presents six motivational reading selections, followed by reading and writing practice.

The book contains a number of distinctive features:

1 **Attention to attitude.** In its opening pages, the book helps students recognize and deal with their attitude about writing. Attitude is shown to be an important part of learning to write well.

2 **Focus on process.** Students are encouraged to see writing as a multi-stage process that moves from prewriting to proofreading.

3 **A sequence of learning activities.** A careful sequence of interesting activities helps students learn and master the principles of effective writing, one step at a time.

4 **Emphasis on specific details.** In particular, the activities will help basic writing students understand the nature of specific details and how to generate and use them. As writing teachers well know, learning to write concretely is a key step for students to master in becoming effective writers.

5 **A handbook that teaches.** To help students learn, the *handbook* is organized as follows:

   • To emphasize the most vital skills, the handbook is divided into two sections. The first section presents information and extended practice for sixteen key skills. The second section includes the basics of other skills, along with short practices. Students can be referred to this section as needed and as time permits.

   • The key skills are organized in a manner conducive to learning. The first page of each chapter begins with an informal test—and then provides the answers and explanations. This page gives students a quick view of key points in the chapter and prepares them to sharpen their understanding of the skill.

The next several pages of each chapter present the basics about the skill. Lively examples clarify the skills; brief exercises give practice in them. Answers at the back of the book allow students to correct their own work, teaching themselves as they go.

The last four pages of every chapter contain four tests on the skill. Half of the items in Tests 1 and 3 are accompanied by hints designed to help students think through each kind of correction. More self-teaching is therefore assured.

In addition, student mastery of the skills advances from the sentence to the multi-sentence level. In Tests 1 and 2, students practice the skills in single sentences; in Tests 3 and 4, they work with short paragraphs.

6 **Motivational readings.** The final part of the book contains six high-interest readings that deal with self-knowledge and the pursuit of learning. Class use has shown that these readings help inspire and motivate students to do their best as they work on becoming more effective writers, readers, and learners.

7 **Exercises on key reading and thinking skills.** Following each motivational selection are reading comprehension and technique questions to help students understand the message and makeup of the reading. Discussion questions provoke deeper understanding and help prepare students to think about the writing assignments that follow.

8 **A variety of writing assignments.** Paragraph writing assignments follow the activities in Part One as well as each of the readings in Part Three. These assignments allow students to explore interesting, relevant topics while practicing the writing process learned in Part One and the grammar, punctuation, and usage skills learned in Part Two.

Two helpful learning aids accompany the book. An *Instructor's Edition* includes the student text along with a full answer key, two more mastery tests for many of the handbook skills, and diagnostic and achievement tests for use with the handbook. A software package called *English Skills Software* contains additional mastery tests for many of the skills in the handbook and is available in IBM or Macintosh format. Both aids are provided at no charge to adopters of the book.

In short, *Basic Writing Skills with Readings* offers an unusually clear rhetoric, a handbook with a self-teaching approach, inspiring reading selections, and helpful supplements. It is a basic writing text ideally suited to today's students.

Finally, this book is the result of a team effort. Our thanks go to Janet M. Goldstein for her design and editing skills and to Beth Johnson and Amy K. Fisher for their help in developing examples and practice materials in the text.

R. Kent Smith
John Langan
Carole Mohr

Introduction

Do you feel a bit uneasy when you sit down to write? Perhaps you are preparing a job application letter, working on a college paper, writing a report on the job, or getting off a note to a relative or friend. Are you uncertain, for example, about the best way to begin or about just where to place punctuation marks? If you have doubts when expressing yourself on paper, this book is for you. *Basic Writing Skills with Readings* will help you learn the basics of effective writing. Step by step, you will master the core of rules you need to become a confident writer.

Here is one way to use the book:

1 **Look at the table of contents on pages v–vi.** You'll see that *Basic Writing Skills with Readings* is divided into three parts. Part One is a guide to the goals of effective writing followed by a series of activities to help you practice and master those goals. Part Two is a convenient handbook of grammar, punctuation, and usage skills. Part Three presents six inspiring readings, along with questions to sharpen your reading skills and assignments to improve your writing.

2 **Begin with Part One.** Read the first chapter carefully. Then work through the series of activities in the second chapter. Your instructor may direct you to certain exercises, depending on your needs. After completing the activities, begin work on the paragraph-writing assignments at the end of the chapter.

3 **Work through the handbook in Part Two.**

   • You'll notice that the handbook is divided into two sections. Concentrate mainly on the first section, which provides explanations and practice for sixteen key grammar, punctuation, and usage skills. The second section includes the basics of other skills and can be covered as time permits.

   • Start each key skill by taking the "Seeing What You Know" test and checking your answers. You'll quickly see what you know and don't know about the skill in question.

   • Then work through the rest of the chapter. Each chapter includes examples that clarify the skill and brief exercises for practice. Answers at the back of the book allow you to correct your own work, teaching yourself as you go.

- The last four pages of each chapter contain four tests on the skill. Tests 1 and 3 include hints that will help you understand and answer half of the items on the tests. To increase your mastery of the skill, take advantage of these hints.

4 Read the selections in Part Three.   The selections will help inspire and motivate you in your own pursuit of learning. After you read a selection, work through the reading comprehension, technique, and discussion questions that follow. They will help you understand, appreciate, and think about the selection. Then write a paragraph on one of the three writing assignments provided.

As you work on a paragraph, refer as needed to the guidelines for effective writing in Part One and the grammar, punctuation, and usage rules in Part Two. Doing so will help make basic writing rules an everyday part of your writing.

Basic Writing Skills with Readings has been designed to benefit you as much as possible. Its format is straightforward, its explanations are clear, its readings are compelling, and its practices and tests will help you learn through doing. *It is a book that has been created to reward effort,* and if you provide that effort, you can make yourself a competent and confident writer.

R. Kent Smith
John Langan
Carole Mohr

Part One

Effective Writing

A Brief Guide to Effective Writing

This chapter will show you how to write an effective paragraph. The principles you learn here will help you write longer papers as well. Answered in turn are the following questions:

1 Why does your attitude about writing matter?

2 What is a paragraph?

3 What are the goals of effective writing?

4 How do you reach the goals of effective writing?

WHY DOES YOUR ATTITUDE ABOUT WRITING MATTER?

Your attitude about writing is an important part of your learning to write well. To get a sense of just how you regard writing, read the following statements. Put a check beside those statements with which you agree. This activity is not a test, so try to be as honest as possible.

_____ 1. A good writer should be able to sit down and write a paper straight through without stopping.

_____ 2. Writing is a skill that anyone can learn with practice.

_____ 3. I'll never be good at writing because I make too many spelling, grammar, and punctuation mistakes.

_____ 4. Because I dislike writing, I always start a paper at the last possible minute.

_____ 5. I've always done poorly in English, and I don't expect that to change.

Now read the comments on the next page about the five statements. The comments will help you see if your attitude is hurting or helping your efforts to become a better writer.

1. *A good writer should be able to sit down and write a paper straight through without stopping.*

   The statement is not true. Writing is, in fact, a process. It is not done in one easy step, but in a series of steps, and seldom at one sitting. If you cannot do a paper all at once, that simply means you are like most of the other people on the planet. It is harmful to carry around the false idea that writing should be an easy matter.

2. *Writing is a skill that anyone can learn with practice.*

   This statement is absolutely true. Writing is a skill, like driving or word processing, that you can master with hard work. If you want to learn to write, you can. It is as simple as that. If you believe this, you are ready to learn how to become a competent writer.

   Some people hold the false belief that writing is a natural gift which some have and others do not. Because of this belief, they never make a truly honest effort to learn to write—and so they never learn.

3. *I'll never be good at writing because I make too many spelling, grammar, and punctuation mistakes.*

   The first concern in good writing should be content—what you have to say. Your ideas and feelings are what matter most. You should not worry about spelling, grammar, and punctuation rules while working on content.

   Unfortunately, some people are so self-conscious about making mistakes that they do not focus on what they want to say. They need to realize that a paper is best done in stages, and that the rules can and should wait until a later stage in the writing process. Through review and practice, you will eventually learn how to follow the rules with confidence.

4. *Because I dislike writing, I always start a paper at the last possible minute.*

   This is all-too-common behavior. You feel you are going to do poorly, and then behave in a way to insure you will do poorly! Your attitude is so negative that you defeat yourself—not even allowing enough time to really try.

   Again, what you need to realize is that writing is a process. Because it is done in steps, you don't have to get it right all at once. If you allow yourself enough time, you'll find a way to make a paper come together.

5. *I've always done poorly in English, and I don't expect that to change.*

   How you may have performed in the *past* does not control how you can perform in the *present*. Even if you did poorly in English in high school, it is in your power to make it one of your best subjects in college. If you believe writing can be learned and then work hard at it, you *will* become a better writer.

In conclusion, your attitude is crucial. If you believe you are a poor writer and always will be, chances are you will not improve. If you realize you can become a better writer, chances are you will improve. Depending on how you allow yourself to think, you can be your own best friend or your own worst enemy.

WHAT IS A PARAGRAPH?

A **paragraph** is a series of sentences about one main idea, or **point**. A paragraph typically starts with a point, and the rest of the paragraph provides specific details to support and develop that point.

Consider the following paragraph written by a student named Wanda.

A Terrible Roommate

Taking in Helen as a roommate was a mistake. For one thing, Helen was a truly noisy person. She talked loudly, she ate loudly, and she snored loudly. She never just watched TV, listened to the radio, or put a cassette in the stereo. Instead, she did all three at once. I would walk into the apartment with my hands clapped over my ears and turn off the first noisemaking machine I reached. Then I would hear her cry out, "I was listening to that." Secondly, Helen had no sense of privacy. If she wanted to speak to me, she would find me no matter where I was or what I was doing. She walked in on me while I was dressing. She sat down on my bed for a chat while I was napping. Once she even wandered in while I was taking a bath. And finally, Helen had too many visiting relatives. There were over ten of them, and they all felt perfectly at home in our apartment. I often came into the apartment after an evening out and practically tripped over one of Helen's sisters, cousins, or nephews asleep on our living room floor. When they visited, they would stay for days, eating our groceries and tying up the bathroom and telephone. Helen is gone now, and I've had to take a second job to handle the rent. It's worth it.

The above paragraph, like many effective paragraphs, starts by stating a main idea, or point. In this case, the point is that taking in Helen as a roommate was a bad idea. A point is a general idea that has an opinion injected into it.

In our everyday lives, we constantly make points about all kinds of matters. We express such opinions as "That was a terrible movie" or "My psychology instructor is the best teacher I have ever had" or "My sister is a generous person" or "Eating at that restaurant was a mistake" or "That team should win the playoff game" or "Waitressing is the worst job I ever had" or "Our state should allow the death penalty" or "Cigarette smoking should be banned everywhere." In *talking* to people, we don't always give the reasons for our opinions. But in *writing*, we *must* provide the reasons to support our ideas. Only by supplying solid evidence for any point that we make can we communicate effectively with readers.

An effective paragraph, then, must not only make a point but must support it with **specific evidence**—reasons, examples, and other details. Such specifics help prove to readers that the point is a reasonable one. Even if readers do not agree with the writer, at least they have in front of them the evidence on which the writer has based his or her opinion. Readers are like juries; they want to see the evidence so that they can make their own judgments.

➤ Take a moment now to examine the evidence that Wanda has provided to back up her point about Helen as a roommate. Complete the following outline of Wanda's paragraph by summarizing in a few words her reasons and the details that develop them. The first reason and its supporting details are summarized for you as an example.

> *Point:* Taking in Helen as a roommate was a mistake.
>
> > *Reason 1:* Noisy person
> >
> > *Details that develop reason 1:* Talked, ate, snored, and played things loudly.
> >
> > *Reason 2:* _____
> >
> > *Details that develop reason 2:* _____
> >
> > _____
> >
> > *Reason 3:* _____
> >
> > *Details that develop reason 3:* _____
> >
> > _____

As the outline makes clear, Wanda provides three reasons to support her point about rooming with Helen: (1) Helen was noisy, (2) she had no sense of privacy, and (3) she had too many visiting relatives. Wanda also provides vivid details to back up each of her three reasons. Her reasons and descriptive details enable readers to see why she feels that rooming with Helen was a mistake.

To write an effective paragraph, then, aim to do what Wanda has done: begin by making a point, and then go on to support that point with specific evidence.

WHAT ARE THE GOALS OF EFFECTIVE WRITING?

Now that you have considered an effective student paragraph, it is time to look at four goals of effective writing:

1 Make a point. It is often best to state that point in the first sentence of your paper, just as Wanda has in her paragraph about her roommate. The sentence that expresses the main idea, or point, of a paragraph is called the **topic sentence**. Activities on pages 26–29 in the next chapter of this book will help you learn how to write a topic sentence.

2 Support the point. To do so, you need to provide specific reasons, examples, and other details that explain and develop the point. The more precise and particular your supporting details are, the better your readers can "see," "hear," and "feel" them. Activities on pages 21–26 and 29–42 in the next chapter of this book will help you learn how to be specific in your writing.

3 Organize the support. There are two common ways to organize the support in a paragraph. You can use either a listing order or a time order. At the same time, you should use suitable signal words, known as **transitions**.

> *a. Listing order.* The writer organizes the supporting evidence in a paper by providing a list of two or more reasons, examples, or other details. Often the most important or interesting item is saved for last because the reader is most likely to remember the last thing read.

Transition words that show a listing order include the following:

for one thing	secondly	another	next	last of all
first of all	also	in addition	moreover	finally

➤ The paragraph about Helen uses a listing order: it lists three reasons why Helen was a bad roommate, and each of those three reasons is introduced by one of the above transitions. In the spaces below, write in the three transitions:

_____   _____   _____

The first reason in the paragraph about Helen is introduced with *for one thing*; the second reason by *secondly;* and the third reason by *finally.*

b. Time order. Supporting details are presented in the order in which they occurred. *First* this happened; *next* this; *after* that, this; and so on. Many paragraphs, especially ones that tell stories or give a series of directions, are organized in a time order.

Transition words that show time relationships include the following:

first	before	after	when	then
next	during	now	while	finally

➤ Read the playful paragraph below. It is organized in a time order. See if you can underline the six transition words that show the time relationships.

There are a few steps to follow if you want to be sure you are not hired for a job. First, go to the job interview in your basketball clothes. In fact, bring your basketball along. That will make it very clear that you're just stopping in on the way to someplace more important. If you can possibly arrange it, be accompanied by a couple of your buddies. While you're being interviewed, they can hang around the reception area, commenting on what a dump the office is. During the interview, sigh loudly at the interviewer's stupid questions. Ask if you can smoke. Clip your nails. Demand to know what the job pays. After you hear what the salary is, express disbelief at the low figure. Comment that a real cheapskate must run the company. Then explain that you're only waiting for work to tide you over, and that your cousin will be getting you a really high-paying job at his place. Finally, tell the interviewer not to call you too early with a decision. Explain that you party late every night and only get out of bed around noon.

The writer makes the main point of the paragraph in the first sentence: "There are a few steps to follow if you want to be sure you are not hired for a job." The support for this point is the suggested things to do at the interview. Those actions are presented in the order in which they are meant to occur. The time relationships between some are highlighted by these transitions: *first, while, during, after, then,* and *finally.*

More About Transitions

Transitions are words and phrases that make clear the relationships between ideas. They are like signposts that guide travelers, showing them how to move smoothly from one spot to the next. Be sure to take advantage of transitions. They will help organize and connect your ideas, and they will help your readers follow the direction of your thoughts.

➤ To see how transitions help, put a check beside the item in each pair that is easier to read and understand.

_____ I begin each day by writing down a list of the things I need to do. I decide which items are most important.

_____ I begin each day by writing down a list of the things I need to do. Then I decide which items are most important.

_____ One way to lose friends is to always talk and never listen. It is a mistake to borrow money and never pay it back.

_____ One way to lose friends is to always talk and never listen. Another mistake is to borrow money and never pay it back.

In each pair, the second item is easier to read and understand. In the first pair, the time word *then* makes the relationship between the sentences clear. The writer first gets down a list of things to do and *then* decides on which are most important. In the second pair, the listing word *another* makes it clear that the writer is going on to a second way to lose friends.

Activities on pages 42–47 will give you practice in the use of listing order and time order, as well as transitions, to organize the supporting details of a paragraph.

4 Write error-free sentences. If you use correct spelling and follow grammar, punctuation, and usage rules, your sentences will be clear and well written. But by no means must you have all that information in your head. Even the best of writers need to use reference materials to be sure their writing is correct. So keep a good dictionary and grammar handbook nearby when you write your papers.

In general, however, save them for after you've gotten your ideas firmly down on paper. You'll see in the next part of this guide that Wanda made a number of sentence errors as she worked on her paragraph. But she simply ignored them until she got to a later draft of her paper, when there was time enough to make the needed corrections.

HOW DO YOU REACH THE GOALS OF EFFECTIVE WRITING?

Even professional writers do not sit down and automatically, in one draft, write a paper. Instead, they have to work on it a step at a time. Writing a paper is a process that can be divided into the following steps:

> **Step 1:** Getting Started Through Prewriting
>
> **Step 2:** Preparing a Scratch Outline
>
> **Step 3:** Writing the First Draft
>
> **Step 4:** Revising
>
> **Step 5:** Proofreading

These steps are described on the following pages.

Step 1: Getting Started Through Prewriting

What you need to learn, first, are strategies for working on a paper. These strategies will help you do the thinking needed to figure out both the point you want to make and the support you have for that point.

There are several **prewriting strategies**—ones that you use before writing the first draft of your paper.

- Freewriting
- Questioning
- Clustering
- List making

Freewriting

Freewriting is just sitting down and writing whatever comes into your mind about a topic. Do this for ten minutes or so. Write without stopping, and without worrying in the slightest about spelling, grammar, or the like. Simply get down on paper all the information about the topic that occurs to you.

Below is the freewriting done by Wanda on problems with her roommate Helen. Wanda had been given the assignment, "Write about a problem with a friend, family member, or roommate." Wanda felt right away that she could write about her roommate. She began prewriting as a way to explore her topic and generate details on it.

Example of Freewriting

One thing I would like to write about is my roommate. What a charakter. I learned my lesson with her, I am going to think twice before taking on a roomate again. She folowed me everywhere. Once when I was taking a bath. She didnt like to be alone. I could be taking a nap and she would just walk right in, I'd wake up and there she would be. Talking away. I had to lock doors all the time. To my bedroom and to my bathroom. Then I hurt her feelings. She did pay her rent on time. I'll say that for her. And she was a good cook. But other things were too much. She was on the phone a lot. She had more family than anyone I ever knew. It seemed like they were living their. I got sick and tired of all the people around. She even had keys made up for them and gave them the keys! I really blowed up with her when that happen. There were always dishes in the sink. I would do mine, she not hers. She was a messy person. Cloths all over her bedroom. Stuff was always turned on. She liked things noisee. The TV was always blaring when I walked in. Give me a break, woman. I got back from a crazy day at school wanting some peace and quite. But what do I get? I needed to get her out of my life.

Notice that there are spelling, grammar, and punctuation problems in Wanda's freewriting. Wanda is not worried about such matters, nor should she be. She is just concentrating on getting ideas and details down on paper. She knows that it is best to focus on one thing at a time. At this stage, she just wants to write out thoughts as they come to her, to do some thinking on paper.

You should take the same approach when freewriting: explore your topic without worrying at all about being "correct." Figuring out what you want to say should have all your attention in this early stage of the writing process.

Questioning

Questioning means that you think about your topic by writing down a series of questions and answers about it. Your questions can start with words like *what, when, where, why,* and *how.*

Here are some questions that Wanda might have asked while developing her paper:

Example of Questioning

- *Why did I have a problem with Helen?* She was hard to live with.

- *How was she hard to live with?* Followed me around everywhere; I had no privacy. Also, she was noisy.

- *When did I have no privacy?* When I got back from school and wanted to be quiet and alone; when her relatives came.

- *Where did I have no privacy?* In my bedroom while I was napping; when her relatives were covering the floor when I walked in.

- *When was she noisy?* When I got back from school and when I'd try to study at night.

- *Where was she noisy?* The noise could be heard anywhere in the apartment.

Clustering

Clustering is another strategy that can be used to generate material for a paper. It is helpful for people who like to do their thinking in a visual way.

In **clustering**, you begin by stating your subject in a few words in the center of a blank sheet of paper. Then as ideas come to you, put them in ovals, boxes, or circles around the subject and draw lines to connect them to the subject. Put minor ideas or details in smaller boxes or circles, and use connecting lines to show how they relate as well.

Keep in mind that there is no right or wrong way of clustering. It is a way to think on paper about how various ideas and details relate to one another. Below is an example of clustering that Wanda could have done to develop her ideas.

Example of clustering

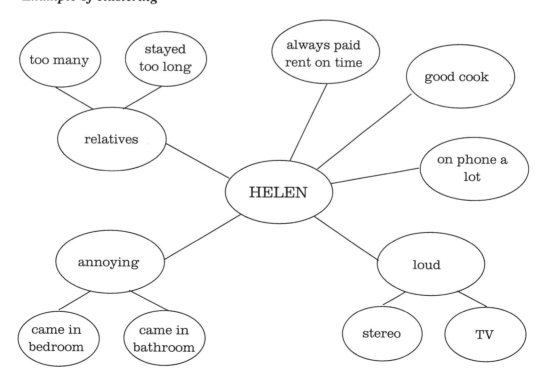

Notice that the clustering, like the freewriting, includes details that do not end up in the final paragraph. Wanda decided later not to develop the idea that Helen spent a lot of time on the phone. And she realized that the details about Helen's paying the rent on time and being a good cook were not relevant to her point. It is natural for a number of such extra or unrelated details to appear as part of the prewriting process. The goal of prewriting is to get a lot of information down on paper. You can then shape, add to, and subtract from your raw material as you take your paper through the series of writing drafts.

List making

In **list making**, a strategy also known as **brainstorming**, you make a list of ideas and details that could go into your paper. Simply pile these items up, one after another, without worrying about putting them in any special order. Try to accumulate as many details as you can think of.

After Wanda did her freewriting about her roommate, she made up the following list of details.

Example of list making

```
Helen was always around
followed me into the bathroom
came into the bedroom when I was sleeping
walked in on me while I was dressing
I couldn't be alone when I wanted to
started locking doors behind me
talked a lot on the phone
talked when I was going out the door to school
had a lot of relatives
three sisters and they all visited
also cousins she was close to
I would come home and relatives would be there
sometimes they were there and Helen wasn't
she had keys made for some of them
ate out sometimes because no room to cook in kitchen
lot of cooking smells in the house
a very good cook
never charged me for food she bought
also good in paying her rent on time
but hard to relax around
played TV all the time
played stereo at the same time
everything about Helen was loud
even her clothes were loud
```

One detail led to another as Wanda expanded her list. Slowly but surely, more supporting material emerged that she could use in developing her paper. By the time she was done with her list, she was ready to plan an outline of her paragraph and to write her first draft.

Important Notes About Prewriting Strategies

Some writers may use only one of the above prewriting strategies. Others may use bits and pieces of all four of them. Any one strategy can lead to another. Freewriting may lead to questioning or clustering, which may then lead to a list. Or a writer may start with a list and then use freewriting or questioning to develop items on the list. During this early stage of the writing process, as you do your thinking on paper, anything goes. You should not expect a straight-line progression from the beginning to the end of your paper. Instead, there probably will be a constant moving back and forth as you work to discover your point and just how you will develop it.

Keep in mind that prewriting can also help you choose from among several topics. Wanda might not have been so sure about which person to write about. Then she could have made a list of possible topics—names of people with whom she has had problems. After selecting two or three names from the list, she could have done some prewriting on each to see which seemed most promising. After finding a likely topic, Wanda would have continued with her prewriting activities until she had a solid main point and plenty of support.

Finally, remember that you are not ready to begin writing a paper until you know your main point and many of the details that can be used to support it. Don't rush through prewriting. It's better to spend more time on this stage than to waste time writing a paragraph for which you have no solid point and too little interesting support.

Step 2: Preparing a Scratch Outline

A **scratch outline** is a brief plan for the paragraph. It shows at a glance the point of the paragraph and the support for that point. It is the logical backbone upon which the paper is built.

This rough outline often follows freewriting, questioning, clustering, and/or list making. Or it may gradually emerge in the midst of these strategies. In fact, trying to outline is a good way to see if you need to do more prewriting. If a solid outline does not emerge, then you know you need to do more prewriting to clarify your main point or its support. Once you have a workable outline, you may realize, for instance, that you want to do more list making to develop one of the supporting details in the outline.

In Wanda's case, as she was working on her list of details, she suddenly discovered what the plan of her paragraph could be. She went back to the list, crossed out items that she now realized did not fit, and added the comments shown on the next page.

Example of a list with added comments

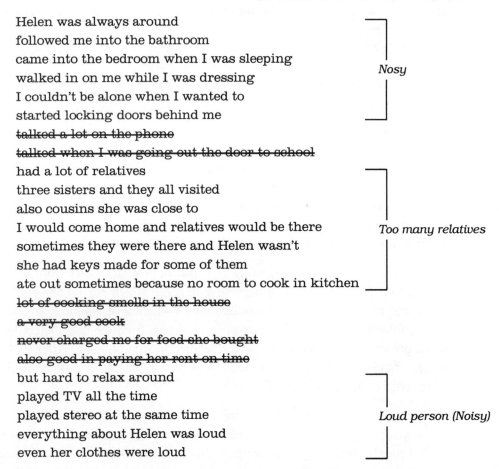

I had a bad roommate—three reasons:

Helen was always around
followed me into the bathroom
came into the bedroom when I was sleeping
walked in on me while I was dressing   *Nosy*
I couldn't be alone when I wanted to
started locking doors behind me
~~talked a lot on the phone~~
~~talked when I was going out the door to school~~
had a lot of relatives
three sisters and they all visited
also cousins she was close to
I would come home and relatives would be there   *Too many relatives*
sometimes they were there and Helen wasn't
she had keys made for some of them
ate out sometimes because no room to cook in kitchen
~~lot of cooking smells in the house~~
~~a very good cook~~
~~never charged me for food she bought~~
~~also good in paying her rent on time~~
but hard to relax around
played TV all the time
played stereo at the same time   *Loud person (Noisy)*
everything about Helen was loud
even her clothes were loud

Under the list, Wanda was now able to prepare her scratch outline:

Example of a scratch outline

I had a bad roommate.

1. Too noisy

2. Too nosy (no sense of privacy)

3. Too many relatives (put last—worst reason)

After all her preliminary writing, Wanda sat back pleased. She knew she had a promising paper—one with a clear point and solid support. Wanda was now ready to write the first draft of her paper, using her outline as a guide.

Step 3: Writing the First Draft

When you do a first draft, be prepared to put in additional thoughts and details that didn't emerge in your prewriting activity. And don't worry if you hit a snag. Just leave a blank space or add a comment such as "Do later" and press on to finish the paper. Also, don't worry yet about grammar, punctuation, or spelling. You don't want to take time correcting words or sentences that you may decide to remove later. Instead, make it your goal to develop the content of your paper with plenty of specific details.

Here is Wanda's first draft:

First draft

Last fall, I decided that I needed to save money by sharing my apartment with someone. I put an ad in the paper and chose the first person who called which was Helen. She was the loudest person I have ever known over the age of five. She talked loud, and she was a noisy eater. When you tried to sleep at night you sure knew what a loud snorer she was. The only other person who snored that loud was my father, and he would wake up everyone in the family. The TV was always on, it was loud. The same thing with the stereo. There was always noise when I walked into the apt. I would have to tell her to turn something off. Then she would compane I was too demandin. Helen never gave me much privicy. She would come into the bedroom when I was naping. I'd be aware that someone was standing there. As soon as I woke she would start talking. ADD MORE DETAILS LATER. Her relatives seemed to come out of the woodwork. I'd walk in and they'd be covering the chairs and sofa and carpet. They were frendly people but too much. They'd be eating in the kitchen. Or watching TV. Or be in the bathroom when I wanted to go in. All this was too much.

After Wanda finished the draft, she was able to put it aside until the next day. You will benefit as well if you can allow some time between finishing a draft and starting to revise.

Step 4: Revising

Revising is as much a stage in the writing process as prewriting, outlining, and doing the first draft. **Revising** means that you rewrite a paper, building upon what has been done to make it stronger and better. One writer has said about revision, "It's like cleaning house—getting rid of all the junk and putting things in the right order." A typical revision means writing at least one or two more drafts.

Here is Wanda's second draft.

Second draft

Taking in Helen as a roomate was a mistake. For one thing Helen was noisy. She talked and ate loudly, and she snored loudly. She never just had on the TV, listened to the radio, or a cassete in the tape deck. She did all three at once. I would walk into the apt. with my hands over my ears and turn off the first noisy machine I reached. I would hear her cry out I was listening to that. The second bad thing about Helen was that she had no sense of privicy. She walked in on me when I was dressing. She sat down on my bed for a chat while I was naping. She even came into the bathroom once when I was taking a bath. The third thing about Helen was that she had too many relatives. I counted over ten and they all came to the apartment. After a night out I would come in and trip over relatives asleep on the living room floor. Relatives would stay eating grocerys and tying up the bathroom and telephone. Helen is gone now, and I've had to take a second job to handle the rent.

Notice that in redoing the draft, Wanda started by clearly stating the point of her paragraph. Also, she inserted clear transitions to set off the three reasons why Helen was a bad roommate. She omitted the detail about her father snoring, which was not relevant to a paragraph focusing on Helen. She added more details, so that she would have enough support for each of her three reasons. She also began to correct some of her spelling mistakes and added a final sentence to round off the paragraph.

Wanda then went on to revise the second draft. Since she was doing her paper on a word processor, she was able to print it out quickly. She double-spaced the lines, allowing room for revisions, which she added in longhand as part of her third draft. (Note that if you are not using a word processor, you may want to do each draft on every other line of a page, so that there is room to revise. Also, write on only one side of a page, so that you can see your entire paper at one time.) Shown below are some of the changes that Wanda made in longhand as she worked on her third draft.

Part of third draft

                roommate
Taking in Helen as a ~~roomate~~ was a mistake. For one thing‚ Helen

  a truly person.   *loudly, she*
was ‸noisy‸. She talked ‸~~and~~ ate loudly, and she snored loudly. She never

     watched   *put*   *Instead, s*
just ~~had on~~ the TV, listened to the radio, or ‸a cassete in the tape deck. ‸$̶S̶$he

                               apartment   *clapped*
did all three at once. I would walk into the ~~apt.~~ with my hands‸over my

                 noisemaking   *Then*
ears and turn off the first ~~noisy~~ machine I reached. ‸I would hear her cry

      "   "   *Secondly,*
out, "I was listening to that." ~~The second bad thing about~~ Helen ~~was that~~

       privacy
~~she~~ had no sense of ~~privicy~~. . . .

After writing out the above and other changes, Wanda typed them into her word processor and printed out the almost-final draft of her paper. She was now ready to do a careful proofreading.

Step 5: Proofreading

Proofreading, the final stage in the writing process, means checking a paper carefully for spelling, grammar, punctuation, and other errors. You are ready for this stage when you are satisfied with your choice of supporting details, the order in which they are presented, and the way they and your topic sentence are worded.

At this point in her work, Wanda used her dictionary to do final checks on her spelling. She used a grammar handbook to be sure about her grammar, punctuation, and usage. Wanda also read through the paper carefully, looking for typing errors, omitted words, and any other errors she may have missed before. Such proofreading is often hard to do—students have spent so much time with their work, or so little, that they want to avoid proofing. But done carefully, this important final step will insure that your paper looks as good as possible.

Some Proofreading Hints

One helpful trick at this stage is to read your paper out loud. You will probably hear awkward wordings and become aware of spots where the punctuation needs to be improved. Make the changes needed for your sentences to read smoothly and clearly.

Another helpful technique is to take a sheet of paper and cover your paragraph so that you can expose and check carefully just one line at a time.

A third strategy is to read your paper backward, from the last sentence to the first. Doing so helps keep you from getting caught up in the flow of the paper and missing small mistakes, which is easy to do since you're so familiar with what you meant to say.

(Pages 247–260 will give you practice in proofreading for specific problems.)

A LOOK AHEAD

The next chapter provides a series of activities to help you master three of the four goals in effective writing: (1) making a point, (2) supporting the point with specific details, and (3) organizing the support. Part Two of this book and a dictionary will help you with the fourth goal—writing error-free sentences. Part Three of the book presents six reading selections that will develop both your reading and your writing skills. The readings will also serve to inspire and motivate you in your pursuit of learning.

CHAPTER REVIEW

Answer the true-false or multiple choice question or fill in the missing word. Doing so will help you check your understanding of the material presented in this chapter.

1. *True or false?* _____ Writing is a skill that anyone can learn with practice.

2. An effective paragraph is one that
   a. makes a point.
   b. provides specific support.
   c. makes a point *and* provides specific support.
   d. none of the above.

3. The sentence that states the main idea of a paragraph is known as the

   _____ sentence.

4. Prewriting can help a writer find
   a. a good topic to write about.
   b. a good main point to make about the topic.
   c. enough details to support the main point.
   d. all of the above.

5. *True or false?* _____ During the freewriting process, you should not concern yourself with spelling, punctuation, or grammar.

6. One prewriting technique that everyone should use at some stage of the writing process is to prepare a plan for the paragraph known as a(n)

   _____.

7. When you start writing, your first concern should be
   a. spelling.
   b. content.
   c. grammar.
   d. punctuation.

8. Two common ways of organizing a paragraph are using a _____

   order and a _____ order.

9. The words *first, next, then, also, another,* and *finally* are examples of

   signal words, commonly known as _____.

10. The purpose of proofreading is to check a paper for errors in
    a. grammar.
    b. punctuation.
    c. usage and spelling.
    d. all of the above.

Practice in Effective Writing

The following series of activities will strengthen your understanding of the writing guidelines presented in the first chapter. Through practice, you will gain a better sense of the goals of effective writing and how to reach those goals. You will also help prepare yourself for the writing assignments that follow the activities.

Your instructor may ask you to do the series of activities in sequence, from beginning to end, or may select the activities that are most suited to your particular needs.

1 UNDERSTANDING GENERAL VERSUS SPECIFIC

A paragraph is made up of a main idea, which is general, and the specific ideas that support it. So to write well, you must understand the difference between general and specific ideas.

It is helpful to realize that you use general and specific ideas all the time in your everyday life. For example, in planning your food shopping, you may tell yourself, "I need some vegetables. I guess I'll buy green peppers, tomatoes, and onions." In such a case, *vegetables* is the general idea, and *green peppers, tomatoes,* and *onions* are the specific ideas.

Or if you are looking for a part-time job, you may think, "What features do I want for that job? I want an hourly pay of at least six dollars, hours from one to five in the afternoon, and a travel time each way of no more than thirty minutes." In this case, *the desired features of a part-time job* is the general idea, and *pay, hours,* and *travel time* are the specific ideas.

Or if you are talking to a friend about a math teacher you feel is poor, you may say, "She acts bored in class, she often arrives late, and she never returns homework." In this case, the general idea is *the math teacher is poor*, and the specific ideas are the three reasons you named.

The four activities here will give you experience in recognizing general-specific relationships. They will also provide a helpful background for all the information and activities that follow.

➤ *Activity 1*

Each group of words consists of one general idea and four specific ideas. The general idea includes all the specific ideas. Underline the general idea in each group.

> ***Example*** cooking   dusting   vacuuming   <u>chore</u>   washing dishes

1. wrench   drill   hammer   screwdriver   tool   pliers

2. bruise   fracture   injury   scrape   cut

3. crime   robbery   kidnapping   murder   rape

4. gas   food   expense   rent   taxes

5. come here   stop   go   command   hurry

6. sneakers   boots   high heels   sandals   footwear

7. entertainment   television   concerts   movies   card games

8. long lines   stuck doors   junk mail   slow waiters   annoyances

9. time savers   microwave ovens   take-out food   high-speed trains   express mail

10. nail biting   tardiness   smoking   interrupting   bad habits

➤ *Activity 2*

In each item below, one idea is general and the others are specific. The general idea includes the specific ones. In the spaces provided, write in two more specific ideas that are covered by the general idea.

> ***Example*** *General:*   beverage
>
> *Specific:*   iced tea, water, _____*soda*_____, _____*grape juice*_____

1. *General:*   snacks

   Specific: pretzels, popcorn, _____, _____

2. *General:*   subject

   Specific: English, biology, _____, _____

3. *General:*   sports

   Specific: baseball, soccer, _____, _____

4. *General:*   cooking methods

   Specific: boil, steam, _____, _____

5. *General:* reading material

   Specific: textbook, comic book, _____, _____

6. *General:* seafood

   Specific: clams, lobster, _____, _____

7. *General:* emotion

   Specific: anger, embarrassment, _____, _____

8. *General:* negative personal qualities

   Specific: greed, cowardice, _____, _____

9. *General:* positive personal qualities

   Specific: reliability, determination, _____, _____

10. *General:* greetings

    Specific: "How are you," "Hello," _____, _____

➤ *Activity 3*

Read each group of specific ideas below. Then circle the letter of the general idea that tells what the specific ideas have in common. Note that the general idea should not be too broad or too narrow. Begin by trying the example item, and then read the explanation that follows.

> ***Example*** *Specific ideas:* egg salad; tuna salad; bacon, lettuce, and tomato; peanut butter and jelly
>
> The general idea is:
> a. foods.
> b. sandwich fillings.
> c. salads used as sandwich fillings.

Explanation

It is true that the specific ideas are all food, but they have in common something even more specific—they are all common sandwich fillings. Therefore answer *a* is too broad, and the correct answer is *b*. Answer *c* is too narrow because it doesn't cover all of the specific ideas. While two of them are salads used as sandwich fillings, two of them are not salads.

1. *Specific ideas:* Easter, Thanksgiving, Valentine's Day, New Year's Day

   The general idea is:
   a. days.
   b. holidays.
   c. religious holidays.

2. *Specific ideas:* hide and seek, tag, jacks, hopscotch

   The general idea is:
   a. games.
   b. toys.
   c. children's games.

3. *Specific ideas:* runny nose, coughing, sneezing, sore throat

   The general idea is:
   a. cold symptoms.
   b. symptoms.
   c. throat problems.

4. *Specific ideas:* yes, no, maybe, OK

   The general idea is:
   a. negative answers.
   b. positive answers.
   c. answers.

5. *Specific ideas:* OPEN, STOP, FIRE EXIT, YIELD

   The general idea is:
   a. words.
   b. words on signs.
   c. words on traffic signs.

6. *Specific ideas:* leaking toilet, no hot water, broken window, roaches

   The general idea is:
   a. problems.
   b. kitchen problems.
   c. apartment problems.

7. *Specific ideas:* tornado, earthquake, sunrise, spring

   The general idea is:
   a. natural disasters.
   b. natural events.
   c. events.

8. *Specific ideas:* big and small, short and tall, fat and lean, kind and mean

   The general idea is:
   a. words.
   b. descriptions of sizes.
   c. opposites.

9. *Specific ideas:* count to ten, take a deep breath, go for a walk

   The general idea is:
   a. actions.
   b. ways to calm down.
   c. ways to calm down just before a test.

10. *Specific ideas:* putting sticky tape on someone's chair, putting a "kick me" sign on someone's back, putting hot pepper in someone's cereal

The general idea is:
a. jokes.
b. practical jokes.
c. practical jokes played on teachers.

➤ Activity 4

In the following items, the specific ideas are given but the general ideas are unstated. Fill in the blanks with the unstated general ideas.

Example *General idea:* _____ *Bodies of water* _____

   Specific ideas: sea   ocean
                      lake   river

1. *General idea:* _____

   Specific ideas: doughnuts   bacon and eggs
                      cereal   pancakes

2. *General idea:* _____

   Specific ideas: chess   checkers
                      Monopoly   dominoes

3. *General idea:* _____

   Specific ideas: rye   six-grain
                      whole wheat   pumpernickel

4. *General idea:* _____

   Specific ideas: salesperson   welder
                      hair stylist   insurance agent

5. *General idea:* _____

   Specific ideas: snow   milk
                      wedding dress the President's house

6. *General idea:* _____

   Specific ideas: "Your mother stinks."   "You look like an ape."
                      "Your father's a bum."   "Your car is a real junk heap."

7. *General idea:* _____

   Specific ideas: snakes   heights
                      flying in an airplane being in small spaces

8. *General idea:* _____

   Specific ideas: "I like your dress."
   "Your new haircut looks terrific."
   "You look great in red."
   "You did a fine job on last week's paper."

9. *General idea:* _____

   Specific ideas: order the invitations   get the tuxedos
   get the bride's gown   find a photographer

10. *General idea:* _____

   Specific ideas: Roll the dough in a circle.
   Cover the dough with tomato sauce.
   Cover the sauce with mushrooms and onions.
   Then add grated mozzarella cheese.

2   UNDERSTANDING THE PARAGRAPH

A **paragraph** is made up of a main idea and a group of related sentences that develop that main idea. The main idea appears in a sentence known as the **topic sentence**.

It is helpful to remember that the topic sentence is a *general* statement. The other sentences provide specific support for the general statement.

➤ *Activity*

Each group of sentences below could be written as a short paragraph. Circle the letter of the topic sentence in each case. To find the topic sentence, ask yourself, "Which is a general statement supported by the specific details in the other three statements?"

Begin by trying the example item below. First circle the letter of the sentence you think expresses the main idea. Then read the explanation.

Example   a. If you stop carrying matches or a lighter, you can cut down on impulse smoking.
   b. If you sit in no-smoking areas, you will smoke less.
   c. You can behave in ways that will help you smoke less.
   d. By keeping a record of when and where you smoke, you can learn the most tempting situations and then avoid them.

Explanation

Sentence *a* explains one way to smoke less. Sentences *b* and *d* also provide specific ways to smoke less. In sentence *c*, however, no one specific way is explained. The words "ways that help you smoke less" refer only generally to such methods. Therefore sentence *c* is the topic sentence; it expresses the author's main idea. The other sentences support that idea by providing examples.

1. a. "I couldn't study because I forgot to bring my book home."
   b. "I couldn't take the final because my grandmother died."
   c. Students use some common excuses with instructors.
   d. "I couldn't come to class because I had a migraine headache."

2. a. The brakes are badly worn.
   b. My old car is ready for the junk pile.
   c. The car floor has rusted through, and water splashes on my feet from a wet highway.
   d. My mechanic says its engine is too old to be repaired, and the car isn't worth the cost of a new engine.

3. a. Tobacco is one of the most addictive of all drugs.
   b. Selling cigarettes ought to be against the law.
   c. Non-smokers are put in danger by breathing the smoke from others' cigarettes.
   d. Cigarette smoking kills many more people than all illegal drugs combined.

4. a. Part-time workers are easily laid off.
   b. Most part-time workers get no fringe benefits.
   c. The average part-timer earns three dollars less an hour than a full-timer.
   d. Part-time workers have second-class status.

5. a. The last time I ate at the diner, I got food poisoning and was sick for two days.
   b. The city inspector found roaches and mice in the diner's kitchen.
   c. Our town diner is a health hazard and ought to be closed down.
   d. The toilets in the diner often back up, and the sinks have only a trickle of water.

3   UNDERSTANDING THE TOPIC SENTENCE

As already explained, most paragraphs center around a main idea that is often expressed in a topic sentence. An effective topic sentence does two things. First, it gives the topic of the paragraph. Second, it expresses the writer's attitude or opinion or idea about the topic. For example, look at the following topic sentence:

• Falling in love involves enormous risks.

In this topic sentence, the topic is *falling in love*; the writer's idea about the topic is that falling in love *involves enormous risks*.

➤ *Activity*

For each topic sentence below, underline the topic and double-underline the point of view that the writer takes toward the topic.

> *Examples* <u>Our vacation</u> <u><u>turned out to be a disaster</u></u>.
>
> <u>The daily life of students</u> <u><u>is filled with conflicts</u></u>.

1. Gambling can be addictive.

2. My mother has always been generous.

3. Politicians are often self-serving.

4. The national speed limit should be raised.

5. Serious depression has several warning signs.

6. Insects serve many useful purposes.

7. Doctors are often insensitive.

8. Our dreams may contain symbols.

9. Owning a pet has a number of benefits.

10. High school students should be required to wear uniforms.

4   IDENTIFYING TOPICS, TOPIC SENTENCES, AND SUPPORT

The following activity will sharpen your sense of the differences among topics, topic sentences, and supporting sentences.

➤ *Activity*

Each group of items below includes one topic, one main idea (expressed in a topic sentence), and two supporting details for that idea. In the space provided, label each item with one of the following:

> *T* — for the topic
> *MI* — for the main idea
> *SD* — for the supporting details

1. _____ Staying in the sun too long can cause sunstroke.

   _____ People develop skin cancer after years of working on their suntans.

   _____ Time in the sun.

   _____ Spending time in the sun can be dangerous.

2. _____ One pitcher smooths the dirt on the pitcher's mound before he throws each pitch.

   _____ One infielder sits in the same spot on the dugout bench during every game.

   _____ Some baseball players think that certain superstitious habits help them win games.

   _____ Superstitious baseball players.

3. _____ The creakings of a house settling may sound like a monster coming out of a grave.

   _____ Nighttime noises can be frightening to children.

   _____ Gusts of wind rattling a bedroom window can sound like invaders about to break in.

   _____ Noises at night.

4. _____ Imagine your former sweetheart wearing a diaper or covered with smelly garbage.

   _____ Recovering from a broken romance.

   _____ Certain methods can help you recover from a broken romance.

   _____ Each time you find yourself thinking of the other person, stop yourself by banging a fist on the table.

5. _____ TV has begun to deal with sex in a more realistic way.

   _____ Couples on TV now openly discuss topics such as birth control.

   _____ Bedroom scenes are now being shown in detail on some TV shows.

   _____ TV's treatment of sex.

5 RECOGNIZING SPECIFIC DETAILS I

Specific details are examples, reasons, particulars, and facts. Such details are needed to support and explain a topic sentence effectively. They provide the evidence needed for us to understand, as well as to feel and experience, a writer's point.

Here is a topic sentence followed by two sets of supporting sentences. Which set provides sharp, specific details?

Topic sentence: Some poor people must struggle to make meals for themselves.

a. They gather up whatever free food items they can find in fast-food restaurants and take them home to use however they can. Instead of planning well-balanced meals, they base their diet on anything they can buy that is cheap and filling.

b. Some add hot water to the free packets of ketchup they get at McDonald's to make tomato soup. Others buy cans of cheap dog food and fry it like hamburger.

Explanation

The second set provides specific details: instead of a general statement about "free food items they find in fast-food restaurants and take . . . home to use however they can," we get a vivid detail we can see and picture clearly: "free packets of ketchup they get at McDonald's to make tomato soup."

Instead of a general statement about how the poor will "base their diet on anything they can buy that is cheap and filling," we get exact and vivid details: "Others buy cans of cheap dog food and fry it like hamburger."

Specific details are often like the information we find in a movie script. They provide us with such clear pictures that we could make a film of them if we wanted to. You would know just how to film the information given in the second cluster. You would show a poor person breaking open a McDonald's packet of ketchup and mixing it with water to make a kind of tomato soup. You would show someone opening a can of dog food and frying its contents like hamburger.

In contrast, the writer of the first cluster fails to provide the specific information needed. If you were asked to make a film based on the first cluster, you would have to figure out for yourself just what particulars you were going to show.

When you are working to provide specific supporting information in a paper, it might help to ask yourself, "Could someone easily film this information?" If the answer is "yes," you probably have good details.

➤ *Activity*

Each topic sentence below is followed by two sets of supporting details. Write *S* (for *specific*) in the space next to the set that provides specific support for the point. Write *G* (for *general*) next to the set that offers only vague, general support.

1. *Topic sentence:* My roommate is a messy person.

   _____ a. He doesn't seem to mind that he can't find any clean clothes or dishes. He never puts anything back in its proper place; he just drops it wherever he happens to be. His side of the room looks as if a hurricane had gone through.

   _____ b. His coffee cup is covered inside with a thick layer of green mold. I can't tell you what color his easy chair is; it has disappeared under a pile of dirty laundry. When he turns over in bed, I can hear the crunch of cracker crumbs beneath his body.

Hint: Which supporting set could you make a film of?

2. *Topic sentence:* Roberta is very aggressive.

_____ a. Her aggressiveness is apparent in both her personal and professional life. She is never shy about extending social invitations. And while some people are turned off by her aggressive attitude, others are impressed by it and enjoy doing business with her.

_____ b. When she meets a man she likes, she is quick to say, "Let's go out sometime. What's your phone number?" In her job as a furniture salesperson, she will follow potential customers out onto the sidewalk as she tries to convince them to buy.

3. *Topic sentence:* Our new kitten causes us lots of trouble.

_____ a. He has shredded the curtains in my bedroom with his claws. He nearly drowned when he crawled into the washing machine. And my hands look like raw hamburger from his playful bites and scratches.

_____ b. It seems he destroys everything he touches. He's always getting into places he doesn't belong. Sometimes he plays too roughly, and that can be painful.

4. *Topic sentence:* My landlord is a softhearted person.

_____ a. Even though he wrote them himself, he sometimes ignores the official apartment rules in order to make his tenants happy.

_____ b. Although the lease agreement states, "No pets," he brought my daughter a puppy after she told him how much she missed having one.

5. *Topic sentence:* The library is a distracting place to try to study.

_____ a. It's hard to concentrate when a noisy eight-person poker game is going on on the floor beside you. It's also distracting to overhear remarks like, "Hey, Baby, what's your mother's address? I want to send her a thank-you card for having such a beautiful daughter."

_____ b. Many students meet in the library to do group activities and socialize with one another. Others go there to flirt. It's easy to get more interested in all that activity than in paying attention to your studies.

6 RECOGNIZING SPECIFIC DETAILS II

➤ *Activity*

At several points in the following paragraphs you are given a choice of two sets of supporting details. Write *S* (for *specific*) in the space next to the set that provides specific support for the point. Write *G* (for *general*) next to the set that offers only vague, general support.

Paragraph 1

My daughter's boyfriend is a good-for-nothing young man. After knowing him for just three months, everyone in our family is opposed to the relationship.

For one thing, Russell is lazy.

_____ a. He is always finding an excuse to avoid putting in an honest day's work. He never pitches in and helps with chores around our house, even when he's asked directly to do so. And his attitude about his job isn't any better. To hear him tell it, he deserves special treatment in the workplace. He thinks he's gone out of his way if he just shows up on time.

_____ b. After starting a new job last week, he announced this Monday that he wasn't going to work because it was his <u>birthday</u>—just as if he is somebody special. And when my husband asked Russell to help put storm windows on the house next Saturday, Russell answered that he uses his weekends to catch up on sleep.

Another quality of Russell's which no one likes is that he is cheap.

_____ c. When my daughter's birthday came around, Russell said he would take her out to Baldoni's, a fancy Italian restaurant. Then he changed his mind. Instead of spending a lot of money on a meal, he said, he wanted to buy her a really nice pair of earrings. So my daughter cooked dinner for him at her apartment. But there was no present, not even a little one. He claims he's waiting for a jewelry sale at Macy's. I don't think my daughter will ever see that "nice gift."

_____ d. He makes big promises about all the nice things he's going to do for my daughter, but he never comes through. His words are cheap, and so is he. He's all talk and no action. My daughter isn't greedy, but it hurts her when Russell says he's going to take her someplace nice or give her something special and then nothing happens.

Worst of all, Russell is mean.

_____ e. Russell seems to get special pleasure from hurting people when he feels they have a weak point. I have heard him make remarks that to him were just funny but that were really very insensitive. You've got to wonder about someone who needs to be ugly to other people just for the sake of being powerful. Sometimes I want to let him know how I feel. Everyone in the family is waiting anxiously for the day when my daughter will see Russell the way the rest of us see him.

_____ f. When my husband was out of work, Russell said to him, "Well, you've got it made now, living off your wife." After my husband glared at him, he said, "Why're you getting sore? I'm just kidding." Sometimes he snaps at my daughter, saying things like "Don't make me wait—there are plenty of other babes who would like to take your place." At such times I want to blow off his head with a bazooka. Everyone in the family is waiting anxiously for the day when my daughter will see Russell the way the rest of us see him.

Paragraph 2

Many adult children move back in with their parents for some period of time. Although living with Mom and Dad again has some advantages, there are certain problems that are likely to arise.

One common problem is that children may expect their parents to do all the household chores.

_____ a. They never think that they should take on their share of work around the house. Not only do they not help with their parents' chores; they don't even take responsibility for the extra work that their presence creates. Like babies, they go through the house making a mess that the parents are supposed to clean up. It's as if they think their parents are their servants.

_____ b. They expect meals to appear on the table as if by magic. After they've eaten, they go off to work or play, never thinking about who's going to do the dishes. They drop their dirty laundry beside the washing machine, assuming that Mom will attend to it and return clean, folded clothes to their bedroom door. And speaking of their bedroom: every day they await the arrival of Mom's Maid Service to make the bed, pick up the floor, and dust the furniture.

Another problem that frequently arises is that parents forget their adult children are no longer adolescents.

_____ c. Parents like this want to know everything about their adult children's lives. They don't think their kids, even though they are adults, should have any privacy. Whenever they see their children doing anything, they want to know all the details. It's as though their children are still teenagers who are expected to report all their activities. Naturally, adult children get irritated when they are treated as if they were little kids.

_____ d. They may insist upon knowing far more about their children's comings and goings than the children want to share. For example, if such parents see their adult son heading out the door, they demand to know: Where is he going? Who will he be with? What will he be doing? What time will he be back? In addition, they may not let their adult child have any privacy. If their daughter and a date are sitting in the living room, for instance, they may join them there and start peppering the young man with questions about his family and his job, as if they were interviewing him for the position of son-in-law.

Finally, there may be financial problems when an adult child returns to live at home.

_____ e. Having an extra adult in the household creates extra expenses. But many adult children don't offer to help deal with those extra costs. Adult children often eat at home, causing the grocery bill to climb. They may stay in a formerly unused room, which now needs to be heated and lit. They produce extra laundry to be washed. They use the telephone, adding to the long-distance bill. For all these reasons, adult children should expect to pay a reasonable room and board fee to their parents.

_____ f. It's expensive to have another adult living in the household. Adult children would be paying a lot of bills on their own if they weren't staying with their parents. It's only fair that they share the expenses at their parents' house. They should consider all the ways that their living at home is increasing their parents' expenses. Then they should insist upon covering their share of the costs.

7 PROVIDING SPECIFIC DETAILS

➤ *Activity*

Each of the sentences that follow contains a general word or words, set off in *italic* type. Substitute sharp, specific words in each case.

> ***Example*** Before dinner I had *several things to do.*
>
> *Before dinner I had to wash the lunch dishes, do some homework,*
>
> *and call a garage about getting my car serviced.*

1. To pass the time in the hospital waiting area, I browsed through some *reading matter.*

   _____

   _____

2. When my marriage broke up, I felt *various emotions.*

   _____

   _____

3. In the car accident I suffered *a number of injuries.*

    _____

    _____

4. At the carnival we went on *several rides.*

    _____

    _____

5. While watching TV I like to eat *salty snacks.*

    _____

    _____

6. The cafeteria offered *several choices* for dessert.

    _____

    _____

7. Before we play cards, remove those *things* from the table.

    _____

    _____

8. My brother's room has *a lot of electronic equipment.*

    _____

    _____

9. *Bugs* invaded our kitchen and pantry this summer.

    _____

    _____

10. All last week, *the weather was terrible.*

    _____

    _____

8   SELECTING DETAILS THAT FIT

The details in your paper must all clearly relate to and support your opening point. If a detail does not support your point, leave it out. Otherwise, your paper will lack unity. For example, see if you can circle the letter of the two sentences that do *not* support the topic sentence below.

Topic sentence: Rita is a kind friend.

   a. When one of her friends is sick, Rita offers to help out by doing any needed grocery shopping.

   b. She has been known to go back to a store the day after buying something to return the excess change a clerk mistakenly gave her.

   c. Rita remembers her friends' birthdays and often arranges some sort of celebration.

   d. Although she makes a modest salary, Rita donates generously to various charities.

   e. She listens to her friends' troubles with patience and understanding.

Explanation

Returning money to a store clerk is not support for the idea that Rita is a kind *friend*, so sentence *b* does not support the topic sentence. Also, while Rita's donations to various charities (sentence *d*) help show she is generous, they do not support the idea of her being a kind friend. The other three statements all clearly back up the topic sentence—they are about how Rita treats her friends kindly.

➤ *Activity*

Circle the two items that do *not* support the topic sentence in each group below.

   1. *Topic sentence:* I'm a perfect example of someone who has "math anxiety."

       a. Fear of math is almost as widespread as fear of public speaking.

       b. I feel dread every time I sit down to take our Friday math quiz.

       c. During the math midterm, I "froze" and didn't even try to answer most of the questions.

       d. I also have a great deal of anxiety when I sit down to write a paper.

       e. I turned down a salesclerk job because I would have had to figure out how much change customers should get back.

   2. *Topic sentence:* Carpooling has various benefits for students.

       a. Their gas and parking expenses are lower in a car pool.

       b. Recent government regulations require some workers to use a car pool.

    c. Students who are not driving can study or sleep on the way.

    d. Traveling with other students provides companionship and support.

    e. Car pools become more popular during hard economic times.

3. *Topic sentence:* Drinking coffee can have unpleasant effects.

    a. Some people don't like the taste of decaffeinated coffees.

    b. Coffee in the evening can interfere with sleep at night.

    c. As addictions go, coffee is less dangerous than tobacco.

    d. Too much coffee can cause the hands to shake.

    e. Drinking too much coffee can lead to a faster heartbeat and lightheadedness.

4. *Topic sentence:* Some people have very poor telephone manners.

    a. They never identify themselves, but just begin the conversation.

    b. They often make their calls on cordless phones.

    c. They have an unlisted telephone number.

    d. They talk to people around them at the same time that they're talking on the phone.

    e. They often call around 6 p.m., which is most people's dinner hour.

5. *Topic sentence:* Convenience stores live up to their name.

    a. Convenience stores are close to home.

    b. At certain times of the day, there may be only one clerk available to both serve people and handle the cash register.

    c. Some convenience-store chains sell products under their own brand name.

    d. Convenience stores are open till late or all night.

    e. Parking is right outside.

9   PROVIDING DETAILS THAT FIT

➤ *Activity 1*

Each topic sentence below is followed by one item of support. See if you can add a second item in each case. Make sure your item truly supports the topic sentence.

1. *Topic sentence:* Lunch at that cafeteria is terrible.

    a. The french fries are always lukewarm and soggy.

    b. _____

2. *Topic sentence:* My little sister's room was a mess.

    a. Two of her dresses were lying on the floor, unbuttoned and inside out.

    b. _____

3. *Topic sentence:* The student lounge is an impossible place to try to study.

    a. A television is always blaring in one corner of the lounge.

    b. _____

4. *Topic sentence:* I had to deal with some rude behavior today.

    a. A teacher cut me off in the middle of a question.

    b. _____

5. *Topic sentence:* When I want people to like me, I do several things.

    a. I ask them a lot of questions about themselves, such as what they're taking in school.

    b. _____

➤ Activity 2

See if you can add two items of support for each of the topic sentences below.

1. *Topic sentence:* The car was extensively damaged in the accident.

    a. The windshield and the driver's side windows were shattered.

    b. _____

    c. _____

2. *Topic sentence:* I spent the night preparing for the history exam.

    a. From 10 p.m. to 2 a.m., I studied all the notes I took in class.

    b. _____

    c. _____

3. *Topic sentence:* My parents were very strict when I was growing up.

    a. I was allowed to watch TV for one hour a day, period.

    b. _____

    c. _____

4. *Topic sentence:* Yesterday there was a robbery at the bank where I work.

   a. Two men wearing aviator sunglasses pointed guns at us.

   b. _____

   c. _____

5. *Topic sentence:* There was a lot of storm damage in the town.

   a. Half of the basements in the town were flooded.

   b. _____

   c. _____

10   PROVIDING DETAILS IN A PARAGRAPH

➤ *Activity*

The following paragraph needs specific details to back up its three supporting points. In the spaces provided, write two or three sentences of convincing details for each supporting point.

An Unpleasant Eating Experience

My family and I will never eat again at the new neighborhood restaurant.

First of all, the service was poor. _____

_____

_____

_____

_____

Second, the prices were very high. _____

_____

_____

_____

_____

Most of all, the food was not very good. _____

_____

_____

_____

_____

11 OMITTING AND GROUPING DETAILS WHEN PLANNING A PAPER

One common way to develop material for a paper is to make up a list of details about your topic. The next steps are to (1) omit details that don't truly support your topic and (2) group together remaining details in logical ways. The ability to omit details that don't fit and to group together related details is part of learning how to write effectively.

See if you can figure out a way of putting the following details into three groups. Put an *A* in front of the details that go with one group, a *B* in front of the details that go with a second group, and a *C* in front of the details that make up a third group. Cross out the four details that do not relate to the topic sentence.

Topic sentence: The vacation was a disaster.

_____ Rental agent a cousin of mine

_____ The house a real disappointment

_____ Bedrooms the size of closets

_____ Rain four of the seven days we were there

_____ Daughter badly sunburned on one hazy day

_____ Dismal weather

_____ Glorious sunset only the last night we were there

_____ Air very humid

_____ Husband caught a virus and had days of digestive problems

_____ House not close to the lake but a half-mile hike

_____ Air conditioning did not work

_____ Too cold to go out in the evenings

_____ Large color television that worked well

_____ Medical problems

_____ Son badly cut his finger and had to get stitches at local hospital

_____ Landlord was sympathetic and gave us a discount

Explanation:

After thinking about the list for a while, you probably realized that the details about the house form one group: the house was a disappointment because it was not close to the lake, its bedrooms were the size of closets, and the air conditioning did not work. Details about the bad weather form another group: a lot of rain, humid air, and cold evenings. Finally, there are details about medical problems: a bad sunburn, a virus, and a cut finger.

The main idea—that the vacation was a disaster—can be supported with three kinds of evidence: a disappointing rental house, dismal weather, and medical problems. The other four items in the list do not logically go with any of these three groups and so should be omitted.

The two activities that follow will give you practice in omitting and grouping details.

➤ *Activity 1*

See if you can figure out a way of putting the following details into three groups. Put an *A* in front of the details that go with one group, a *B* in front of the details that go with a second group, and a *C* in front of the details that make up a third group. Cross out the four details that do not relate to the topic sentence.

Topic sentence: My return to school at the age of 38 has created special challenges for my family.

_____ School means extra work for my husband, Jack.

_____ Jack has to help kids with their homework.

_____ The children have been on the honor roll at school all year.

_____ Often impossible for me to be with the kids when they're sick.

_____ Could not attend my daughter's birthday party this year.

_____ School cuts into my time with my children.

_____ Jack gets tired of hearing stories of fellow students he doesn't know.

_____ Most of my fellow students are in their 20's.

_____ Jack has to bathe children and put them to bed.

_____ He worries I will get a "crush" on my teacher.

_____ Cooking dinner is something Jack now must do.

_____ No quiet time after dinner for Jack and me to talk about our day.

_____ School sometimes creates a strain between Jack and me.

_____ I haven't been to one of my son's Little League games.

_____ My employer pays most of my tuition.

_____ Jack once took an accounting course at the same college I attend.

➤ *Activity 2*

Follow the directions for Activity 1.

> *Topic sentence:* Living at home while going to school can be a very good idea.

_____ Home a quieter place to study than a noisy college dorm.

_____ It can produce better grades.

_____ Some students live at apartments near a college.

_____ It can be good for the relationship between a student and parents.

_____ Parents can begin to know student as an adult instead of a child.

_____ Parents and student will more easily find time just to talk.

_____ Parents usually charge a low fee for room and board.

_____ Some students live at home until they marry.

_____ Living at home means not paying to furnish an apartment or dorm room.

_____ It's economical to split the grocery bill with parents.

_____ It can be cheaper to live at home than on one's own.

_____ Students living at home will need a car or access to buses that go to school.

_____ At home, students aren't distracted by campus social activities.

_____ College roommates may encourage more goofing off than studying.

_____ College activities can help students meet new friends.

_____ Students can begin to appreciate parents as people, not just as parents.

12 USING TRANSITIONS

As already stated, transitions are signal words that help readers follow the direction of the writer's thought. To see the value of transitions, look at the two versions of the short paragraph below. Check the version that is easier to read and understand.

_____ To study a textbook more effectively, follow a few helpful steps. Preview the reading, taking a couple of minutes to get a quick sense of what the selection is about. Read and mark the selection, using a highlighter pen to set off important points. Write up a set of study notes that summarize the most important ideas in the selection. Go over and over the ideas in your notes until you know the material.

_____ To study a textbook more effectively, follow a few helpful steps. First, preview the reading, taking a couple of minutes to get a quick sense of what the selection is about. Next, read and mark the selection, using a highlighter pen to set off important points. Then write up a set of study notes that summarize the most important ideas in the selection. Finally, go over and over the ideas in your notes until you know the material.

You no doubt chose the second version. The time transitions—*first, next, then, finally*—emphasize the order in which the steps are to be done. The transitions also make clear when one step ends and the other begins.

➤ *Activity*

The following paragraphs use a listing order or a time order. Fill in the blanks with appropriate transitions from the box above each paragraph. Use every transition once.

In addition	First of all	Finally

1. My blind date with Walter was truly dreadful. _____, he was the rudest date I've ever had. Although he'd said he would pick me up at 7, he showed up at 7:35. Then he just sat in the driveway, gunning his engine. When he realized I wasn't going to walk out to the car, he came to the door and shouted through it, "Hey! You ready or what?" _____, he was just plain dumb. Throughout the evening, I tried everything to get a conversation going. But whenever I mentioned a book, a movie, a sport, or a news event, he would say, "Never heard of it." _____, he was cheap. When we sat down in the restaurant, he handed me a menu and said, "Don't order anything over five dollars." I learned a valuable lesson from my date with Walter—always bring enough money so you can take a bus home.

Then	While	After	When

2. To relieve the stress I feel after a day of work and school, I take the following steps. To start with, I get off the bus a mile from my apartment. I find a brisk walk helps me shake off the dragged-out feeling I often have at the day's end. _____ I get home, I make myself a cup of tea and lie down on the couch with my feet up. _____ I lie there, I often look through a catalog and imagine having the money to buy all the nice things I see. _____, if I've had an especially hard day, I run a deep bath with plenty of nice-smelling bath oil in it. _____ a good long soak in the hot water, I find the cares of the day have drifted away.

Another	Last of all	For one thing

3. There are several reasons why high schools should require students to wear uniforms. _____, uniforms would save money for parents and children. It would be a big relief for everyone if they could simply buy two or three inexpensive uniforms, instead of constantly shelling out for designer jeans and other high-priced clothes. _____ advantage of uniforms is that students would not have to spend time worrying about clothes. They would get up every day knowing what they were wearing to school, so they could concentrate more on schoolwork and less on making a fashion statement. _____, uniforms would make the division between rich and poor students less obvious. If wealthy students didn't show off their expensive clothes, and students from modest backgrounds didn't feel second-rate because of their lower-cost wardrobes, everyone would get along better.

Before	As	While	Then	When

4. An incident happened yesterday that made me very angry. I got off the bus and started walking the four blocks to my friend's house. _____ I walked along, I noticed a group of boys gathered on the sidewalk about a block ahead of me. _____ they saw me, they stopped talking. Suddenly nervous, I thought about crossing the street to avoid them. But as I came nearer and heard them start to whistle, a different feeling came over me. Instead of being afraid, I was suddenly angry. Why should I have to worry about being hassled just because I was a woman? I stared straight at the boys and continued walking. _____ the remarks started. "Oooh, baby. Looking fine today," said one. I ignored him. Next another one made a dirty remark about my underwear.

_____ I knew what I was doing, I turned on him. "Do you have a mother? Or any sisters?" I demanded. He looked astonished and didn't answer me. I went on. "Is it OK with you if men speak to them like that? Doesn't it bother you that they can't walk down the street without some creep bothering them?" _____ I was speaking, the other boys backed away. The one I was facing gave a nervous-sounding laugh, then backed away too. I kept walking. An hour later, I was still shaking with anger.

13 ORGANIZING DETAILS IN A PARAGRAPH

The supporting details in a paragraph must be organized in a meaningful way. The two most common methods of organizing details are to use a listing order and a time order. The activities that follow will give you practice in both methods of organization.

➤ *Activity 1*

Use *listing order* to arrange the scrambled list of sentences below. Number each supporting sentence 1, 2, 3, . . . so that you go from the least to the most important item.

Note that transitions will help by making clear the relationships between sentences.

Topic sentence: My after-school job has provided me with important benefits.

_____ Since the job is in the morning, it usually keeps me from staying up too late.

_____ Without the money I've earned, I would not have been able to pay my tuition.

_____ A second value of the job is that it's helped me make new friends.

_____ For one thing, it's helped me manage my time.

_____ One of my co-workers loves baseball as much as I do, and we've become sports buddies.

_____ The biggest advantage of the job is that it's allowed me to stay in school.

➤ *Activity 2*

Follow the directions for Activity 1.

Topic sentence: There are several reasons why people daydream.

_____ Some production line workers, for instance, might dream about running the company.

_____ Being without something also leads to daydreaming.

_____ For example, an angry student might dream about dropping his instructor out of a classroom window.

_____ A starving person will dream about food, or a poor person will dream about owning a house or car.

_____ One cause of daydreaming is boring jobs that are bearable only when workers imagine themselves doing something else.

_____ A final reason for daydreaming is to deal with angry feelings.

➤ *Activity 3*

Use *time order* to arrange the scrambled sentences below. Number the supporting sentences in the order in which they occur in time (1, 2, 3 . . .).

Note that transitions will help by making clear the relationships between sentences.

Topic sentence: There are several steps you can take to find an apartment.

_____ Check the classified ads and two or three real estate offices for apartments within your price range and desired location.

_____ When you have chosen your apartment, have a lawyer or a person who knows leases examine your lease before you sign it.

_____ Then make up a list of the most promising places.

_____ As you inspect each apartment, make sure that faucets, toilets, stove, and electrical outlets are working properly.

_____ After you have a solid list, visit at least five of the most promising apartments.

➤ *Activity 4*

Follow the directions for Activity 3.

Topic sentence: The story of a man named Gary can be an inspiration to many.

_____ By age seventeen he regularly came to school drunk.

_____ Gary's moment of truth came at age twenty-five, when he barely escaped death in a drunk-driving incident.

_____ After an intensive three-month treatment, he was free of alcohol for the first time in over ten years.

_____ Gary began stealing liquor from his parents when he was fourteen.

_____ He took advantage of being alcohol-free and returned to college and received a degree.

_____ Now he works as a counselor in the same treatment center that gave him his second chance.

_____ In his early twenties, he realized he was completely dependent on alcohol.

_____ Soon after the accident, he committed himself to a local alcohol-recovery center.

14   PREWRITING

These activities will give you practice in some of the prewriting strategies you can use to generate material for a paper.

➤ Activity 1: Freewriting

On a sheet of paper, freewrite for several minutes on the best or worst job you ever had. Don't worry about grammar, punctuation, or spelling. Without stopping, try to write about whatever comes into your head concerning your best or worst job.

➤ Activity 2: Questioning

On another sheet of paper, answer the following questions about your job.

- When did you have the job?
- Where did you work?
- What did you do?
- Whom did you work for?
- Why did you like or dislike the job? (Give one reason and some details that support that reason.)
- What is another reason you liked or disliked the job? What are some details that support the second reason?
- Can you think of a third reason you liked or did not like the job? What are some details that support the third reason?

➤ *Activity 3: Clustering*

In the center of a blank sheet of paper, write "best job" or "worst job" and circle it. Then, around the circle, add reasons and details about the job. Use a series of boxes, circles, or other shapes, along with connecting lines, to set off the reasons and details. In other words, try to think about and explore your topic in a very visual way.

➤ *Activity 4: List Making*

On separate paper, make a list of details about the job. Don't worry about putting them in a certain order. Just get down as many details about the job as occur to you. The list can include specific reasons you liked or did not like the job and specific details supporting those reasons.

15   OUTLINING, DRAFTING, AND REVISING A PAPER

Here you will get practice in the writing steps that follow prewriting: outlining, drafting, and revising the paper.

➤ *Activity 1: Scratch Outline*

Based on the list you have prepared, see if you can prepare a scratch outline made up of the three main reasons you liked or did not like the job.

_____ was the best or worst job I ever had.

Reason 1: _____

Reason 2: _____

Reason 3: _____

➤ *Activity 2: First Draft*

Now write a first draft of your paper. Begin with your topic sentence stating that a certain job was the best or worst one you ever had. Then state the first reason why it was such a job, followed by specific details that support that reason. Next, state the second reason, followed by specific details supporting that reason. Finally, state the third reason, followed with support.

Don't worry about grammar, punctuation, or spelling. Just concentrate on getting down on paper the details about the job. You may find it helpful to look at the first draft by Wanda (page 17) on why Helen was a terrible roommate.

➤ *Activity 3: Revising the Draft*

Ideally, you will have a chance to put the paper aside for a while before doing the second draft. In your second draft, try to do all of the following:

- Add transition words such as *first of all, another, and finally* to introduce each of the three reasons you liked or disliked the job.
- Omit any details that do not truly support your topic sentence.
- Add more details as needed, making sure you have plenty of specific support for each of your three reasons.
- In general, improve the flow of your writing.
- Be sure to include a final sentence that rounds off the paper, bringing it to a close.

➤ *Activity 4: Proofreading*

When you have your almost-final draft of the paper, proofread it in the following ways:

- Using your dictionary (or a spell-check program on your word processor), check any words that you think might be misspelled.
- Using Part Two of this book, check your paper for sentence-skills mistakes.
- Read the paper aloud, listening for awkward wordings and places where the meaning is unclear. Make the changes needed for the paper to read smoothly and clearly. Even better, see if you can get another person to read the draft aloud to you. The spots that this person has trouble reading are spots where you may have to do some rewriting.
- Take a sheet of paper and cover your paper, so that you can expose and carefully check one line at a time. Or, read the paper backwards, from the end of the paragraph to the beginning. Look for typos, omitted words, and other remaining errors.

Don't fail to do a careful proofreading. You may be tired of working on the paper at this point, but you want to make the extra effort needed to make the paper as good as possible. A final push can mean the difference between a higher and a lower grade.

16   DRAFTING AND REVISING PAPERS: MORE WRITING ASSIGNMENTS

Note: Your instructor may ask you to do some of the following paragraph writing assignments. Be sure to refer to the guidelines on the three preceding pages as you do your writing. Also, check the rules for paper form on pages 58–59.

➤ *Assignment 1: A Good or Bad Day in Your Life*

Write in detail about a recent good or bad day in your life—your activities, feelings, and experiences during the day. You might begin by making a list of things that you did, felt, saw, thought, heard, and said during that day. Your aim is to accumulate a great many details that you can draw upon later as you begin writing your paper. Making a long list is an excellent way to get started.

Then select and develop those details that best support the idea that the day was a good one or a bad one. Organize your paragraph using a time order—*first* this happened, *then* this, *next* this, and so on.

➤ Assignment 2: Directions to a Place

Write a set of specific directions on how to get from the English classroom to your house. Imagine you are giving these directions to a stranger who has just come into the room and who wants to deliver a million dollars to your home. You want, naturally, to give *exact* directions, including various landmarks that may guide the way, for the stranger does not know the area.

To help you write the paper, first make up a list of all the directions involved. Also, use words like *next, then,* and *after* to help the reader follow clearly as you move from one direction to the next.

➤ Assignment 3: Best or Worst Childhood Experience

Some of our most vivid memories are of things that happened to us as children, and these memories don't ever seem to fade. In fact, many elderly people say that childhood memories are clearer to them than things that happened yesterday. Think back to one of the best or worst experiences you had as a child. Try to remember the details of the event—sights, sounds, smells, textures, tastes.

You might begin by freewriting for ten minutes or so about good or bad childhood experiences. That freewriting may suggest to you a topic you will want to develop.

After you have decided on a topic, try to write a clear sentence stating what the experience was and whether it was one of the best or worst of your childhood. For example, "The time I was beaten up coming home from my first day in fifth grade was one of my worst childhood moments."

You may then find it helpful to make a list in which you jot down as many details as you can remember about the experience. Stick with a single experience, and don't try to describe too much. If a week you spent at summer camp was an unpleasant experience, don't try to write about the entire week. Just describe one horrible moment or event.

When you write the paper, use a time order to organize details: *first* this happened, *then* this, *next* this, and so on.

As you write, imagine that someone is going to make a short film based on your paragraph. Try to provide vivid details, quotations, and pictures for the filmmaker to shoot.

➤ *Assignment 4: A Problem on Campus*

Students on every college campus seem to have certain complaints about their school. They feel there are problems with grades, teachers, buildings, registration procedures, or security, for example. Write a paragraph about a problem on your campus.

You might begin by asking yourself a series of questions: What are some problems on campus? When do they occur? Where do they occur? Why do they occur? How do they affect people? As you answer such questions, you will gradually get a sense of a particular problem you may be able to write about.

State the problem in the first sentence of your paragraph. For example, you could begin, "The school library at Lincoln College is a distracting place to study." Then provide solid supporting details that support your statement. In your concluding sentence, you might mention a possible solution.

➤ *Assignment 5: A Special Photograph*

We tend to take photographs for granted, but they are magical things. They freeze moments forever, capturing small pieces of time within their borders. Find a photograph that has special meaning for you. Write a paper which describes the photograph and explains why it is special to you.

You might want to first describe the event, place, person or persons that the photograph shows. Then explain the special significance that the photograph has for you. Attach the photograph (or a photocopy of it) to the final draft of your paper.

➤ *Assignment 6: Hindsight*

Occasionally, we call someone a "Monday-morning quarterback." By this we mean that it's easy to say what *should* have been done after an event (or game) is over. But while we're in the midst of our daily lives, it's hard to know which is the right decision to make or what is the right course of action. We've all looked back and thought, "I wish I'd done . . ." or "I wish I'd said . . ."

Think back to a year or two ago. What is the best advice someone could have given you then? Freewrite for ten minutes or so about how your life might have changed if you have been given that advice.

Then go on to write a paper that begins with a topic sentence something like this, "I wish someone had told me a year ago to cut back a little on my work hours while I'm in college."

➤ *Assignment 7: Things to Accomplish in the Next Year*

Everyone has goals. Some goals, like graduating from college, are realistic; others, like winning a lottery, are mainly fantasy. Think about what you would like to accomplish between today and one year from today. Make the goals realistic ones which you might actually accomplish through determination, persistence, and hard work.

Start by making a list of a number of goals that would make sense for you in the next year. Here is one student's list:

- Get A's or B's in at least half my classes
- Lose ten pounds
- Get a better part-time job
- Take a typing course
- Stay away from people who are bad influences
- Cut down my TV time to ten hours a week
- Focus more on the future and less on old family problems
- Begin an exercise schedule
- Stop smoking

Begin your paper with a general point, such as, "There are three goals I intend to accomplish in the following year." Choose the goals from the list you've written, and develop each with specific details. For instance, the student mentioned above developed the idea of getting a better part-time job by writing, "For the past six months I've been working fifteen hours a week at the Burger Hut restaurant near my home. I get paid only an hourly rate there. One of my goals is to get another restaurant job where I can make money through tips as well."

Arrange the items in an order that makes sense to you. Save what you feel is the most important goal for last.

➤ Assignment 8: Parents and Children

It has been said that the older we get, the more we see our parents in ourselves. Indeed, any of our habits (good and bad), beliefs, and temperaments can often be traced to one of our parents.

Write a paragraph in which you describe three characteristics you have "inherited" from a parent. You might want to think about your topic by asking yourself a series of questions: "How am I like my mother (or father)?" "When and where am I like her (or him)?" "Why am I like her (or him)?"

One student who did such a paper used as her topic sentence the following statement: "Although I hate to admit it, I know that in several ways I'm just like my mom." She then went on to describe how she works too hard, worries too much, and judges other people too harshly. Another student wrote, "I resemble my father in my love of TV sports, my habit of putting things off, and my reluctance to show my feelings." Be sure to include examples for each of the characteristics you mention.

A FINAL NOTE

Detailed writing assignments follow each of the six readings in Part Three of the book. As you work on a given assignment, you will find it helpful to turn back to the writing guidelines on pages 47–49.

Part Two

Handbook of Grammar, Punctuation, and Usage Skills

Basic Punctuation and Paper Form

Seeing What You Know

A. Add the period (**.**), question mark (**?**), or exclamation mark (**!**) needed to end each of the following sentences. Use each punctuation mark once.

1. Those tomato plants need to be watered

2. When did you buy your motorcycle

3. Get away from that hornets' nest

B. Below is the beginning of a student essay on study groups. Circle the number of the title and first line that you think are punctuated correctly.

1.

	"Studying in Groups"
	Studying in groups has several advantages. First of all...

2.

	Studying in Groups.
	Studying in groups has several advantages. First of all...

3.

	Studying in Groups
	Studying in groups has several advantages. First of all...

Understanding the Answers

A. 1. Those tomato plants need to be watered**.**

This sentence makes a statement. Statements end with a period.

2. When did you buy your motorcycle**?**

This sentence asks a question. A direct question always gets a question mark.

3. Get away from that hornets' nest**!**

This sentence expresses strong feeling. Statements that express very strong feeling, such as fear, surprise, or urgency, end with an exclamation point.

B. Number 3 is correctly punctuated.

Titles should not be surrounded by quotation marks or followed by a period. A line should be skipped between the title and the first line. The first sentence of a paragraph should be set in from the margin about half an inch.

As you work your way through *Basic English Brushup*, your writing will become more and more skillful. This chapter reviews the basic punctuation you need to begin writing school papers. It also shows the form to use when writing your papers.

BEGINNING A SENTENCE

Begin each sentence with a **capital letter**.

- **My** four brothers share one bedroom.
- **A**bout 20 percent of the Earth is permanently frozen.
- **We** record movies overnight and watch them on the weekends.

ENDING A SENTENCE

The Period (.)

Use a **period** at the end of a statement, a mild command, or an indirect question.

- The children jumped over all the rain puddles.

  (A statement)

- Hand me the red pen.

  (A mild command)

- I wonder if there will be a surprise quiz today.

  (An indirect question)

The Question Mark (?)

Use a **question mark** after a sentence that asks a question.

- Are you ready for the exam?
- How did the car get scratched?
- "Can I have your phone number?" Susanne asked Phil.

Indirect questions tell the reader about questions rather than ask them directly. They end with periods, not question marks.

- The teacher asked if we were ready for the exam.
- I wonder how the car got scratched.
- Susanne asked Phil if she could have his phone number.

The Exclamation Point (!)

Use an **exclamation point** after a word or statement that expresses extreme emotion or that gives a strong command.

- Help!
- Wow!
- I just got a huge raise!
- Stop that thief!
- Don't you dare touch that dial!

Note: Exclamation points lose their power if they are used too frequently. Use them only when you wish to emphasize strong emotion.

➤ *Practice 1*

Rewrite each of the following sentences on the line provided. Add the capital letter as well as the period, question mark, or exclamation point needed in each sentence.

1. my car has trouble starting on cold mornings

   _____

2. how many courses are you taking this semester

   _____

3. that helicopter is going to crash

   _____

4. please fill out an application, and then take a seat

   _____

5. look out—he's got a gun

   _____

6. iced tea was first served at the 1904 World's Fair

   _____

7. can I use your computer

   _____

8. I asked my brother if I could use his computer

   _____

PREPARING A PAPER

Here are important guidelines for writing a paper.

The Title

Most of your school papers will begin with a title. The title of a typed paper should be about an inch and a half from the top of the page. The title of a handwritten paper should be on the top line of the first page. For example, here are the title and the opening part of a paper on the topic of shyness.

	A Shy Brother
	My older brother is the shyest person I know. Whenever
	there are more than two people in a group, he will stop talking.
	He has never raised his hand to answer a question in class...

Looking at the above example, identify each of the following statements as either true or false.

_____ 1. The title should be set off in quotation marks.

_____ 2. The title should have a period after it.

_____ 3. The title should be capitalized.

_____ 4. The title should be centered on the page.

_____ 5. A line should be skipped between the title and the first sentence.

You should have answered false for the first two items and true for the last three. Here is a checklist that summarizes how to handle a title:

• Type the title about an inch and a half below the top of the first page. For handwritten papers, put the title on the top line of the first page.
• Center the title.
• Do not use quotation marks around the title or put a period after the title.
• Capitalize each word in the title. (The only exceptions are small words such as *of, in,* or *for* in the middle of a title.)
• Skip a line between the title and the first sentence of the paper.

Indenting the First Line

The first line of a paragraph should be indented—that is, set in—about one-half inch from the left-hand margin. (Note the indentation of the first line of the paper on shyness.) Do not indent the other sentences in a paragraph.

Margins

Leave enough margin on all four sides of a paper to avoid a crowded look. The standard margins are about an inch and a half on the top and left side of the paper and an inch on the right and at the bottom.

Other Guidelines

1. Use full-sized paper (8½ by 11 inches).

2. Write or type on only one side of the paper.

3. Ideally, type your paper using double-spacing. But if you are writing by hand, do the following:

   • Use blue or black ink—never pencil.

   • Use wide-lined paper, or write on every other line of narrow-lined paper.

   • Write letters and punctuation marks as clearly as you can, taking care to distinguish between small and capital letters.

➤ *Practice 2*

What **five** corrections are needed in the student paper shown below? Explain the corrections in the spaces provided.

	Family meetings
	My family has found various ways to get along well. One way is having
	family meetings. We meet twice a month to discuss and handle our
	problems before they get out of hand. This has saved the members of
	my family a great deal of aggravation. For instance, when my brother . . .

1. _____

2. _____

3. _____

4. _____

5. _____

CHAPTER REVIEW

Answer each question by filling in the correct word or words in the space provided.

1. The first word of every sentence begins with a _____.

2. A sentence that makes a statement should end in a _____.

3. *True or false?* _____ A sentence that expresses extreme emotion should end in a period.

4. The _____ of a paper should be be centered on the page.

5. The first line of a paragraph should be _____.

Name_____   Section _____ Date _____

Score: (Number right) _____ x 10 = _____%

➤ *Basic Punctuation and Paper Form: Test 1*

A. Rewrite each of the following sentences on the line provided. Add the capital letter as well as the period, question mark, or exclamation point needed in each sentence.

Note: Hints are given for half of the sentences.

1. have you ever seen a shooting star
   This sentence asks a direct question.

   _____

2. why isn't Nina speaking to you

   _____

3. this ring sparkles in the sunlight
   The sentence makes a statement about the ring.

   _____

4. the tide gradually washed away the sandcastle

   _____

5. don't eat that bug in your salad
   This sentence expresses a strong emotion.

   _____

6. oh, no, the senator has collapsed

   _____

7. my son wondered if our fat male cat was pregnant
   This statement is an indirect question.

   _____

8. the salesman asked if he could come inside

   _____

B. What **two** corrections are needed in the student paper shown below? Explain the corrections in the spaces provided.

	"Our Worst Family Vacation"
	My family's trip to the Grand Canyon was a horrible experience for
	a number of reasons. First, our van broke down halfway there…

9. _____

10. _____

Name _____ Section _____ Date _____

Score: (Number right) _____ x 10 = _____ %

➤ *Basic Punctuation and Paper Form: Test 2*

A. Rewrite each of the following sentences on the line provided. Add the capital letter as well as the period, question mark, or exclamation point needed in each sentence.

1. how do I turn this computer on

   _____

2. potatoes were first discovered by the Spanish

   _____

3. run—the tornado is coming our way

   _____

4. tiny bugs have eaten the leaves of that plant

   _____

5. where are you going to college

   _____

6. I've just been bitten by a poisonous snake

   _____

7. do you know you just stepped on my glasses

   _____

8. call me when you get back in town

   _____

B. What **two** corrections are needed in the student paper shown below? Explain the corrections in the spaces provided.

	My Favorite Possession.
	Even though it is a dangerous machine, my motorcycle provides me
	with wonderful benefits. For one thing, driving a motorcycle is easy on
	the wallet. I can travel nearly sixty miles on just one gallon of gas…

9. _____

10. _____

Name_____ Section _____ Date _____

Score: (Number right) _____ x 10 = _____ %

➤ *Basic Punctuation and Paper Form: Test 3*

A. (1–5.) There are **five** errors in basic punctuation in the student paragraph below:

- 2 missing capital letters   • 1 missing period   • 1 missing question mark
- 1 missing exclamation point

Add the missing capital letters and marks of punctuation.

Hint: Use a sheet of paper to cover the paragraph. Then expose and read one line at a time, looking for the errors listed.

	"How I Raise My Children."
	I am raising my children very differently than my parents raised
	me. for one thing, there is only one situation in which I'll hit my
	kids. That is when they've done something dangerous, like run
	into traffic. even then, I would only smack them once on the rear
	end. My parents, though, would bellow about any little thing,
	"You're going to get it this time" They would then chase me
	around with a belt and use it when they caught me. Another
	thing I do with my kids is listen respectfully to them At times they
	ask silly things like "Why is that bird blue" But I don't ignore
	them or make fun of them. My parents, on the other hand, were
	likely to laugh at me when I asked simple childhood questions.

B. The student paragraph also contains **five** mistakes in paper form. List these mistakes in the spaces below.

6. _____

7. _____

8. _____

9. _____

10. _____

Name_____   Section _____   Date _____

Score: (Number right) _____ x 10 = _____ %

➤ *Basic Punctuation and Paper Form: Test 4*

A. (1–5.) There are **five** errors in basic punctuation in the student paragraph below:

- 2 missing capital letters   • 1 missing period   • 1 missing question mark
- 1 missing exclamation point

Add the missing capital letters and marks of punctuation.

	"My Worst Vacation."
	My worst vacation took place when some friends offered our
	family their house on a lake. Unfortunately, two days before we
	arrived, a bad storm hit We thought that since the house was not
	damaged, our vacation could go on. but once we were at the
	lake, we found no electricity and the beach half under water. My
	dad and I spent half our first day trying to buy basic necessities
	such as ice. store owners asked us, "Are you folks kidding"
	They then explained that they had been sold out for days. We
	drove unhappily back to the house, only to hear my mother
	calling out to us, "Hurry up inside The twins are sick." Sure
	enough, my little brothers were both throwing up. What a
	wonderful week it was—not.

B. The student paragraph also contains **five** mistakes in paper form. List these mistakes in the spaces below.

6. _____

7. _____

8. _____

9. _____

10. _____

Parts of Speech

Seeing What You Know

Fill in each answer space with a word that makes sense within the sentence.

1. A _____ was blown across our yard during the wind storm.

2. Ray saw a good used car on Monday and drove _____ home that evening.

3. Carla _____ the heavy bag of groceries.

4. The rug _____ the hotel lobby is ugly.

5. Our boss wore a _____ suit to work today.

6. Michele drove _____ on the ice-covered road.

7. My father made breakfast, _____ I washed the dishes.

Understanding the Answers

1. To complete this sentence, you must use a **noun**. A noun names a person, place, or thing. Among the possible choices are *chair, ball,* or *tire.*

2. To complete this sentence, use a **pronoun**. A pronoun is a word that stands for a noun. The words *the car* would fit in the slot, but the sentence is less wordy with the pronoun *it.*

3. To complete this sentence, use a **verb**. A verb is a word that gives the action of the sentence. You could use a verb such as *dropped, carried,* or *packed.*

4. Use the word *in* to complete this sentence. The word *in* is a **preposition**. It connects the word *lobby* to the word *rug* to tell us that the rug is located in the hotel lobby.

5. You need an **adjective** to complete this sentence. An adjective is a word that describes a noun. In this case, you need a word to describe the noun *suit.* Among the many possible choices are *old, new,* or *brown.*

6. To complete this sentence, you need an **adverb**. An adverb is a word that describes a verb, adjective, or another adverb. In this case, the adverb describes the verb *drove.* You could, for instance, use *slowly* or *carefully.*

7. You can use either *and* or *so* here. These words are known as **conjunctions**. They connect parts of a sentence. Here, the conjunction connects *My father made breakfast* to *I washed the dishes.*

Words—the building blocks of sentences—can be divided into seven major parts of speech.* **Parts of speech** are classifications of words according to their meaning and use in a sentence. The parts of speech are as follows:

nouns	**prepositions**	**adverbs**
pronouns	**adjectives**	**conjunctions**
verbs		

This chapter will explain each of these seven parts of speech.

1   NOUNS

A **noun** is a word that is used to name something: a person, a place, an object, or an idea. Here are some examples of nouns:

Nouns

woman	city	pancake	freedom
Janet Reno	street	diamond	possibility
Michael Jordan	Chicago	Corvette	mystery

Most nouns begin with a lowercase letter and are known as **common nouns.** These nouns name general things.

Some nouns, however, begin with a capital letter. They are called **proper nouns.** While a common noun refers to a person or thing in general, a proper noun names someone or something specific. For example, *woman* is a common noun—it doesn't name a particular woman. On the other hand, *Janet Reno* is a proper noun because it names a specific woman.

➤ *Practice 1*

Insert a noun into each of the following blanks.

1. The shoplifter stole a _____ from the department store.

2. _____ threw the football to me.

3. Tiny messages were scrawled on the _____.

4. A _____ crashed through the window.

5. Give the _____ to Ellen.

---

*There is also an eighth part of speech called an **interjection**. Interjections are words that can stand independently and are used to express emotion. Examples are *oh, wow, ouch,* and *oops.* These words are usually not found in formal writing.

Singular and Plural Nouns

Singular nouns name one person, place, object, or idea. **Plural nouns** refer to two or more persons, places, objects, or ideas. Most singular nouns can be made plural with the addition of an *s*.

Some nouns, like *box*, have irregular plurals. You can check the plural of nouns you think may be irregular by looking up the singular form in a dictionary.

Singular	*Plural*
goat	goats
alley	alleys
friend	friends
truth	truths
box	boxes

➤ *Practice 2*

Underline the three nouns in each sentence. The nouns you find may be singular or plural.

1. Two bats swooped over the heads of the frightened children.

2. The artist has purple paint on her sleeve.

3. The lost dog has fleas and a broken leg.

4. Gwen does her homework in green ink.

5. Some farmers plant seeds by moonlight.

2 PRONOUNS

A **pronoun** is a word that stands for a noun. Pronouns eliminate the need for constant repetition. Look at the following sentences:

- The phone rang, and Bill answered the phone.
- Lisa met Lisa's friends in the record store at the mall. Lisa meets Lisa's friends there every Saturday.
- The waiter rushed over to the new customers. The new customers asked the waiter for menus and coffee.

Now look at how much clearer and smoother the sentences sound with pronouns.

- The phone rang, and Bill answered **it**.

(The pronoun *it* is used to replace the word *phone*.)

- Lisa met **her** friends in the record store at the mall. **She** meets **them** there every Saturday.

    (The pronoun *her* is used to replace the word *Lisa's*. The pronoun *she* replaces *Lisa*. The pronoun *them* replaces the words *Lisa's friends*.)

- The waiter rushed over to the new customers. **They** asked **him** for menus and coffee.

    (The pronoun *they* is used to replace the words *the new customers*. The pronoun *him* replaces the words *the waiter*.)

Following is a list of commonly used pronouns:

Pronouns

I	you	he	she	it	we	they
me	your	him	her	its	us	them
my	yours	his	hers		our	their

➤ *Practice 3*

Fill in each blank with the appropriate pronoun.

1. Andrew feeds his pet lizard every day before school. _____ also gives _____ flies in the afternoon.

2. The female reporter interviewed the striking workers. _____ told _____ about their demand for higher wages and longer breaks.

3. Students should save all returned tests. _____ should also keep _____ review sheets.

4. The pilot announced that we would fly through some air pockets. _____ said that we should be past _____ soon.

5. Randy returned the calculator to Sheila last Friday. But Sheila insists _____ never got _____ back.

3 VERBS

Every complete sentence must contain at least one verb. There are two types of verbs: action verbs and linking verbs.

Action Verbs

An **action verb** tells what is being done in a sentence. For example, look at the following sentences:

- Mr. Jensen **swatted** at the bee with his hand.
- Rainwater **poured** into the storm sewer.
- The children **chanted** the words to the song.

In these sentences, the verbs are *swatted, poured,* and *chanted.* These words are all **action verbs**; they tell what is happening in each sentence. (You will learn more about action verbs in "Subjects and Verbs" on page 85.)

➤ *Practice 4*

Insert a word into each blank. That word will be an action verb; it will tell what is happening in the sentence.

1. The surgeon _____ through the first layer of skin.

2. The animals in the cage _____ all day.

3. The elderly woman on the street _____ me for directions.

4. The boy next door _____ our lawn every other week.

5. The instructor _____ the student papers.

Linking Verbs

Some verbs are **linking verbs**. These verbs link (or join) a noun to something that is said about it. For example, look at the following sentence:

- The clouds **are** steel gray.

In this sentence, *are* is a linking verb. It joins the noun *clouds* to words that describe it: *steel gray.*

Other common linking verbs include *am, is, was, were, look, feel, sound, appear, seem,* and *become.* (Linking verbs are explained further in "Subjects and Verbs" on pages 86–87.)

➤ *Practice 5*

Into each slot, insert one of the following linking verbs: *am, feel, is, look, were.* Use each linking verb once.

1. I _____ anxious to get my test back.

2. The important papers _____ in a desk drawer.

3. The grapes _____ as if they are not quite ripe.

4. The grocery store _____ usually open until 11 p.m.

5. Whenever I _____ angry, I go off by myself to calm down.

Helping Verbs

Sometimes the verb of a sentence consists of more than one word. In these cases, the main verb will be joined by one or more **helping verbs**. Look at the following sentence.

- The basketball team **will be leaving** for their game at six o'clock.

In this sentence, the main verb is *leaving*. The helping verbs are *will* and *be*.

Other helping verbs include *do, has, have, may, would, can, must, could,* and *should.* (You will learn more about helping verbs in "Subjects and Verbs" on pages 87–88.)

➤ *Practice 6*

Into each slot, insert one of the following helping verbs: *does, must, should, could,* and *has been.* Use each helping verb once.

1. You _____ start writing your paper this weekend.

2. The victim _____ describe her attacker in great detail.

3. You _____ rinse the dishes before putting them into the dishwasher.

4. My neighbor _____ arrested for drunk driving.

5. The bus driver _____ not make any extra stops.

4 PREPOSITIONS

A **preposition** is a word that connects a noun or a pronoun to another word in the sentence. For example, look at the following sentence:

- A man **in** the bus was snoring loudly.

In is a preposition. It connects the noun *bus* to *man.* Here is a list of common prepositions:

Prepositions

about	before	down	like	toward
above	behind	during	of	under
across	below	except	off	up
after	beneath	for	on	with
among	beside	from	over	without
around	between	in	through	
at	by	into	to	

The noun or pronoun that a preposition connects to another word in the sentence is called the **object** of the preposition. A group of words that begins with a preposition and ends with its object is called a **prepositional phrase**. The words *in the bus*, for example, are a prepositional phrase.

Now read the following sentences and explanations.

- An ant was crawling **up the teacher's leg**.

Explanation: The noun *leg* is the object of the preposition *up*. *Up* connects *leg* with the word *crawling*. The prepositional phrase *up the teacher's leg* describes *crawling*. It tells just where the ant was crawling.

- The man **with the black moustache** left the restaurant quickly.

Explanation: The noun *moustache* is the object of the preposition *with*. The prepositional phrase *with the black moustache* describes the word *man*. It tells us exactly which man left the restaurant quickly.

- The plant **on the windowsill** was a present **from my mother**.

Explanation: The noun *windowsill* is the object of the preposition *on*. The prepositional phrase *on the windowsill* describes the word *plant*. It describes exactly which plant was a present.

There is a second prepositional phrase in this sentence. The preposition is *from,* and its object is *mother.* The prepositional phrase *from my mother* explains *present.* It tells who gave the present.

➤ *Practice 7*

Into each slot, insert one of the following prepositions: *of, by, with, in*, and *without*. Use each preposition once.

1. The letter from his girlfriend had been sprayed _____ perfume.

2. The weedkiller quickly killed the dandelions _____ our lawn.

3. _____ giving any notice, the tenant moved out of the expensive apartment.

4. Donald hungrily ate three scoops _____ ice cream and an order of French fries.

5. The crates _____ the back door contain glass bottles and old newspapers.

5 ADJECTIVES

An **adjective** is a word that describes a noun (the name of a person, place, or thing). Look at the following sentence.

- The dog lay down on a mat in front of the fireplace.

Now look at this sentence when adjectives have been inserted.

- The **shaggy** dog lay down on a **worn** mat in front of the fireplace.

The adjective *shaggy* describes the noun *dog*; the adjective *worn* describes the noun *mat*. Adjectives add spice to our writing. They also help us to identify particular people, places, or things.

Adjectives can be found in two places in a sentence:

1 An adjective may come before the word it describes (a **damp** night, the **moldy** bread, a **striped** umbrella).

2 An adjective may come after a linking verb. The linking verb may be a form of the verb *be* (he is **furious**, I am **exhausted**, they are **hungry**). Other linking verbs include *feel, look, sound, smell, taste, appear, seem,* and *become* (the soup tastes **salty**, your hands feel **dry**, the dog seems **lost**).

➤ *Practice 8*

Write an adjective in each slot.

1. The _____ pizza was eaten greedily by the _____ teenagers.

2. Melissa gave away the sofa because it was _____ and

   _____ .

3. Although the alley is _____ and _____ , Karen often takes it as a shortcut home.

4. The restaurant throws away lettuce that is _____ and

   tomatoes that are _____ .

5. When I woke up in the morning, I had a _____ fever and

   a(n) _____ throat.

6 ADVERBS

An **adverb** is a word that describes a verb, an adjective, or another adverb. Many adverbs end in the letters *ly*. Look at the following sentence:

- The canary sang in the pet store window as the shoppers greeted each other.

Now look at this sentence after adverbs have been inserted.

- The canary sang **softly** in the pet store window as the shoppers **loudly** greeted each other.

The adverbs add details to the sentence. They also allow the reader to contrast the singing of the canary to the noise the shoppers are making.

Look at the following sentences and the explanations of how adverbs are used in each case.

- The chef yelled **angrily** at the young waiter.

  (The adverb *angrily* describes the verb *yelled*.)

- My mother has an **extremely** busy schedule on Tuesdays.

  (The adverb *extremely* describes the adjective *busy*.)

- The sick man spoke **very** faintly to his loyal nurse.

  (The adverb *very* describes the adverb *faintly*.)

Some adverbs do not end in *-ly*. Examples include *very, often, never, always,* and *well.*

➤ *Practice 9*

Fill in each slot with an adverb.

1. The water in the pot boiled _____.

2. Carla _____ drove the car through _____ moving traffic.

3. The telephone operator spoke _____ to the young child.

4. The game show contestant waved _____ to his family in the audience.

5. Wes _____ studies, so it's no surprise that he did _____ poorly on his finals.

7 CONJUNCTIONS

Conjunctions are words that connect. There are two types of conjunctions, coordinating and subordinating.

Coordinating Conjunctions (Joining Words)

Coordinating conjunctions join two equal ideas. Look at the following sentence:

- Kevin **and** Steve interviewed for the job, **but** their friend Anne got it.

In this sentence, the coordinating conjunction *and* connects the proper nouns *Kevin* and *Steve*. The coordinating conjunction *but* connects the first part of the sentence, *Kevin and Steve interviewed for the job*, to the second part, *their friend Anne got it.*

On the next page is a list of all the coordinating conjunctions. In this book, they will simply be called *joining words.*

Coordinating Conjunctions (Joining Words)

and	so	nor	yet
but	or	for	

➤ *Practice 10*

Write a coordinating conjunction in each slot. Choose from the following: *and, but, so, or,* and *nor.* Use each conjunction once.

1. Either Jerome _____ Alex scored the winning touchdown.

2. I expected roses for my birthday, _____ I received a vase of plastic tulips from the discount store.

3. The cafeteria was serving liver and onions for lunch, _____ I bought a sandwich at the corner deli.

4. Marian brought a pack of playing cards _____ a pan of brownies to the company picnic.

5. Neither my sofa _____ my armchair matches the rug in my living room.

Subordinating Conjunctions (Dependent Words)

When a **subordinating conjunction** is added to a sentence, the words can no longer stand alone as an independent sentence. In other words, they are no longer a complete thought. For example, look at the following sentence:

- Karen fainted in class.

See what happens to the sentence when a subordinating conjunction is added:

- When Karen fainted in class

Now the words cannot stand alone as a sentence. They are dependent on other words to complete the thought:

- When Karen fainted in class, we put her feet up on some books.

On the next page are some common subordinating conjunctions. (In this book, they will simply be called *dependent words.*)

Subordinating Conjunctions (Dependent Words)

after	even if	unless	where
although	even though	until	wherever
as	if	when	whether
because	since	whenever	while
before	though		

Here are some more sentences with subordinating conjunctions:

• **After** she finished her last exam, Joanne said, "Now I can relax."

(*After she finished her last exam* is not a complete thought. It is dependent on the rest of the words to make up a complete sentence.)

• Lamont listens to books on tape **while** he drives to work.

(*While he drives to work* cannot stand by itself as a sentence. It depends on the rest of the sentence to make up a complete thought.)

• **Since** apples were on sale, we decided to make an apple pie for dessert.

(*Since apples were on sale* is not a complete sentence. It depends on *we decided to make an apple pie for dessert* to complete the thought.)

➤ Practice 11

Write a subordinating conjunction in each slot. Choose from the following: *even though, because, until, when,* and *before.* Use each conjunction once.

1. The bank was closed down by federal regulators _____ it lost more money than it earned.

2. _____ Paula wants to look mysterious, she wears dark sunglasses and a scarf.

3. _____ the restaurant was closing in fifteen minutes, customers sipped their coffee slowly and continued to talk.

4. _____ anyone could answer it, Carl rushed to the phone and whispered, "It's me."

5. The waiter was instructed not to serve any food _____ the guest of honor arrived.

CHAPTER REVIEW

Identify each part of speech by writing in the letter of the correct definition.

_____ 1. noun   a. A word that connects

_____ 2. pronoun   b. A word that describes a noun

_____ 3. verb   c. A word that describes a verb, an adjective, or
                                 an adverb

_____ 4. preposition   d. A word that expresses action or that links

_____ 5. adjective   e. The name of a person, place, thing, or idea

_____ 6. adverb   f. A word that connects a noun or pronoun to
                                 another word

_____ 7. conjunction   g. A word that stands for a noun

Name_____   Section _____   Date _____

Score: (Number right) _____ x 10 = _____%

➤ *Parts of Speech: Test 1*

Note: Hints are given for half of the items.

A. Fill in each slot with a word that makes sense in the sentence. The part of speech of the word needed in each case is given in parentheses.

1. The sailors *(preposition)* _____ the ship's deck could see a giant

   (noun) _____ in the water below.
   In the first slot, write a word connecting *sailors* to *deck*. (*Deck* is the object of the missing preposition.)

2. My nephew drinks three glasses of soda *(coordinating conjunction)*

   _____ then burps as *(adverb)* _____ as he can.
   This sentence has two action verbs (*drinks, burps*). Write a word in the first slot that connects the two actions.

3. The star pitcher for the women's softball team *(verb)* _____ as

   (pronoun) _____ accepted the trophy.
   In the first slot, write a word telling what the star pitcher did.

B. In each sentence below, **two** words have been boldfaced. Identify each word as one of the following: *noun, pronoun, verb, preposition, adjective, adverb, conjunction.*

4. A lonely stray cat **meowed** softly from **under** a bush in the garden.

   meowed: _____   *under:* _____
   Meowed is what the stray cat did.

5. The coach became **angry** when he learned that three of **his** players had decided to skip practice.

   angry: _____   *his:* _____
   Angry describes the coach.

Name_____   Section _____ Date _____

Score: (Number right) _____ x 10 = _____%

➤ *Parts of Speech: Test 2*

A. Fill in each slot with a word that makes sense in the sentence. The part of speech of the word needed in each case is given in parentheses.

1. The child whimpered *(adverb)* _____ as the school nurse

   examined his *(adjective)* _____ elbow.

2. A hairy *(noun)* _____ crawled slowly along the side

   (preposition) _____ the shed.

3. The pilot *(verb)* _____ as the plane bounced through

   (adjective) _____ wind currents.

B. In each sentence below, **two** words have been boldfaced. Identify each word as one of the following: *noun, pronoun, verb, preposition, adjective, adverb, conjunction.*

4. The guitar **is** dented and scratched, but its sound is **clear** and soothing.

   is: _____   *clear:* _____

5. Since my grandmother bought a red convertible, **she** drives her friends **to** the beach every day.

   she: _____   *to:* _____

Name_____ Section _____ Date _____

Score: (Number right) _____ x 10 = _____%

➤ *Parts of Speech: Test 3*

Note: Hints are given for half of the items.

A. Fill in each slot with a word that makes sense in the sentence. The part of speech of the word needed in each case is given in parentheses.

1. Two cars had crashed on the *(adjective)* _____ road. Pieces

    of *(noun)* _____ were scattered all over the highway.
    In the first slot, write a word describing the road on which the crash had occurred.

2. The job applicant *(adverb)* _____ took a last look at herself

    in the mirror. Then she left the ladies' room and *(verb)* _____
    toward the office where the job interview would take place.
    Add a word in the first slot describing how she looked at herself.

B. In each short passage below, **two** words have been boldfaced. Identify each word as one of the following: *noun, pronoun, verb, preposition, adjective, adverb, conjunction.*

3. Business has been bad this year, **so** all the mall stores are having sales this week. Shoppers can save up to 50 percent **on** furniture and clothing.

    so: _____   *on:* _____
    So connects the first part of the sentence, *Business has been bad this year*, to the second part, *all the mall stores are having sales this week.*

4. Each morning, the bus makes many sudden stops on its **busy** route. Despite all the stops, passengers sleep, read the newspaper, and even drink hot **coffee**.

    busy: _____   *coffee:* _____
    Busy describes the bus's route in the morning.

5. Several grade school children knocked over some tombstones in the graveyard. They also **stomped** on the flowers planted there. When the police caught them, they said their friends had dared **them** to do it.

    stomped: _____   *them:* _____
    Stomped is what the children did.

Name_____ Section _____ Date _____

Score: (Number right) _____ x 10 = _____%

➤ *Parts of Speech: Test 4*

A. Fill in each slot with a word that makes sense in the sentence. The part of speech of the word needed in each case is given in parentheses.

1. Lena thought she had lost her *(noun)* _____. She looked all

   over the garage floor and *(preposition)* _____ the car seats. Then she found them in her pocket.

2. A bright light shines on the patient's body. As machines *(adverb)*

   _____ keep track of the patient's heart rate, a nurse hands

   the surgeon a *(adjective)* _____ scalpel. With great care, the surgeon marks the patient's chest for the first cut.

B. In each short passage below, **two** words have been boldfaced. Identify each word as one of the following: *noun, pronoun, verb, preposition, adjective, adverb, conjunction.*

3. The woman at the deli is very **good** at her job. She can spread mustard on a ham sandwich, add up a customer's bill, **and** answer the phone—all at the same time.

   good: _____   *and:* _____

4. Be careful when you **travel** down Maple Road. There are deep potholes for the first half mile. Then the road makes a sharp curve. Finally, there is a railroad crossing. Often, however, the warning lights don't work, so listen **closely** before you cross.

   travel: _____   *closely:* _____

5. **During** the storm, the family huddled together in their basement. As the winds howled, they told ghost stories by candlelight. Later, the frightened children thought **they** heard screams in the wind.

   During: _____   *they:* _____

Subjects and Verbs

Seeing What You Know

In each blank, insert a word that makes sense. Then read the explanations below.

1. The little _____ on the corner _____ for the bus.

2. A _____ in the back of the classroom _____ a very strange question.

3. The white _____ suddenly _____ into the middle lane.

4. _____ should never _____ during a job interview.

Understanding the Answers

Each word that you have added is either the subject or the verb of the sentence. Here are some completed versions of the sentences:

1. The little **children** *(subject)* on the corner **waited** *(verb)* for the bus.

    Children are what the sentence is about. *Waited* is what they did.

2. A **student** *(subject)* in the back of the classroom **asked** *(verb)* a very strange question.

    A *student* is what the sentence is about. *Asked* (a question) is what he or she did.

3. The white **truck** *(subject)* suddenly **moved** *(verb)* into the middle lane.

    The *truck* is what the sentence is about. *Moved* is what the truck did.

4. **People** *(subject)* **should** never **argue** *(verb)* during a job interview.

    People are the ones the sentence is about. *Should argue* is what the sentence says people should never do during an interview. (*Never* is not part of the verb.)

Subjects and verbs are the basic parts of any sentence. This chapter explains what subjects and verbs are and how to find them.

FINDING THE SUBJECT

Look at the following sentences. Which word do you think is the subject of each?

- Gloria wrote her answers on the blackboard.
- The balloons drifted slowly to earth.
- He won a stuffed bear at the carnival.
- Danger goes hand in hand with police work.

The **subject** of a sentence is the person, place, thing, or idea that the sentence is about. The subject can be called the "who or what" word. To find a sentence's subject, ask yourself, "Who or what is this sentence about?" or "Who or what is doing something in this sentence?"

Let's look again at the sentences above.

- Who is the first one about? *Gloria.* (That's who wrote.)
- What is the second one about? *Balloons.* (They're what drifted slowly.)
- Who is the third one about? *He.* (That's who won a stuffed bear.)
- What is the fourth one about? *Danger.* (That's what goes hand in hand with police work.)

So in the sentences above, the subjects are *Gloria, balloons, he,* and *Danger.*

Each of these subjects is either a **noun** (the name of a person, place, or thing—including a quality or idea) or a **pronoun.** As you may recall from "Parts of Speech," a pronoun is a word—such as *I, you he, she it, we,* or *they*—that stands for a noun. *The subject of a sentence will always be either a noun or a pronoun.*

➤ Practice 1

Add an appropriate word to each blank. The word that you insert will be the subject of the sentence. It will tell *who or what* the sentence is about.

1. A _____ crept through the dark house.

2. Only three _____ are left in the refrigerator.

3. A _____ suns himself on a log.

4. David's gold _____ glittered in the sunlight.

5. My _____ reminded me to wear suntan lotion.

6. Several _____ were crowded into the small cage.

7. _____ ate the raspberries right from the box.

8. _____ is my favorite school subject.

9. Without a sound, a _____ grabbed the field mouse by the neck.

10. My mother never went to college. _____ has always felt bad about that.

The Subject and Prepositional Phrases

The subject of a sentence is never part of a prepositional phrase. As you may recall from "Parts of Speech," a **prepositional phrase** is a group of words that begins with a preposition (a word like *in, from, of,* or *with*) and ends with a noun or pronoun (the object of the preposition). Here are a few examples of prepositional phrases:

- in the house
- from the bakery
- of the world
- with your permission

Following is a list of some common prepositions:

Prepositions

about	before	down	like	toward
above	behind	during	of	under
across	below	except	off	up
after	beneath	for	on	with
among	beside	from	over	without
around	between	in	through	
at	by	into	to	

Now look at the sentence below. What is the subject? Write your answer here:

_____.

- A bunch of green grapes fell onto the supermarket floor.

The answer is *bunch*, but many people would be tempted to choose *grapes*. In this case, however, *grapes* is part of the prepositional phrase "of green grapes," so it cannot be the subject.

As you look for the subject of a sentence, it may help to cross out the prepositional phrases. For example, look at the following sentences. In each sentence, find the prepositions and cross out the prepositional phrases. Then underline the subject.

- The models at the fashion show dressed in brightly-colored suits.

  The prepositions are *at* and *in.* So the prepositional phrases *at the fashion show* and *in brightly-colored suits* should be crossed out. Then you are left with the sentence *The models dressed.* Now you can ask yourself, "*Who* dressed?" The answer, *models*, is the subject of this sentence.

- The man, with shaking hands, poured the pills from the brown bottle.

  The prepositions are *with* and *from.* Cross out *with shaking hands* and *from the brown bottle*, and you are left with the sentence *The man poured the pills.* Ask yourself, "*Who* poured the pills?" The answer, *man*, is the subject of the sentence.

- A student in the class fell asleep during the long lecture.

  In and *during* are prepositions. You should have crossed out the prepositional phrases *in the class* and *during the long lecture.* When you do this, you are left with the sentence *A student fell asleep.* Ask yourself, "*Who* fell asleep?" The answer, *student*, is the subject of the sentence.

➤ *Practice 2*

Cross out the one prepositional phrase in each sentence. Then underline the subject of the sentence.

> *Example*   The pack ~~of cookies~~ disappeared quickly.

1. The blueberries in this pie are bitter.

2. A crowd swarmed around the injured boy.

3. The woman with a pierced nose is my hairdresser.

4. Leaves from our neighbor's tree covered our lawn.

5. During the school play, Betsy lost her voice.

6. A flyer was stuck in our mailbox door.

7. The dust under your bed contains tiny creatures.

8. Some of our roof shingles are loose.

9. Strange shows are broadcast on late-night TV.

10. One of my best friends is a computer programmer.

A Note on Singular and Plural Subjects

In addition to spotting subjects, you should note whether a subject is **singular** (one) or **plural** (more than one). Most plural subjects simply end in *s*:

Singular: The **car** in front of us is speeding.

Plural: The **cars** in front of us are speeding.

Some plural subjects are irregular:

Singular: The **child** is crying.

Plural: The **children** are crying.

Other plural subjects are known as compound (more than one) subjects:

Compound: The **car** and the **truck** in front of us are speeding.

FINDING THE VERB

Every complete sentence contains a verb. In general, there are two types of verbs: action verbs and linking verbs.

Action Verbs

Action verbs express action; they tell what the subject is doing. You can find an action verb by asking "What does the subject do?" For example, look again at the following four sentences:

- Gloria wrote her answers on the blackboard.
- The balloons drifted slowly to earth.
- He won a stuffed bear at the carnival.
- Danger goes hand in hand with police work.

See if you can write in the answer to the following questions:

- In the first sentence, what did Gloria do? She _____.
- In the second sentence, what did the balloons do? They _____.
- In the third sentence, what did "he" do? He _____.
- In the last sentence, what does danger do? It _____.

In each case, you can find the verbs by answering the question, "What does the subject of the sentence do?" The verbs above are *wrote, drifted, won*, and *goes*.

If you have trouble finding the verb of a sentence, here is one other way to identify a verb: Try putting a pronoun such as *I, you, he, she, it,* or *they* in front of the word you suspect is a verb. If the word is a verb, the resulting sentence will make sense. Notice, for instance, that for the sentences above, *she wrote, they drifted, he won,* and *it goes* all make sense.

➤ *Practice 3*

Write a word into each blank. The word that you insert will be an action verb. It will tell what the subject does or did.

1. A mosquito _____ over the sleeping boy.

2. For exercise, I _____.

3. Paul _____ the ball over the wooden fence.

4. The cattle _____ during the hot summer afternoon.

5. The customer in the back booth _____ about her turkey sandwich.

6. The tiny boat _____ on the stormy lake.

7. During his biology lecture, Mickey often _____.

8. The jury _____ carefully to both sides of the story.

9. Emma _____ during the scary parts of horror movies.

10. For fun, we _____ all the way home from the corner store.

Linking Verbs

While many verbs show action, some verbs simply link, or join, the subject to words that describe the subject. Such verbs are known as **linking verbs**. Look at the following sentences, and see if you can underline the linking verbs.

- Anger is sometimes a healthy emotion.
- The runners were anxious before the race.
- George looks uncomfortable in a suit and tie.

You should have underlined the word *is* in the first sentence. This word links *anger* to information about it—that it is *sometimes a healthy emotion.*

In the second sentence, you should have underlined the word *were*. This word links the subject, *runners*, to an idea about them—that they were *anxious.*

In the third sentence, you should have underlined the word *looks. Looks* links the subject, *George*, to an idea about him—that he appears to be *uncomfortable.*

Most linking verbs are forms of the verb *be*. Here are the forms of *be*, which is the most used verb in the English language:

Forms of the Linking Verb **Be**

am	were	has been
is	will be	had been
are	have been	will have been
was		

In addition to *be*, other words that can be linking verbs are listed on the next page. See if you notice what these seven verbs have in common:

Other Linking Verbs

look	taste	appear
sound	feel	seem
smell		

The verbs have in common the fact that they all involve our five senses of sight, hearing, taste, smell, and touch.

➤ *Practice 4*

Underline the one word that is a linking verb in each of the following sentences.

1. That nurse was kind.

2. The kitchen smells spicy.

3. Lisa and I are roommates.

4. Velvet feels soft and silky.

5. The chocolate cookies taste salty and dry.

6. After jogging, I am always hungry.

7. Those dishes just out of the dishwasher still look dirty.

8. Since his divorce, Nate seems unhappy.

9. The cashier at our supermarket is a student at Jefferson High School.

10. During the hot, dry summer, the farmers were worried about their crops.

Helping Verbs

Most of the verbs you have looked at so far have been just one word—*wrote, drifted, won, is, look,* and so on. But many verbs consist of a main verb plus one or more **helping verbs**.

- Greg has visited the learning skills lab.
- The couple could have danced all night.
- Those pants should be washed.

See if you can answer the following questions.

- The subject of the first sentence is *Greg*. What does the sentence say about Greg?

  It says that Greg _____.

- The subject of the second sentence is *couple*. What does the sentence say about the couple?

It says that the couple _____.

- The subject of the third sentence is *pants*. What does the sentence say about the pants?

It says that those pants _____.

The first sentence says that Greg *has visited* the lab. *Visited* is the main verb, and *has* is the helping verb.

The second sentence says that the couple *could have danced* all night. *Danced* is the main verb, and *could* and *have* are the helping verbs.

The third sentence says that the pants *should be washed*. *Washed* is the main verb, and *should* and *be* are the helping verbs.

Remember, then, that a complete verb can be made up of a main verb plus one or more helping verbs. Here is a list of common helping verbs.

Helping Verbs

is	have	do	must
are	has	does	might
am	had	did	may
was	have been	could	
were	has been	can	
will	had been	should	

➤ *Practice 5*

Fill in the blanks under each sentence.

1. As usual, my brother was complaining about his homework.

   Helping verb(s): _____   *Main verb:* _____

2. The students will decorate the classroom for the teacher's surprise party.

   Helping verb(s): _____   *Main verb:* _____

3. The dental appointment should take about an hour.

   Helping verb(s): _____   *Main verb:* _____

4. You should have washed the borrowed sweater.

   Helping verb(s): _____   *Main verb:* _____

5. Margaret has planted parsley and other herbs in her back yard.

   Helping verb(s): _____   *Main verb:* _____

6. The chicken in the refrigerator should be eaten soon.

   Helping verb(s): _____   *Main verb:* _____

7. The video game machine will accept only quarters.

   Helping verb(s): _____ *Main verb:* _____

8. Kelly could have been killed by the drunk driver.

   Helping verb(s): _____ *Main verb:* _____

9. My girlfriend must have forgotten our date this evening.

   Helping verb(s): _____ *Main verb:* _____

10. The star basketball player at our college might have injured himself seriously.

    Helping verb(s): _____ *Main verb:* _____

Other Notes About Verbs

Here is some added information that will help when you look for verbs in a sentence.

1 The verb of a sentence never begins with the word *to*.

- The instructor **agreed** to provide ten minutes for study before the quiz.

  (Although *provide* is a verb, *to provide* cannot be the verb of a sentence. The verb of this sentence is *agreed*.)

2 A word ending in *-ing* cannot by itself be the verb of the sentence. It can be part of the verb, but it needs a helping verb before it.

- Jackie **is starting** a card-playing club in her neighborhood.

  (*Starting* by itself would not make sense as a verb. It would be incorrect to say, "Jackie starting a card-playing club in her neighborhood.")

3 Certain words—such as *not, just, never, only,* and *always*—may appear between the main verb and the helping verb. Such words are never part of the verb.

- Our canary **does** not **sing** in front of visitors.
- I **will** never **eat** at that restaurant again.
- You **should** always **wear** your seat belt in a moving vehicle.

➤ Practice 6

In the space provided, write the complete verb in each sentence.

1. My uncle is not wearing his toupee anymore.

   Complete verb: _____

2. The children hurried to finish their art projects by the end of the class.

   Complete verb: _____

3. A truck driver is waiting at the front door with a delivery.

   Complete verb: _____

4. You should never ride your bike in the streets without a helmet.

   Complete verb: _____

5. Carolyn will always love her ex-husband.

   Complete verb: _____

6. The teacher has promised to return the papers by Friday.

   Complete verb: _____

7. The noodles should not be boiled more than seven minutes.

   Complete verb: _____

8. Marilyn is sipping fresh coconut juice.

   Complete verb: _____

9. Those pants should never have been washed in hot water.

   Complete verb: _____

10. For two months I have been trying to rid the apartment of cockroaches.

    Complete verb: _____

CHAPTER REVIEW

Answer each question by filling in the correct word or words in each space provided.

1. A _____ and a _____ are the basic parts of any sentence.

2. The subject of a sentence is never found in a _____ phrase.

3. *True or false?* _____ Verbs that join the subject to a word or words that describe the subject are known as helping verbs.

4. Words such as *look, smell,* and *appear* are known as _____ _____.

5. A complete _____ can be made up of a main verb and one or more helping verbs.

Name_____   Section _____   Date _____

Score: (Number right) _____ x 5 = _____%

➤ *Subjects and Verbs: Test 1*

For each sentence, cross out the prepositional phrase or phrases. Then underline the subject once and the verb twice. Remember to underline all the parts of the verb.

Note: Hints are given for half of the sentences.

1. Laura told the joke with a straight face.

   With is a preposition; *with a straight face* is a prepositional phrase. The sentence is about *Laura. Told* (the joke) is what she did.

2. A red kite danced in the gentle breeze.

3. The plant in the window has died.

   In the window is a prepositional phrase. The sentence is about the *plant. Has died* (*died* plus the helping verb *has*) is what the sentence says about the plant.

4. We will spend our vacation at home.

5. In some countries, snails are a favorite food.

   In some countries is a prepositional phrase. The sentence is about *snails.* The linking verb *are* joins the subject to words that describe it: *a favorite food.*

6. For many Americans, money is success.

7. My young son is wearing his helmet and shoulder pads to the picnic.

   To the picnic is a prepositional phrase. The sentence is about the *son.* The complete verb is a combination of the helping verb *is* and the *-ing* word *wearing.*

8. Several guests at the party were singing with the band.

9. After my last final, I plan to sleep for a week.

   There are two prepositional phrases: *after my last final* and *for a week.* Once they are crossed out, *I plan to sleep* remains. *I* is the one doing something in the sentence. Since *sleep* has the word *to* in front of it, it cannot be the verb of the sentence.

10. At the age of forty-six, Ray learned to read.

Name _____ Section _____ Date _____

Score: (Number right) _____ x 5 = _____%

➤ *Subjects and Verbs: Test 2*

For each sentence, cross out the prepositional phrase or phrases. Then, on the lines provided, write the subject and verb of the sentence. Remember to include all the parts of the verb.

1. The coffee from the leaking pot stained the carpet.

   Subject: _____   *Verb:* _____

2. I will study after work.

   Subject: _____   *Verb:* _____

3. My cousins in Louisiana formed a gospel music group.

   Subject: _____   *Verb:* _____

4. The green book on the shelf belongs to the library.

   Subject: _____   *Verb:* _____

5. A warm sweatshirt with a hood feels good on a chilly day.

   Subject: _____   *Verb:* _____

6. The cardboard boxes by the river are home to several people.

   Subject: _____   *Verb:* _____

7. For my little brother and sister, happiness is a McDonald's restaurant.

   Subject: _____   *Verb:* _____

8. At exactly noon, my summer vacation will begin.

   Subject: _____   *Verb:* _____

9. The rug-cleaning people should have been here by now.

   Subject: _____   *Verb:* _____

10. The source of electricity for the house is solar batteries.

    Subject: _____   *Verb:* _____

Name_____ Section _____ Date _____

Score: (Number right) _____ x 5 = _____%

➤ *Subjects and Verbs: Test 3*

Cross out the prepositional phrases. Then on the lines below each two-sentence passage, write the subject and verb of each sentence. Remember to write all the parts of each verb.

Note: Hints are given for half of the sentences.

1. Between you and me, I dislike Rita. Her opinion of herself is too high.

   a. *Subject:* _____ *Verb:* _____
      Between you and me is a prepositional phrase. The sentence is about *I*, the speaker of the sentence. *Dislike* is what the speaker does.

   b. *Subject:* _____ *Verb:* _____

2. The children gathered around the movie poster. They pointed at the picture of Superman.

   a. *Subject:* _____ *Verb:* _____
      Around the movie poster is a prepositional phrase. The *children* are the ones doing something. *Gathered* is what they did.

   b. *Subject:* _____ *Verb:* _____

3. An ambulance passed me at top speed. After a minute, a fire truck followed with its siren screaming.

   a. *Subject:* _____ *Verb:* _____
      At is a preposition. The sentence is about an *ambulance. Passed* is what it did.

   b. *Subject:* _____ *Verb:* _____

4. Today's lunch specials are cheese omelet and chef's salad. The soup of the day is vegetable beef.

   a. *Subject:* _____ *Verb:* _____
      The sentence is about *specials.* The linking verb *are* joins the subject with words that describe it.

   b. *Subject:* _____ *Verb:* _____

5. Most of the students in this class hold part-time jobs. In addition, several of them have children at home.

   a. *Subject:* _____ *Verb:* _____
      Of the students and *in this class* are prepositional phrases. After crossing them out, what remains is *Most hold part-time jobs.* Now it is clear that the sentence is about *most* (of the students). *Hold* (part-time jobs) is what they do.

   b. *Subject:* _____ *Verb:* _____

Name_____   Section _____ Date _____

Score: (Number right) _____ x 5 = _____%

➤ *Subjects and Verbs: Test 4*

Cross out the prepositional phrases. Then on the lines below each two-sentence passage, write the subject and verb of each sentence. Remember to write all the parts of each verb.

1. Many passengers slept during the long bus trip. Others read in the dim light.

    a. *Subject:* _____   *Verb:* _____

    b. *Subject:* _____   *Verb:* _____

2. The handwriting on this essay looks terrible. In the future, you should type your essays.

    a. *Subject:* _____   *Verb:* _____

    b. *Subject:* _____   *Verb:* _____

3. Lani has been elected to city council. Her election surprised many people.

    a. *Subject:* _____   *Verb:* _____

    b. *Subject:* _____   *Verb:* _____

4. The small country store sells groceries and gasoline. It has been owned by the same woman for forty years.

    a. *Subject:* _____   *Verb:* _____

    b. *Subject:* _____   *Verb:* _____

5. On Sunday nights, we usually play games with friends. Some of our favorite games are Monopoly, checkers, and poker.

    a. *Subject:* _____   *Verb:* _____

    b. *Subject:* _____   *Verb:* _____

Verb Tenses

Seeing What You Know

Each sentence below shows a common verb tense. See if you can write each verb in the space or spaces provided. (The number of spaces tells how many parts there are to each verb.)

1. The truck climbs slowly up the steep hill.   *Present tense verb:* _____

2. A fire alarm sounded during the night.   *Past tense verb:* _____

3. Anne will add the nuts last to the cookie dough.
   Future tense verb: _____ _____

4. My parents have worked for the same company for twenty years.   *Present perfect tense verb:* _____ _____

5. Julie had driven an old Ford before winning her new Jeep.   *Past perfect tense verb:* _____ _____

6. I will have taken four writing courses by the time of graduation.   *Future perfect tense verb:* _____ _____ _____

7. The pitcher is throwing curve balls and sinkers.
   Present progressive tense verb: _____ _____

8. That diner was losing business steadily before the fire.   *Past progressive tense verb:* _____ _____

9. By tomorrow afternoon, I will be sleeping on the beach.   *Future progressive tense verb:* _____ _____ _____

Understanding the Answers

1. *Climbs* is a verb in the present tense.
2. *Sounded* is a verb in the past tense.
3. *Will add* is a verb in the future tense.
4. *Have worked* is a verb in the present perfect tense.
5. *Had driven* is a verb in the past perfect tense.
6. *Will have taken* is a verb in the future perfect tense.
7. *Is throwing* is a verb in the present progressive tense.
8. *Was losing* is a verb in the past progressive tense.
9. *Will be sleeping* is a verb in the future progressive tense.

All verbs have different **tenses**—forms that indicate the *time* the sentence is referring to. This chapter begins with the four principal verb parts that are the basis for all of the tenses. Then it goes on to describe the most common verb tenses in English:

Six main tenses:	present, past, future
	present perfect, past perfect, future perfect
Three progressive tenses:	present progressive, past progressive, future progressive

This chapter also explains how to avoid a few common verb errors.

THE FOUR PRINCIPAL PARTS OF VERBS

All of the verb tenses come from one of the four principal parts of verbs. Those principal parts are as follows:

1   Basic Form

The **basic form** is the form in which verbs are listed in the dictionary. It is used for the present tense for all subjects except third-person singular subjects.

- I **ask** questions in class.

The present tense for third-person singular subjects is formed by adding *-s* to the basic form.

- Sue **asks** questions in class.

2   Past Tense Form

The **past tense form** of most verbs is formed by adding *-ed* or *-d* to the basic form.

- We **asked** the teacher to postpone the test.
- I **raised** the garage door with the remote control.

3   Present Participle

The **present participle** is the *-ing* form of a verb. The present participle is the form that is used with the helping verbs *am, is, are, was,* or *were* to show continuing action.

- Jim is **asking** the teacher something in the hallway.
- As I was **raising** the garage door, the wind blew buckets of rain into the garage.

4   Past Participle

The **past participle** of a verb is usually the same as its past tense form. The past participle is the form that is used with the helping verbs *have, has,* and *had* and with *am, is, are, was,* or *were.*

- The teachers have **asked** us to study in groups.

- The garage door was **raised** with the remote control.

Here, for example, are the principal parts of three regular verbs:

Basic Form	Past Tense Form	Present Participle	Past Participle
work	worked	working	worked
smile	smiled	smiling	smiled
wonder	wondered	wondering	wondered

(Irregular verbs, which have irregular forms for the past tense form and past participle, are explained in the next chapter, starting on page 111.)

SIX MAIN TENSES

There are six main tenses in English. They are **present, past, future, present perfect, past perfect,** and **future perfect**.

Look at the following chart. It shows the six basic tenses of the verb *work.*

Tense	Example
Present	**I work.**
Past	**I worked.**
Future	**I will work.**
Present Perfect	**I have worked.**
Past Perfect	**I had worked.**
Future Perfect	**I will have worked.**

These tenses are explained in more detail on the pages that follow.

Present Tense

Verbs in the **present tense** express present action or habitual action. (A habitual action is one that is often repeated.)

- Our dog **smells** the neighbor's barbecue.

  (present action)

- Jay **works** as a waiter on weekends.

  (habitual action)

The forms of present tense verbs are shown with the verb *work* in the box on the next page. Do you notice the difference between the singular third-person form and the other present tense forms?

Present Tense Forms

	Singular	Plural
First person	I work	we work
Second person	you work	you work
Third person	he, she, it works	they work

Present tense verbs for the third person singular end with an -*s*. Here are some other third person sentences:

- She reads about a book a week.
- It takes me a month to read a book.
- Dan drives an hour to school every day.
- His old car averages only ten miles a gallon.

In a third person sentence, the subject is *he, she, it,* or any single person or thing other than the speaker (first person) or the person spoken to (second person). (See also "Subject-Verb Agreement" on page 124.)

➤ *Practice 1*

Fill in each space with the present tense form of the verb shown in the margin.

drill   1. The dentist _____ the cavity as his assistant watches.

practice   2. Ling _____ her typing every day.

ring   3. Those church bells _____ on the hour.

make   4. He suddenly _____ a U-turn.

dig   5. Some workers _____ through the stones and rubble.

trim   6. I _____ my fingernails before playing the piano.

clean   7. Nanette _____ her apartment every Saturday.

tell   8. The nurse _____ the patient to make a fist.

discover   9. My sister often _____ loose change in her coat pockets.

remember   10. The children _____ the fights their parents used to have.

Past Tense

Verbs in the **past tense** express actions that took place in the past.

- Last year, Jay **worked** as a messenger.
- One day our dog **chased** a raccoon.

The past tense is usually formed by adding -*ed* or -*d* to the end of the basic form of the verb. (The -*d* ending is used when the basic form ends in *e*.) In the above sentences, the -*ed* and -*d* endings are added to the basic forms of the verbs *work* and *chase*.

Note: People sometimes drop the -*ed* or -*d* ending in their everyday speech. They then tend to omit those endings in their writing as well. For example, someone might say

- I finish the paper an hour before class.

instead of

- I **finished** the paper an hour before class.

In written English, however, the -*ed* or -*d* ending is essential.

➤ *Practice 2*

Fill in each space with the past tense form of the verb shown in the margin.

seem   1. The movie _____ to end suddenly.

sail   2. The ship _____ to the Bahamas last week.

wonder   3. Alisha _____ where she had put her car keys.

knock   4. Last night someone _____ on the door.

name   5. Jean _____ the spotted puppy "Freckles."

jump   6. My little son _____ up when I entered the room.

talk   7. The students _____ easily with the new instructor.

check   8. I _____ the air in my car tires before I went on vacation.

wipe   9. The man _____ the lipstick off his cheek with his shirt sleeve.

play   10. Stan _____ his guitar in a concert last summer.

Future Tense

Verbs in the **future tense** describe future actions.

- Next summer, Jay **will work** at a camp.

The future tense is formed by adding the word *will* or *shall* to the basic form of the verb.

➤ *Practice 3*

Fill in the space with the future tense form of the verb shown in the margin.

play   1. Stan _____ his guitar in a concert tonight.

plant   2. The lumberjacks _____ new trees here next spring.

iron   3. I _____ my shirt before going to work tomorrow.

attend   4. Penny _____ San Antonio Community College in the fall.

circle   5. The instructor _____ any errors she finds in your paper.

THE PERFECT TENSES

The perfect tenses are formed by adding the helping verb *have, has, or had* to the past participle of the verb. The **past participle** of a regular verb is simply the form that ends in *-ed.*

Present Perfect Tense

The **present perfect tense** describes an action that began in the past and either has been finished or is continuing at the present time.

• Jay **has worked** at a number of jobs over the years.

The present perfect tense is made by adding the correct form of the helping verb *have* to the past participle of the verb. Here are the present tense forms of *have*:

Present Tense Forms of **Have**

	Singular	Plural
First person	I have	we have
Second person	you have	you have
Third person	he, she, it has	they have

➤ *Practice 4*

Fill in each space with the present perfect tense form of the verb shown in the margin. One is done for you as an example.

pour   1. The hostess _____*has poured*_____ iced tea for most of her guests.

live   2. My roommate _____ in three different countries.

check 3. Because I'm driving a long distance, I _____ the air in my car tires.

boil 4. The chef _____ the eggs for the salad and is now slicing them.

mix 5. The children _____ together in one box the pieces of three different puzzles.

Past Perfect Tense

The **past perfect** tense describes an action that was completed in the past before another past action.

- Jay **had worked** as a messenger before he located a better job as a waiter.

The past perfect tense is formed by adding *had* to the past participle of a verb.

➤ *Practice 5*

Fill in the space with the past perfect tense form of the verb shown in the margin. Add *had* to the past participle of the verb. One is done for you as an example.

promise 1. Zora ____*had promised*____ to go to the meeting before she realized it was on her birthday.

struggle 2. The man _____ in several part-time jobs before returning to college.

ask 3. Sally _____ two other men to the dance before inviting Dan.

intend 4. I _____ to study after dinner, but then my boss called and asked me to work tonight.

invite 5. Hector _____ his friends to his apartment before he knew that his roommate was ill.

Future Perfect Tense

The **future perfect** tense describes an action that will be completed before some time in the future.

- Jay **will have worked** at a half dozen different jobs before college graduation.

The future perfect tense is formed by adding *will have* to the past participle of a verb.

➤ *Practice 6*

Fill in the space with the future perfect tense form of the verb shown in the margin. Add *will have* to the past participle of the verb. One is done for you as an example.

complete   1. I _____*will have completed*_____ five exams by the end of finals week.

attend   2. By graduation day, I _____ five parties.

finish   3. You eat so slowly that I _____ my ice cream before you begin your spaghetti.

hire   4. The company _____ several new employees by May.

design   5. By the end of the summer, my mother _____ and made my wedding dress.

THE PROGRESSIVE TENSES

As their names suggest, the progressive tenses express actions still *in progress* at a particular time. They are made by adding a form of the helping verb *be* to the *-ing* form of the verb.

Present Progressive Tense

The **present progressive** tense expresses an action taking place at this moment or that will occur sometime in the future.

- Jay **is working** at the restaurant today.
- I **am going** to get home late tonight.

The present progressive tense is formed by adding the correct present tense form of the helping verb *be* to the *-ing* form of the verb.

Present Tense Forms of Be

	Singular	*Plural*
First person	I am	we are
Second person	you are	you are
Third person	he, she, it is	they are

➤ *Practice 7*

Below are five sentences with verbs in the present tense. Cross out each verb and change it to the present progressive in the space provided. One is done for you as an example.

1. The child ~~plays~~ with the puppy. _____*is playing*_____

2. The microwave beeps loudly. _____

3. The roses in the garden bloom. _____

4. I practice my speech tonight. _____

5. The visitors pace in the hospital lobby. _____

Past Progressive Tense

The **past progressive** tense expresses an action that was in progress at a certain time in the past.

- Jay **was working** yesterday.

The past progressive tense is formed by adding the correct past tense form of *be* to the *-ing* form of the verb.

Past Tense Forms of **Be**

	Singular	Plural
First person	I was	we were
Second person	you were	you were
Third person	he, she, it was	they were

➤ *Practice 8*

Below are five sentences with verbs in the past tense. Cross out each verb and change it to the past progressive in the space provided. One is done for you as an example.

1. The child ~~played~~ with the puppy. _____ *was playing* _____

2. The microwave beeped loudly. _____

3. The roses in the garden bloomed. _____

4. I practiced my speech last night. _____

5. The visitors paced in the hospital lobby. _____

Future Progressive Tense

The **future progressive** tense expresses an action that will be in progress at a certain time in the future.

- Jay **will be working** tomorrow.

The future progressive tense is formed by adding *will be* to the *-ing* form of the verb.

➤ *Practice 9*

Below are five sentences with verbs in the future tense. Cross out each verb and change it to the future progressive in the space provided. One is done for you as an example.

1. The child ~~will play~~ with the puppy. _____ *will be playing* _____

2. The microwave will beep loudly. _____

3. The roses in the garden will bloom. _____

4. I will practice my speech tonight. _____

5. The visitors will pace in the hospital lobby. _____

A Note on *-ing* Verbs

Look at the following word groups:

- Jay working tonight.
- The visitors pacing in the hospital lobby.

The above word groups express incomplete thoughts because their verbs are incomplete. The *-ing* form of a verb cannot by itself be the verb of a sentence—it must be accompanied by a helping verb:

- Jay **is working** tonight.
- The visitors **were pacing** in the hospital lobby.

➤ *Practice 10*

Complete each of the following sentences by writing *is, are, was,* or *were* in the space provided.

1. Oscar _____ playing the clarinet in his school band this year.

2. You _____ giggling in your sleep last night.

3. The girl reported that even though she _____ screaming, no one helped her.

4. If you look down the street, you'll see that five boys _____ standing on the corner.

5. The customers _____ complaining about the long wait until a waitress offered them free cups of coffee.

CONSISTENT VERB TENSE

In your writing, avoid illogical or needless shifts in tense. For example, if you are writing a paper with the action in the past tense, don't shift suddenly to the present for no reason. Look at the examples below:

Inconsistent verb tense: In my nightmare, a hairy spider **crawled** up the side of my bed and **races** quickly onto my pillow.

Consistent verb tense: In my nightmare, a hairy spider **crawled** up the side of my bed and **raced** quickly onto my pillow.

There is no reason for the writer to shift suddenly from the past tense *(crawled)* to the present tense *(races)*.

➤ *Practice 11*

In each short passage, there is one illogical or unneeded change in verb tense. Cross out the incorrect verb. Then write the correct form of that verb on the line provided.

_____   1. The ice skater moved smoothly through her routine. On her last jump, however, she lost her balance and crashes to the ice with a thud.

_____   2. On many farms, machines milk the cows. The farmers then send the fresh milk to a processing plant. Workers there heated the milk at high temperatures. The intense heat removes bacteria.

_____   3. When Tina saw flames and smoke coming from her kitchen, she reacted quickly. She picks up her kitten and some pictures of her family. Then she rushed out into the fresh air.

_____   4. Soldiers in the Civil War fought in bloody battles during the day. But at night, they often cross "enemy" lines for a friendly visit.

_____   5. White flowers blossom on the apple trees every spring. Then tiny green apples appeared. Finally, the apples grow into sweet red fruit.

_____   6. My roommate was very annoyed with me last week. I promise him that he could borrow my car, but I forgot to leave him the keys.

_____   7. Arlo works for a small greeting card company. He writes poems for the wedding cards. Then he delivered the cards to the art department, where an artist sketches pictures of wedding bells or flowers.

_____ 8. Last summer, my father went water skiing. After about five attempts, he skied around the entire lake. But when a large wave from another boat surges by, he flipped into the water head first.

_____ 9. The Bensons are going to visit the Grand Canyon this summer. Mrs. Benson is buying extra film, and Mr. Benson is making the hotel reservations. The children work odd jobs. They are planning to buy souvenirs with their earnings.

_____ 10. Last night, I went on the worst date ever. My date, Martin, showed up an hour late. During dinner, all he talked about was himself. Then, just before the waitress brought our check, he disappears. I paid the bill and took a taxi home.

CHAPTER REVIEW

Answer the questions by correctly filling in the blank spaces.

1. There are six basic tenses in English. They are the present, past, _____, present perfect, _____, and future perfect.

2. The past tense is formed with regular verbs by adding _____ or _____ to the basic form of the verb.

3. The _____ tense is formed by adding the word *will* before the basic form of the verb.

4. The _____ tenses are formed by adding a form of the helping verb *have* (*have, has,* or *had*) to the past participle of the verb.

5. The _____ tense describes an action that was completed in the past before another past action.

6. The present progressive tense is formed by adding the correct form of the helping verb *be* to the (*-s, -ing,* or *-ed?*) _____ form of the verb.

Name_____ Section _____ Date _____

➤ *Verb Tenses: Test 1*

Note: Follow the examples given for each group of sentences.

A. In each space, write the **present tense** form of the verb in the margin.

    Examples   *plan*   Carl _____*plans*_____ to enter the contest.

                attend   The students _____*attend*_____ a meeting on the new dress code.

    soar   1. The hawk _____ above the corn field.

    listen   2. The jurors _____ to the witness.

    think   3. Leona _____ she passed her English exam.

B. In each space, write the **past tense** form of the verb in the margin.

    Example   *promise*   My son _____*promised*_____ to wash my car on Saturday.

    scratch   4. The prisoner _____ his initials in the cell wall.

    arrive   5. The bus _____ at our hotel at 7:15 a.m.

    float   6. Five orange slices _____ on top of the red punch.

    struggle   7. The campers _____ through the thick underbrush near the camp.

C. In each space, write the **future tense** form of the verb in the margin.

    Example   *check*   The nurse _____*will check*_____ your blood pressure each day.

    blossom   8. Those trees _____ into fluffy white clouds.

    stand   9. Everyone _____ when the judge enters the courtroom.

    wear   10. Johnny _____ a dinosaur costume to the party.

Name_____ Section _____ Date _____

Score: (Number right) _____ x 10 = _____ %

➤ *Verb Tenses: Test 2*

Note: Follow the examples given for each group of sentences.

A. In each space, write the **present perfect tense** form of the verb in the margin.

Examples   *walk*   Bernice ____*has walked*____ over twenty miles this week.

           look   I ____*have looked*____ all over for my glasses.

wash   1. The students _____ nearly seventy cars to raise money for their class trip.

gain   2. Rodney _____ ten pounds in his first year of college.

learn   3. We _____ about the civil rights movement in our history class this semester.

noticed   4. I _____ changes in you since you started going to the gym.

B. In each space, write the **past perfect tense** form of the verb in the margin.

Example   *walk*   Before her heart attack, Bernice seldom ____*had walked*____ for exercise.

argue   5. Fritz _____ with a friend before the car accident.

warn   6. Before planting a bomb in the warehouse, the criminal _____ the FBI.

manage   7. Chelsea _____ to clean the entire house by the time her parents got home last evening.

C. In each space, write the **future perfect tense** form of the verb in the margin.

Example   *walk*   By the end of this month, Bernice ____*will have walked*____ over one hundred miles.

work   8. I _____ fifty-five hours by the end of the week.

interview   9. By the time she writes her paper, Jodi _____ six nurses.

watch   10. By the end of the day, the children _____ five hours of television.

Name_____ Section _____ Date _____

➤ *Verb Tenses: Test 3*

Note: Follow the examples given for each group of sentences.

A. In each space, write the **present progressive tense** form of the verb in the margin.

Examples	*try*	I _____*am trying*_____ to build up my self-confidence.
	sleep	It's so hot out that Jay _____*is sleeping*_____ in his cool basement.
	eat	The squirrels _____*are eating*_____ all the bird food.

polish 1. Hank _____ his car again.

think 2. You _____ of ways to avoid an argument.

go 3. The students _____ to watch the eclipse of the moon.

plant 4. I _____ fifty red tulips along the driveway.

B. In each space, write the **past progressive tense** form of the verb in the margin.

Examples	*sleep*	Jay _____*was sleeping*_____ when the siren blared.
	whisper	Some people in the theater _____*were whispering*_____ all during the movie.

wait 5. Theo _____ for me to pick him up at the movie.

find 6. Companies _____ coal in this area in the early 1900s.

cry 7. When I got home from school, my son _____.

C. In each space, write the **future progressive tense** form of the verb in the margin.

Example	*use*	In the future, farmers _____*will be using*_____ fewer and fewer chemicals.

visit 8. We _____ California next summer.

discuss 9. The senators _____ the President's tax bill today.

work 10. The actress _____ on a movie during her vacation from her television series.

Name_____ Section _____ Date _____

Score: (Number right) _____ x 10 = _____%

➤ *Verb Tenses: Test 4*

In each short passage, there is one illogical or needless shift in verb tense. Cross out the incorrect verb. Then write the correct form of that verb on the line provided.

_____ 1. The gangster movie started with a car chase, featured a half dozen gun fights, and ends with the death of half the characters.

_____ 2. Josh wanted to attend college, but his parents couldn't afford to send him. So he works for two years after high school graduation. With the money he saved, he attended a community college.

_____ 3. Officer McFry worked the night shift last night. He patrolled the western part of the city. He also watches traffic at the intersection on Main Street. McFry returned home around 6:30 a.m.

_____ 4. Our service group meets at a nursing home once a month. We visit with the patients and plan fun activities for them. We sing, played card games, and do craft projects.

_____ 5. As we walked into the department store, a well-dressed woman from the cosmetics department approached us. Before we could protest, she sprays a cloud of musky-smelling perfume in our direction.

_____ 6. My friends worked at odd jobs this past summer. Carlos worked at a zoo, cleaning out the bird cages. Jenny worked at Pizza Hut. She delivers pizzas every night of the week.

_____ 7. The taxi driver stopped to pick up a couple. The woman smoked a long cigarette. When the driver asked her to put it out, she refuses. Finally, the driver stopped at a corner and asked the couple to get out of the cab.

_____ 8. Melba took an inexpensive vacation this summer. She called parks and museums in the area to find out the cheapest times to visit. To save money, she prepares picnic lunches for her visits.

_____ 9. My sister complains at the drop of a hat. She often runs to her room in a rage. She stayed there for hours feeling sorry for herself.

_____ 10. On the first Thanksgiving, pilgrims celebrated their survival through the winter. They served many foods, but turkey was not one of them. The menu includes duck, goose, seafood, and eels.

Irregular Verbs

Seeing What You Know

In each numbered item, the present tense of a common irregular verb is italicized. See if you can add the past tense and the past participle of the italicized verb in the spaces provided.

Example I *grow* something in my yard each year. Last summer I ___grew___ a vegetable garden. I had ___grown___ sunflowers the year before.

1. We often *see* unusual things at the zoo. Yesterday, we _____ a two-headed snake. We had never _____ such a creature before.

2. Once a week, we *eat* Mexican food. Last night, we _____ burritos. We had _____ burritos the week before, but everyone wanted them again.

3. Each time I visit my sister, I *break* something. Last time, I _____ a wine glass. She keeps a list of all the things I have _____.

4. Please *get* a quart of skim milk. Last time, you _____ two-percent milk by mistake. But I have _____ used to skim milk and don't like anything else.

5. I *do* the dishes while watching TV. Last night, I _____ them during the evening news. I have _____ the dishes in our home ever since I was seven.

Understanding the Answers

Following are the irregular past tense and past participle forms that fit in the five sentences:

Past Tense	Past Participle
1. saw	seen
2. ate	eaten
3. broke	broken
4. got	gotten
5. did	done

This chapter explains the difference between regular and irregular verbs. Then it gives you practice with some common irregular verbs.

REGULAR VERBS

Most English verbs are **regular**. That is, they form their past tense and past participles by adding *-ed* or *-d* to the basic form, as shown in this chart:

Basic Form	Past Tense Form	Past Participle
ask	asked	asked
raise	raised	raised

Note: The present participle of both regular and irregular verbs is formed simply by adding *-ing* to the basic form.

IRREGULAR VERBS

Irregular verbs, however, do not follow the pattern of adding *-ed* or *-d* to the basic form. Instead, their past tense and past participles are formed in other ways. Below are some of the most common irregular verbs. Review them enough to become familiar with them.

Note: When using this chart, keep these two points in mind:

1 If your sentence does not have a helping verb, choose the past tense form.

   • My mother **became** my special friend.

2 If the sentence does have a helping verb, choose the past participle.

   • My mother **has become** my special friend.

Basic Form	Past Tense Form	Past Participle
become	became	become
begin	began	begun
blow	blew	blown
break	broke	broken
bring	brought	brought
catch	caught	caught
choose	chose	chosen
come	came	come
cut	cut	cut
draw	drew	drawn
drink	drank	drunk
drive	drove	driven

Basic Form	Past Tense Form	Past Participle
eat	ate	eaten
fall	fell	fallen
feel	felt	felt
find	found	found
fly	flew	flown
freeze	froze	frozen
get	got	got, gotten
give	gave	given
go	went	gone
grow	grew	grown
hide	hid	hidden
keep	kept	kept
know	knew	known
lay	laid	laid
leave	left	left
lend	lent	lent
lie	lay	lain
lose	lost	lost
make	made	made
read	read	read
ride	rode	ridden
rise	rose	risen
run	ran	run
say	said	said
see	saw	seen
sell	sold	sold
set	set	set
shake	shook	shaken
sit	sat	sat
sleep	slept	slept
speak	spoke	spoken
spend	spent	spent
steal	stole	stolen
swim	swam	swum
take	took	taken
teach	taught	taught
tell	told	told
think	thought	thought
throw	threw	thrown
wear	wore	worn
win	won	won
write	wrote	written

Note: If you think a verb is irregular, and it is not in the above list, look it up in your dictionary. If it is irregular, the principal parts will be listed.

➤ *Practice 1*

In each item, the present tense of an irregular verb is shown in *italic* type. Fill in the missing **past tense form** in the *(a)* slot and the **past participle** in the *(b)* slot. One item is done for you as an example.

1. I *freeze* candy bars so that they'll take longer to eat. Last week I *(a)* _____*froze*_____ several Snickers Bars. In the past year, I probably have *(b)* _____*frozen*_____ a dozen kinds of candy bars.

2. My cousin *drives* a city bus. He *(a)* _____ a taxi cab for years before that. In fact, he has *(b)* _____ for a living all of his adult life.

3. In fifteen minutes, Larry can *draw* a lifelike portrait of anybody. Once, a picture he *(a)* _____ was published in the newspaper. He works in a little booth at the mall, surrounded by portraits he has *(b)* _____.

4. Nadia's parents *speak* Spanish at home. She *(a)* _____ only Spanish until she was four. But for the last twelve years, she has *(b)* _____ English in school.

5. I *take* my nursing certification tests next Saturday. One of my classmates *(a)* _____ them last fall. She told me that they were the toughest tests she had ever *(b)* _____.

6. People often *become* lost in a strange city. When Fran drove to visit her sister in Chicago, she *(a)* _____ confused by a detour. Once she had *(b)* _____ hopelessly lost, she telephoned her sister for help.

7. My wife will not *ride* roller coasters. She *(a)* _____ one once many years ago. When I ask her to give it another chance, she says, "I have *(b)* _____ one, and I hated it. Why would I want to try it again?"

8. My sister reminded me, "Please *bring* paper plates to the picnic." Unfortunately, I *(a)* _____ some that bent and spilled food on people's laps. Luckily, someone else had *(b)* _____ some heavy cardboard plates.

9. Elizabeth cannot *make* up her mind about her job. On Monday, she *(a)* _____ the decision to quit. On Tuesday, she told her boss. On Wednesday, she decided she had *(b)* _____ a mistake and begged for her job back. By Thursday, she wanted to quit again.

10. My uncle *knows* everything about cars. When my car wouldn't start last week, he *(a)* _____ exactly what was wrong. "You should have *(b)* _____ better than to leave the radio on all evening," he scolded me.

➤ Practice 2

Write the correct form of each verb in the space provided.

wrote, written   1. The recipe was _____ on the back of an envelope.

selled, sold   2. Ken _____ his car and now rides his bicycle to work.

wore, worn   3. My favorite blue sweater finally has _____ out.

ate, eaten   4. A mouse has _____ a hole through this bag of dogfood.

lost, losted   5. You could tell by the runner's face that he had _____ the race.

fell, fallen   6. Before the driver could stop, three large boxes had _____ from the back of his truck.

broke, broken   7. When I _____ my leg, my friends scribbled cheerful messages on the cast.

spended, spent   8. Nathan _____ most of his teenage years dressed in black and alone in his bedroom.

began, begun   9. The concert had already _____, but people were still coming to their seats.

hid, hided   10. The news told about a person who foolishly _____ some money in a microwave oven.

went, gone   11. Sandy has _____ to a counselor every week since her parents' divorce.

stole, stealed   12. Some neighborhood kids _____ the flags on all of the mailboxes on our block.

risen, rose   13. By the time the sun had _____, Margie had already run two miles.

taught, teached   14. The deli manager _____ the new workers how to slice meat, make potato salad, and use the food scale.

sleeped, slept   15. Since starting her new job in a law office, Susan has not _____ well.

chose, chosen   16. Polly has _____ the color gray for her bridesmaids' dresses.

shaked, shook   17. The elevator _____ suddenly and then came to a complete stop between the eighth and ninth floors.

throwed, threw   18. The teenagers were fined when they _____ water balloons out of the hotel window.

became, become   19. Rob did not _____ a firefighter until he had passed several written and physical exams.

drank, drunk   20. Our guests have _____ every drop of juice, soda, and milk that was in the house.

Three Problem Verbs

Three irregular verbs that often cause special problems are *be*, *do*, and *have*. Some speakers use nonstandard forms of these verbs. They say, for example, *I be* instead of *I am*, *you was* instead of *you were*, *they has* instead of *they have*, *he do* instead of *he does*, and *she done* instead of *she did*. If you are one of these speakers, pay special attention to these verbs.

Here are the correct present tense and past tense forms of these three verbs.

		Present Tense		*Past Tense*	
Be	I am	we are	I was	we were
	you are	you are	you were	you were
	he, she, it is	they are	he, she, it was	they were
Do	I do	we do	I did	we did
	you do	you do	you did	you did
	he, she, it does	they do	he, she, it did	they did
Have	I have	we have	I had	we had
	you have	you have	you had	you had
	he, she, it has	they have	he, she it had	they had

➤ *Practice 3*

Write the correct form of each verb in the space provided.

has, have   1. Alice _____ the same pants in three colors.

are, is   2. Few people realize that pigs _____ intelligent animals.

do, does   3. Every morning before breakfast, my grandfather _____ fifty push-ups.

was, be   4. By halftime, I _____ sure we would lose the game.

do, does   5. In art class, the children _____ self-portraits with crayons and finger paints.

are, be   6. Local merchants _____ worried about the mall being built outside of town.

has, have   7. Gang members often _____ to perform dangerous stunts to become a part of the group.

was, were   8. During the nineteenth century, children _____ often forced to work twelve-hour days.

did, done   9. The doctor _____ eight tests on his patient before concluding that she had a cold.

was, were   10. The salesman _____ annoyed when a customer put a new pair of shoes on bare feet.

are, is   11. My mother _____ working part-time as a telephone salesperson.

has, have   12. Those sneakers _____ glow-in-the-dark stripes.

was, were   13. Because Dionne _____ the first customer at the new store, she won passes to a weekend concert.

has, have   14. No one _____ ordered the frog legs on the menu.

am, be   15. I _____ always ready for a game of cards.

has, have   16. The veteran pilot _____ landed planes in snow, hail, and thick fog.

do, does   17. My parents _____ not seem to care that I'm very depressed, and that depresses me more.

did, done   18. Even though I _____ the reading for the course, I still felt lost in class.

was, were   19. Martin Luther King, Jr. _____ a believer in protest without violence.

was, were   20. We _____ relieved to see the doctor come out of the operating room with a smile on his face.

CHAPTER REVIEW

Fill in the correct word in each space provided.

1. The past tense of a(n) _____ verb is formed by adding *-ed* or *-d* to the present form.

2. _____ verbs do not follow the usual pattern for the past tense.

3. *True or false?* _____ The past tense of a verb is used with such helping verbs as *am, is, are, was, were, have, has,* and *had.*

4. Complete the missing present-tense forms of the following verbs:

   I am   I do   I have
   you are   you do   you have
   he, she, it _____   he, she, it _____   he, she, it _____

Name_____ Section _____ Date _____

Score: (Number right) _____ x 10 = _____%

➤ *Irregular Verbs: Test 1*

For each sentence below, fill in the correct form of the verb in the space provided.

Note: Hints are given for half of the sentences.

grew, growed   1. The fairy tale was about a magic beanstalk that _____ higher than the clouds.
Grow is an irregular verb. Its past tense is *not* formed by adding *-ed*.

drived, drove   2. The family _____ away without paying for their take-out food.

chose, chosen   3. The children already have _____ teams for the kickball game.
After the helping verb *have*, use the past participle of the irregular verb *choose*.

flew, flown   4. The hot-air balloons had _____ straight into a dangerous storm.

do, does   5. Charles often _____ his grandmother's shopping for her.
Use the standard present tense of *do*.

did, done   6. Many students _____ poorly on the final exam.

telled, told   7. When I let Katy know my secret, she _____ everyone she knew.
Tell is an irregular verb. Its past tense is *not* formed by adding *-ed*.

read, readed   8. Last night, Yoko _____ an entire mystery novel before going to bed.

went, gone   9. The sign on the barber shop door said, "Closed. I have _____ fishing."
After the helping verb *have*, use the past participle of the irregular verb *go*.

wrote, written   10. The pen pals had _____ to each other for years, but they had never met in person.

Name _____ Section _____ Date _____

➤ *Irregular Verbs: Test 2*

For each sentence, fill in the correct form of the verb in the space provided.

rided, rode   1. My sister _____ a horse over the mountain trail.

had, haved   2. Meg _____ a job interview with a catering firm last Saturday.

drank, drunk   3. Everyone who had _____ from that well got a stomachache.

shaked, shook   4. My father _____ the chicken in a bag with breadcrumbs and spices.

leaved, left   5. When the carpenters finished their work, they _____ behind piles of sawdust.

hid, hidden   6. It was rumored that the old man had _____ money inside his pillow.

do, does   7. I do the cooking, and my roommate _____ the cleaning up.

keeped, kept   8. During the war, the soldier _____ a picture of his mother in his shirt pocket.

freezed, frozen   9. My aunt has _____ eight quarts of strawberries so that she can make pies this winter.

was, were   10. We _____ amazed when our gray dog had five tiny white and black puppies.

Name_____ Section _____ Date _____

➤ *Irregular Verbs: Test 3*

Each short passage below contains an error in the past tense and in the past participle of an irregular verb. Find the **two** errors and cross them out. Then write the correct form of the verb in the space provided.

Note: Hints are given for half of the items.

1. It is dangerous to shake a baby. Many babies who have been shook have suffered brain injuries. The adults who shaked these babies seldom meant to cause such harm.

    a. _____

       After the helping verbs *have been*, use the past participle of *shake*.

    b. _____

2. Last Sunday, Grandma invited a dozen people over for dinner. After everything was ate, the men started to go watch TV. "Hold it," said Grandma. "If you eaten, you help clean up."

    a. _____

       After the helping verb *was*, use the past participle of *eat*.

    b. _____

3. I give my little children household chores. This month, my son sets the table, and my daughter do some dusting. Last month, they both done some weeding in the back yard.

    a. _____

       Use the standard present tense of *do*.

    b. _____

4. It really can be more fun to give than to receive. Yesterday I gived my niece a ring of mine that she had always loved. When she saw what I had gave her, her face lit up.

    a. _____

       Use the past tense of the irregular verb *give*.

    b. _____

5. In the winter, I drink about a quart of orange juice a week. But last week when it was so hot, I drinked that much in a day. Once all the orange juice was drank, I started in on ice water and cold milk.

    a. _____

       Use the past tense of the irregular verb *drink*.

    b. _____

Name_____ Section _____ Date _____

Score: (Number right) _____ x 10 = _____%

➤ *Irregular Verbs: Test 4*

Each short passage below contains **two** irregular verb errors. Find these errors and cross them out. Then write the correct form of each verb in the space provided.

1. "Try to fall in love with a rich woman," my mother urged me. But I falled for a starving artist. When I told her I had fallen in love with a poor woman, she sighed, "Your father did the same thing."

   a. _____

   b. _____

2. Randy losed forty pounds by drinking a diet shake instead of eating meals. But in a year, he gained it all back. Kay, on the other hand, became thin by changing her eating habits and exercising. She dropped pounds more slowly, but she has keeped them off.

   a. _____

   b. _____

3. Hawks has keen eyesight. Once I saw a hawk dive from the top of a tall tree to capture a field mouse. The bird had saw the tiny creature running through the tall grass.

   a. _____

   b. _____

4. The two doctors in this office usually see about twenty-five patients each day. But yesterday they seen more than forty. Most of the patients was sick with the flu. Both doctors are planning to take a vacation after the flu season is over.

   a. _____

   b. _____

5. My aunt be a big fan of Elvis Presley. Every time she hears "Love Me Tender," she becomes misty-eyed. Last year, she and my uncle gone on a trip to Graceland, Elvis's home. While there, she bought "Elvis Lives" bumper stickers for herself and all her friends.

   a. _____

   b. _____

Subject-Verb Agreement

Seeing What You Know

Underline the verb form that you think should be used in each of the following sentences. Then read the explanations below.

1. The waitress (pours, pour) over thirty cups of coffee an hour.

2. Many restaurants in this area (serves, serve) low-fat meals.

3. Where (is, are) the ticket stub from the theater?

4. Everybody in my family (loves, love) to get mail.

Understanding the Answers

1. The waitress **pours** over thirty cups of coffee an hour.

   A subject and verb must agree in number. Since the subject, *waitress*, is singular, the singular verb *pours* must be used.

2. Many restaurants in this area **serve** low-fat meals.

   The subject, *restaurants*, is plural, so the plural verb *serve* must be used. *In this area* is a prepositional phrase. The verb must agree with the subject of the sentence, not with a word in the prepositional phrase.

3. Where **is** the ticket stub from the theater?

   Subject and verb must agree in number even when the subject comes after the verb. The subject, *stub*, is singular, so the singular verb *is* must be used.

4. Everybody in my family **loves** to get mail.

   The subject, *everybody*, is an indefinite pronoun that is singular. Therefore it requires the singular verb *loves*.

In a correctly written sentence, the subject and verb **agree** (match) **in number**. Singular subjects have singular verbs, and plural subjects have plural verbs.

In a simple sentence of few words, it may not be difficult to make the subject and verb agree:

- *Mike* often <u>sings</u> in the shower.

(Here and in the rest of the chapter, the *subject* is shown in italic type, and the <u>verb</u> is underlined.)

However, not all sentences are as straightforward as the above example. This chapter will present four types of situations that can cause problems with subject-verb agreement:

1   Present Tense Verbs
2   Words Between the Subject and the Verb
3   Verb Coming Before the Subject
4   Indefinite Pronoun Subjects

1   PRESENT TENSE VERBS

The past tense verb is the same for all subjects, including singular and plural ones:

- Last night, *I* <u>played</u> gin rummy. My *parents* <u>played</u> poker.

However, present tense verbs have two forms. Look at the following short sentences. They demonstrate the pattern of present tense verbs. See if you can find the pattern among the verbs.

Singular		*Plural*
I play.	She plays.	We play.
You play.	He plays.	You play.
	It plays.	They play.

The sentences above illustrate the **pattern of present tense verbs**:

- There is an *s* at the end of present tense verbs for singular subjects other than *I* and *you*.

- There is no *s* at the end of present tense verbs for *I*, *you*, and all plural subjects.

➤ *Practice 1*

Write in the correct form of the verb in the space provided.

sort, sorts   1. The postal worker _____ huge bundles of mail.

sort, sorts   2. The postal workers _____ huge bundles of mail.

listen, listens   3. My daughter _____ to music while studying.

listen, listens   4. My daughters _____ to music while studying.

wriggle, wriggles   5. The worm _____ in the grass.

wriggle, wriggles   6. The worms _____ in the grass.

whistle, whistles   7. The chef _____ while he cooks.

whistle, whistles   8. The chefs _____ while they cook.

argue, argues   9. The actor _____ over his lines.

argue, argues   10. The actors _____ over their lines.

➤ *Practice 2*

Rewrite each of the following sentences in the plural.

> ***Example***   My brother no longer eats meat.
> *My brothers no longer eat meat.*

1. The dog growls softly.

_____

2. Your sneaker needs tying.

_____

3. The pig chews on corn cobs.

_____

4. My niece blows soap bubbles.

_____

5. The porkchop sizzles on the grill.

_____

6. Their son plays football.

_____

7. A guard blocks the door.

_____

8. The shadow gets longer and longer.

_____

9. Our neighbor complains about everything.

_____

10. The instructor reads the school newspaper.

_____

2 WORDS BETWEEN THE SUBJECT AND THE VERB

A verb often comes right after its subject, as in this example:

- The sealed *boxes* <u>belong</u> to my brother.

In many sentences, however, the subject and verb are separated by a prepositional phrase. You may remember that a **prepositional phrase** is a group of words that begins with a preposition and ends with a noun or pronoun. *In, on, for, from, of, to* and *by* are common prepositions. (A longer list of prepositions is on page 70.) Look at the following sentence:

- The sealed *boxes* in the closet <u>belong</u> to my brother.

In this sentence, the subject and verb are separated by the prepositional phrase *in the closet*. In such cases, you must be careful to make the verb agree with the subject—not with a word in the prepositional phrase.

Following are more examples with explanations.

- The *tomatoes* in this salad <u>are</u> brown and mushy.

   (Because the subject, *tomatoes*, is plural, the verb must also be plural. The prepositional phrase, *in this salad*, has no effect on the subject and verb agreement.)

- That silk *flower* by the candles <u>looks</u> real.

   (Because the subject, *flower*, is singular, it needs the singular verb *looks*. *By the candles* is a prepositional phrase.)

- *Books* about baseball <u>fill</u> my son's room.

   (The plural subject *books* takes the plural verb *fill*. *About baseball* is a prepositional phrase.)

(The separation of subjects and verbs by prepositional phrases is also discussed on pages 83–84 in "Subjects and Verbs.")

➤ *Practice 3*

Underline the subject of each sentence. To help you find the subject, cross out the prepositional phrase in each case. Then write the correct verb in the space provided.

taste, tastes   1. The flakes in this cereal _____ like sawdust.

is, are   2. The woman with the dark sunglasses _____ our mayor.

speaks, speak   3. Many people in Europe _____ several languages.

is, are   4. The red-haired boy by the swings _____ my son.

sleep, sleeps   5. A person in my classes _____ through most of the lectures.

3   VERB COMING BEFORE THE SUBJECT

The verb follows the subject in most sentences:

- *Ed* <u>passed</u> the course.
- A *rabbit* <u>lives</u> in my back yard.
- The *plane* <u>roared</u> overhead.

However, in some sentences, the verb comes *before* the subject. These sentences often are questions, or they may begin with prepositional phrases or word groups like *there is* or *here are*.

- What <u>was</u> the *answer* to the fifth question on the test?

  (The verb *was* is singular, so it agrees with the singular subject *answer*. *To the fifth question* and *on the test* are prepositional phrases. The subject of a sentence is never in a prepositional phrase.)

- There <u>goes</u> my *bus*.

  (The verb of this sentence is *goes*. You can find the subject by asking, "What goes?" The answer, *bus*, is the subject.)

- On that shelf <u>are</u> the *reports* for this year.

  (The verb of this sentence is *are*. You can find the subject by asking, "What are on that shelf?" The answer, *reports*, is the subject of this sentence.)

Here's another helpful way to find the subject when the verb comes first: Try to rearrange the sentence so that the subject comes first. The subject may be easier to find when the sentence is in the normal order. For the sentences above, you would then get:

- The *answer* to the fifth question on the test <u>was</u> what?
- My *bus* <u>goes</u> there.
- The *reports* for this year <u>are</u> on that shelf.

➤ *Practice 4*

Underline the subject of each sentence. Then, in the space provided, write the form of the verb that agrees with the subject. (If you have trouble finding the subjects, try crossing out any prepositional phrases.)

is, are   1. Here _____ some messages for you.

is, are   2. Where _____ the box for these crayons?

stands, stand 3. Beside the stream _____ a low wooden fence.

grows, grow 4. In that little garden _____ twenty herbs.

was, were   5. There _____ black clouds in the sky this morning.

4   INDEFINITE PRONOUN SUBJECTS

Indefinite pronouns are pronouns that do not refer to a specific person or thing. The ones in the box below are always singular.

Singular Indefinite Pronouns

each	anyone	anybody	anything
either	everyone	everybody	everything
neither	someone	somebody	something
one	no one	nobody	nothing

In the following sentences, the subjects are singular indefinite pronouns. Each of the verbs is therefore also singular.

- *Neither* of the boys <u>knows</u> his true father.

- Despite the rules, nearly *everyone* in my apartment building <u>owns</u> a pet.

➤ *Practice 5*

Underline the subject of each sentence. Then, in the space provided, write the form of the verb that agrees with the subject.

is, are   1. Everybody at my new school _____ friendly.

feel, feels   2. Neither of those mattresses _____ comfortable.

know, knows   3. Nobody in my family _____ how to swim.

needs, need   4. Each of the children _____ some attention.

sound, sounds 5. Something about Robbie's story _____ suspicious.

CHAPTER REVIEW

Answer the questions by filling in the correct word in each space provided.

1. A singular subject takes a *(singular or plural?)* _____ verb.

    A plural subject takes a *(singular or plural?)* _____ verb.

2. The *(singular or plural?)* _____ of present tense verbs is sometimes formed by adding the letter *s* to the end of the verb.

3. *True or false?* _____ The subject of a sentence is often found in a prepositional phrase.

4. The indefinite pronouns *anyone* and *everybody* take a *(singular or plural?)* _____ verb.

Name_____ Section _____ Date _____

➤ *Subject-Verb Agreement: Test 1*

For each sentence, fill in the correct form of the verb in the margin.

Note: Hints are given for half of the sentences.

smile, smiles   1. The patient _____ weakly.
   The verb for the singular subject *patient* must end in an *s*.

chat, chats   2. The sisters _____ before falling asleep at night.

is, are   3. The enemy in these computer games _____ a pink blob named Fred.
   In these computer games is a prepositional phrase. The subject of the sentence is the singular noun *enemy*, so the verb must also be singular.

belongs, belong   4. The bones in the backyard _____ to our neighbor's dog.

is, are   5. Here _____ a parking space.
   In a sentence that begins with *here*, the subject will often come after the verb. In this case, the subject is *space*.

is, are   6. There _____ sad expressions on the students' faces.

draw, draws   7. Everyone in our art class _____ with a charcoal stick.
   The indefinite pronoun *everyone* is singular and therefore requires a singular verb.

itches, itch   8. Each of these sweaters _____.

is, are   9. Why _____ the lights off?
   In a question, the subject often follows the verb.

was, were   10. What _____ the reasons for the workers' strike?

Name_____ Section _____ Date _____

Score: (Number right) _____ x 10 = _____%

➤ *Subject-Verb Agreement: Test 2*

For each sentence, fill in the correct form of the verb in the margin.

sip, sips   1. The woman _____ a cola while doing her work.

is, are   2. What _____ your middle name?

know, knows   3. Nobody _____ the directions to the park.

is, are   4. The seats on the airplane _____ small and crowded.

slide, slides   5. The raindrops _____ slowly down the window.

was, were   6. Among the guests _____ a private detective.

seems, seem   7. The questions on this test _____ unfair to me.

roll, rolls   8. The garbage cans often _____ down the street.

is, are   9. There _____ many hungry people in America's cities.

play, plays   10. Someone in the apartment upstairs _____ a guitar late at night.

Name_____   Section _____   Date _____

Score: (Number right) _____ x 10 = _____%

➤ *Subject-Verb Agreement: Test 3*

Each of the following passages contains **two** mistakes in subject-verb agreement. Find these two mistakes and cross them out. Then write the correct form of each verb in the space provided.

Note: Hints are given for half of the items.

1. Few people recalls seeing baby pigeons. The reason is simple. Baby pigeons in the nest eats a huge amount of food each day. Upon leaving the nest, they are close to the size of their parents.

    a. _____

    The subject of the first sentence, *people*, is plural. It takes a plural verb.

    b. _____

2. Everything in the mall stores are on sale today. Customers from all over are crowding the aisles. There is terrific bargains in many departments.

    a. _____

    Everything is a singular indefinite pronoun, so it takes a singular verb.

    b. _____

3. I am disappointed in my frozen dinner. The peas looks wrinkled and dry. Mounds of soggy stuffing covers a tiny piece of meat.

    a. _____

    Peas is plural, so its present tense verb must also be plural.

    b. _____

4. The members of the swimming team paces nervously beside the pool. Finally, an official blows a whistle. Into the pool dive a swimmer with large tan arms. He paddles quickly through the water.

    a. _____

    The subject of the first sentence is *members*, which is plural. The verb must also be plural.

    b. _____

5. There are three paths through the woods. There is narrow, rocky parts on two of the paths. The hikers take the easiest one. Around a bend, someone spots a snake. It is lying in the middle of the path, sunning itself. One of the hikers fear snakes. He refuses to go on.

    a. _____

    The subject of the second sentence, *parts*, is plural.

    b. _____

➤ Subject-Verb Agreement: Test 4

Each of the following passages contains **two** mistakes in subject-verb agreement. Find these two mistakes and cross them out. Then write the correct form of each verb in the space provided.

1. Our friends in the country gets rid of the insects in their yard without using poisonous sprays. Instead, they use chickens. The chickens happily eats most of the insects. Our friends also get to enjoy fresh eggs.

   a. _____

   b. _____

2. The paint on the house and barn are peeling. Also, each of the buildings need repairs. However, there is never enough time to do those jobs.

   a. _____

   b. _____

3. "Here rests the bones of evil Ned Sloan. The memory of his evil deeds have not died."

   a. _____

   b. _____

4. One of my professors always listens to students and makes sure they understand the lesson. Each of his students feel free to ask questions. Also, the tests in his classes is always fair and clear.

   a. _____

   b. _____

5. The rain forests of South America is home to many species of frogs. Nobody among the world's scientists know exactly how many. More types are being discovered all the time.

   a. _____

   b. _____

Sentence Types

A. In each blank, add a word that fits the sentence.

1. A _____ landed on my arm.

2. The actor _____ to his fans.

B. Into each sentence, insert the most suitable of the following words: **and, but, so**. Use each word once.

1. Ken's house is new, _____ his wife is new too.

2. There is a hole in the screen, _____ we have to keep the window shut.

3. The principal of the school is strict, _____ she is fair.

C. Into each sentence, insert the most suitable of the following words: **although, if, because**. Use each word once.

1. _____ I get angry at someone, I generally let him or her know it.

2. I scrubbed my kitchen _____ my mother was coming to visit.

3. _____ the restaurant is nothing special, it is always crowded.

Understanding the Answers

A. The first sentence could have been completed with a subject such as *bee*. The second sentence could have been completed with a verb such as *waved*.

Some sentences in English are **simple**, made up of one subject-verb combination expressing a complete thought. The two sentences given are examples.

B. The words that best join together the three pairs of statements are *and* (for the first sentence), *so* (for the second sentence), and *but* (for the third sentence).

Other sentences are **compound**, made up of two or more complete thoughts connected by a joining word such as *and, but,* or *so*. The three sentences in group B are all compound sentences.

C. The words that best fit the sentences in group C are *if* (in the first sentence), *because* (in the second sentence), and *although* (in the third sentence).

Yet other sentences are **complex**, made up of one complete thought and one dependent thought. Dependent thoughts begin with a dependent word such as *although, if,* or *because*. The three sentences in group C are all complex sentences.

The three most basic kinds of sentences in English are simple, compound, and complex sentences. This chapter explains and provides practice in all three sentence types. It also presents two types of words you can use to connect ideas together into one sentence:

1   Joining words (for compound sentences)

2   Dependent words (for complex sentences)

THE SIMPLE SENTENCE

A **simple sentence** has only one subject-verb combination and expresses a complete thought.

- The alarm sounded.
- A jet soared through the darkening sky.
- The tourist should have packed her sunglasses.

A simple sentence may have more than one subject:

- Shorts and T-shirts sway on the clothesline.

   (In this sentence, *shorts* and *T-shirts* are the subjects.)

A simple sentence may have more than one verb:

- The children splashed and squealed in the swimming pool.

   (In this sentence, both *splashed* and *squealed* are the verbs.)

A simple sentence may even have several subjects and verbs:

- Every weekend, Gary, Sam, and Rita go to the movies, eat at a Chinese restaurant, and dance at a club.

   (There are three subjects in this sentence: *Gary, Sam,* and *Rita.* There are also three verbs: *go, eat,* and *dance.*)

➤ Practice 1

Complete the simple sentences below by filling in one or more subjects and/or one or more verbs.

1. _____ is my favorite color.

2. The batter _____ the ball.

3. The _____ gave me regular coffee instead of decaf.

4. The thoughtless driver _____ a paper cup onto the highway.

5. _____ and _____ were blowing across the empty parking lot.

6. _____ and _____ are my least favorite foods.

7. A suitcase _____ off the van and _____ into a ditch.

8. On rainy Saturday mornings, the children _____ cookies and _____ cartoons on television.

9. _____ and I often exercise and _____ together.

10. _____ and _____ went to a movie and then _____ dinner at a local diner.

THE COMPOUND SENTENCE

A **compound** sentence is made up of two or more complete thoughts. For instance, look at the following simple sentences:

- Rose wants chili for dinner.
- She forgot to buy beans.

These two simple sentences can be combined to make one compound sentence:

- Rose wants chili for dinner, **but** she forgot to buy beans.

The process of joining together two ideas of equal importance is known as *coordination.*

Joining Words

In the above example, the simple sentences have been connected by using a comma plus the joining word *but.* There are other joining words (also known as *coordinating conjunctions)* that can be used to connect two ideas. The chart below explains all the joining words.

Joining Words

and	means *in addition*
but	means *however*
so	means *as a result*
for	means *because*
yet	means *however*
or	is used to show alternatives
nor	is used to show a second negative statement

Look at the following uses of the joining words:

- The driver failed to signal, and he went through a stop sign.

    (**And** means *in addition*: The driver failed to signal; *in addition*, he went through a stop sign.)

- I was very tired, but I still had two hours of homework.

    (**But** means *however:* I was very tired; *however*, I still had two hours of homework.)

- The meal was not hot, so we sent it back to the kitchen.

    (**So** means *as a result:* The meal was not hot; *as a result*, we sent it back to the kitchen.)

- I work at home, for I want to be with my two young children.

    (**For** means *because:* I work at home *because* I want to be with my two young children.)

- My brother loves cooking, yet he decided to major in business.

    (**Yet** means *however:* My brother loves cooking; *however*, he decided to major in business.

- You can ride with us to the game, or you can go in someone else's car.

    (**Or** introduces an alternative choice: You can ride with us to the game. *Alternatively,* you can go with someone else.)

- Eli does not eat meat, nor does he eat fish.

    (**Nor** introduces a negative statement that has been added to the first negative statement: Eli does *not* eat meat. He also does *not* eat fish.)

Note how each compound sentence is punctuated: A comma comes right after the first complete thought and before the joining word.

➤ Practice 2

Complete each of the following sentences by adding a second complete thought. Remember that a complete thought must contain a subject and a verb.

1. The class was cancelled, so _____

2. I gave our dog a bath, for _____

3. The beef barley soup smelled delicious, but _____

    _____

4. Kay went to the store during her break, and _____

    _____

5. The man spilled coffee on his new linen slacks, so _____

    _____

6. I did not pass the test, nor _____

7. The telephone rang six times, but _____

8. The party started late, and _____

9. Sheila promised to meet me at the mall at ten, yet _____

_____

10. You could work as a waitress this summer, or _____

_____

➤ *Practice 3*

Use a comma and a suitable joining word to combine each pair of simple sentences into a compound sentence. Choose from the following joining words:

and   **but**   **so**

1. The city workers are on strike.
    The streets are lined with garbage bags.

    _____

    _____

2. The television was on.
    No one was watching it.

    _____

    _____

3. The room is painted yellow.
    It has big, sunny windows.

    _____

    _____

4. A storm was approaching quickly.
    The campers found shelter in a cave.

    _____

    _____

5. Dean likes whole-wheat toast for breakfast.
    Chris prefers sugar-coated cereal.

    _____

    _____

THE COMPLEX SENTENCE

As you have already learned, a compound sentence is made up of two or more complete thoughts. Each thought could stand alone as an independent statement. A **complex sentence**, on the other hand, includes one independent statement and at least one dependent statement, which *cannot* stand alone. Look at the following example:

- Although nearby trees were blown down, our house escaped the tornado.

The second statement in this sentence is independent. It can stand alone as a simple sentence:

- Our house escaped the tornado.

The first statement, however, cannot stand alone. It is dependent—it depends on the rest of the sentence to finish the thought:

- Although nearby trees were blown down

Dependent statements begin with dependent words, such as *although*. They also include a subject and a verb. (The subject of the dependent statement above is *trees*; the verb is *were blown*.)

Now look at another sentence:

- As the kidnapper made demands on the phone, police surrounded the building.

This is also a complex sentence. One part can stand independently as a simple sentence: *Police surrounded the building.* The other part of the sentence has a subject and a verb, but it begins with a dependent word and cannot stand alone: ***as the kidnapper made demands on the phone.***

Here's another complex sentence. See if you can spot the independent and dependent parts of the sentence.

- Paula will not sell her home in the country even if she gets a job in the city.

Paula will not sell her home in the country is the independent part of the sentence. The dependent part begins with the dependent words *even if* and cannot stand alone: ***even if** she gets a job in the city.*

Dependent Words

In the above examples, the dependent words *although, as,* and *even if* make the statements they introduce dependent. There are various other dependent words (also known as subordinating conjunctions). The chart on the next page lists some of the common ones.

Look at the following examples again to understand how to punctuate complex sentences.

- **As** the kidnapper made demands on the phone, police surrounded the building.
- Paula will not sell the farm **even if** she gets a job in the city.

Dependent Words

after	even if	unless	where
although	even though	until	wherever
as	if	when	whether
because	since	whenever	while
before	though		

Notice that when the dependent statement comes first, it is followed by a comma. When the dependent idea comes last, it is generally not separated from the rest of the sentence by a comma.

➤ *Practice 4*

Underline the dependent word in each of the following sentences. Then complete each dependent statement. (Every dependent statement should have a subject and a verb.)

1. Dolores cried when _____

2. Although _____,
   I was too tired to go.

3. Lynn took a shower after _____

4. Because _____,
   I set my alarm for 5 a.m.

5. I was paid for a full week of work even though_____

   _____

6. Until _____, Danny was not
   allowed to stay at home alone.

7. If _____, you should
   get a quart of milk.

8. Since _____,
   I am saving extra money each month.

9. José did some research in the library before _____

   _____

10. Because _____,
    we decided not to go to the rock concert.

➤ *Practice 5*

Combine each pair of simple sentences into a complex sentence. To change a simple sentence into a dependent statement, add a dependent word to it, as shown in the example. Choose a suitable dependent word from the following:

after   **although**   **because**   **since**   **when**   **while**

Finally, be sure to place a comma after a dependent statement when it starts a sentence.

> ***Example***   The sweater is old and faded.
> It is Paula's favorite.
>
> *Although the sweater is old and faded, it is Paula's favorite.*

1. The travelers slept in their station wagon.
   All the motels in the area were full.

   _____

   _____

2. The campers slept.
   Raccoons tore apart their backpacks.

   _____

   _____

3. The band finally began to play.
   We had sat through an hour of recorded music.

   _____

   _____

4. There is a playoff game in the city.
   Traffic is jammed for miles.

   _____

   _____

5. His wife died.
   Mr. Albertson has been lonely.

   _____

   _____

6. A fan just moves the air.
   An air conditioner cools it.

   _____

   _____

7. My father and mother are separated.
   They do not plan to divorce.

   _____

   _____

8. The test was over.
   We decided to get something to eat.

   _____

   _____

9. Julie asked Leonard out on a date.
   Her legs were trembling.

   _____

   _____

10. We're trying not to waste paper.
    We usually use cloth napkins.

    _____

    _____

CHAPTER REVIEW

Circle the letter of the correct answer to each question.

1. The statements in a compound sentence are joined together by a
   a. dependent word.
   b. comma and a joining word.
   c. semicolon.

2. A dependent statement includes a
   a. dependent word.
   b. comma and a joining word.
   c. semicolon.

3. Which sentence is a simple sentence?
   a. Mom did a somersault.
   b. When Mom did a somersault, she hurt her back.
   c. Mom did a somersault, and she hurt her back.

4. Which sentence is a compound sentence?
   a. Mom did a somersault.
   b. When Mom did a somersault, she hurt her back.
   c. Mom did a somersault, and she hurt her back.

5. Which sentence is a complex sentence?
   a. Mom did a somersault.
   b. When Mom did a somersault, she hurt her back.
   c. Mom did a somersault, and she hurt her back.

Name_____ Section _____ Date _____

➤ *Sentence Types: Test 1*

A. Use a comma and a suitable joining word to combine the following pairs of simple sentences into compound sentences. Choose from *and, but,* or *so.*

> *Note:* Hints are given for half of the sentences.

  1. Kwan is quite attractive.
     She thinks she is ugly.
     Add a comma and the joining word *but.*

     _____

  2. This coffee is cold.
     It is too strong.

     _____

  3. The book was very expensive.
     I didn't buy it.
     Add a comma and the joining word *so.*

     _____

  4. Gene laughed throughout the movie.
     His date didn't laugh once.

     _____

B. Use a suitable dependent word to combine the following pairs of simple sentences into complex sentences. Choose from *although, because, since,* and *when.* Place a comma after a dependent statement when it starts a sentence.

> *Note:* Hints are given for half of the sentences.

  5. Strawberries are expensive.
     I don't often buy them.
     Begin the complex sentence with *because.* Place a comma after the dependent statement.

     _____

  6. An elephant's skin is very thick.
     It is sensitive.

     _____

  7. The city pools have been crowded.
     The weather turned hot.
     Start the complex sentence with a complete thought. Then begin the dependent statement with *since.* (No comma is needed.)

     _____

  8. An egg spins faster.
     It is hard-boiled.

     _____

➤ *Sentence Types: Test 2*

A. Use a comma and a suitable joining word to combine the following pairs of simple sentences into compound sentences. Choose from *and, but,* or *so.*

1. The car runs well.
   Its body is rusty.

   _____

2. The electricity was out.
   We had no candles.

   _____

3. The tea stain didn't wash out of my white skirt.
   I dyed the skirt tan.

   _____

4. Thirty percent of M&M's are brown.
   Twenty percent of them are red.

   _____

B. Use a suitable dependent word to combine the following pairs of simple sentences into complex sentences. Choose from *although, because, since,* and *when.* Place a comma after a dependent statement when it starts a sentence.

5. Sandra wanted a good novel to read.
   She went to the library.

   _____

6. I quickly called the police.
   I heard a scream outside.

   _____

7. Mark seems unfriendly.
   He is really just shy.

   _____

8. The ball game was postponed.
   It began to rain heavily.

   _____

Name_____ Section _____ Date _____

Score: (Number right) _____ x 12.5 = _____ %

➤ *Sentence Types: Test 3*

Combine each group of simple sentences into compound or complex sentences. Combine the first two sentences into one sentence, and combine the last two sentences into another sentence. Use any of the following joining words and dependent words.

Joining words:	**and**	**but**	**so**	
Dependent words:	**after**	**although**	**because**	**when**

Here are two comma hints: (1) Use a comma between two thoughts joined by *and, but,* or *so*. (2) Place a comma after a dependent statement when it starts a sentence.

Note: Hints are given for half of the groups.

1. It had rained for three days.
   The sun finally came out.
   We wanted to have a picnic.
   The ground was too wet.
   Use *after* to combine the first two sentences. Use *but* to combine the second two sentences.

   _____

   _____

   _____

2. Roy saw a bright rainbow.
   He ran to get his camera.
   He rushed back to take a picture.
   The rainbow had gone.

   _____

   _____

   _____

3. A cosmetics saleswoman came to my door.
   I pretended not to be home.
   She rang the bell several times.
   She knocked on the door repeatedly.
   Use *when* to combine the first two sentences. Use *and* to combine the second two sentences.

   _____

   _____

   _____

4. Nadine hates her job.
   She won't leave it.
   She likes the pension plan.
   She will stay for twenty years until retirement.

   _____

   _____

   _____

Name_____ Section _____ Date _____

➤ *Sentence Types: Test 4*

Combine each group of simple sentences into compound or complex sentences. Combine the first two sentences into one sentence, and combine the last two sentences into another sentence. Use any of the following joining words and dependent words.

Joining words: **and** **but** **so**
Dependent words: **although** **because** **since** **when**

Here are two comma hints: (1) Use a comma between two thoughts connected by *and, but,* or *so.* (2) Place a comma after a dependent statement when it starts a sentence.

1. The instructor was late to class.
   The classroom was quiet anyway.
   The students were reading their textbooks.
   They were taking an important test that day.

   _____

   _____

   _____

2. I had to meet my girlfriend's mother.
   I was very nervous.
   I was afraid of her opinion of me.
   She was very warm and friendly.

   _____

   _____

   _____

3. Sue Lin left Vietnam in a small, crowded boat.
   She wanted freedom so badly.
   Everyone on the boat faced starvation.
   They were finally rescued by a passing ship.

   _____

   _____

   _____

4. Jack was tired of his appearance.
   He shaved all the hair off his head.
   He bought new clothing in bright colors.
   He added an earring as well.

   _____

   _____

   _____

Sentence Fragments

Seeing What You Know

Underline the statement in each numbered item that you think is *not* a complete sentence. Then read the explanations below.

1. Because I could not sleep. I turned on my light and read.

2. Calling his dog's name. Todd walked up and down the street.

3. My little sister will eat anything. Except meat, vegetables, and fruit.

4. The reporter turned on her laptop computer. Then began to type quickly.

Understanding the Answers

1. *Because I could not sleep* is an incomplete sentence.

   The writer does not complete the thought by telling us what happened because he could not sleep. Correct the fragment by joining it to the sentence that follows it:

   • Because I could not sleep, I turned on my light and read.

2. *Calling his dog's name* is not a complete sentence.

   The word group lacks both a subject and a verb, and it does not express a complete thought. Correct the fragment by adding it to the sentence that follows it:

   • Calling his dog's name, Todd walked up and down the street.

3. *Except meat, vegetables, and fruit* is not a complete sentence.

   Again, the word group lacks a subject and a verb, and it does not express a complete thought. Correct the fragment by adding it to the sentence that comes before it:

   • My little sister will eat anything except meat, vegetables, and fruit.

4. *Then began to type quickly* is not a complete sentence.

   The word group lacks a subject. One way to correct the fragment is to add the subject *she*:

   • Then she began to type quickly.

To be a complete sentence, a group of words must contain a subject and a verb. It must also express a complete thought—in other words, it must make sense by itself. A **sentence fragment** is *less than a sentence* because it lacks a subject or a verb or because it does not express a complete thought.

This chapter describes the most common types of sentence fragments:

1   Dependent-Word Fragments

2   *-Ing* and *To* Fragments

3   Added-Detail Fragments

4   Missing-Subject Fragments

1   DEPENDENT-WORD FRAGMENTS

Some fragments contain a subject and a verb, but they do not express a complete thought. Here are three such fragments:

- Since Laura was tired.
- When the man pointed the gun at us.
- After I turned off the television set.

All of these word groups begin with dependent words—*since, when, after*. All three word groups depend upon another statement to complete the thought. See if you can add words to each fragment that would complete the thought.

- Since Laura was tired, _____.
- When the man pointed the gun at us, _____.
- _____ after I turned off the television set.

Here are some possible completions for the above word groups:

- Since Laura was tired, **she took a nap**.
- When the man pointed the gun at us, **we gave him our money**.
- **I picked up a book** after I turned off the television set.

When you begin a statement with a dependent word, take care that you follow through and complete the thought in the same sentence. Otherwise, a sentence fragment will result. Here is a list of common dependent words:

Dependent Words

after	even if	unless	where
although	even though	until	wherever
as	if	when	whether
because	since	whenever	while
before	though		

➤ *Practice 1*

This practice will give you a sense of the difference between a dependent-word fragment and a complete sentence. Turn each fragment into a sentence by adding a statement that completes the thought.

1. When I rang the doorbell, _____.

2. Because Jill forgot her house keys, _____.

3. _____ while the music played.

4. Unless the rash disappears soon, _____.

5. _____ before I go to sleep at night.

6. Although the report was due yesterday, _____.

7. If you want to take a vacation, _____.

8. _____ after the alarm rang.

9. Since no one was home, _____.

10. As I walked into the classroom, _____.

Correcting Dependent-Word Fragments

A common way to correct a dependent-word fragment is to connect it to the sentence that comes before or after it. For example:

- Since I had lost my house key. I had to break a window.

Since I had lost my house key is a fragment that begins with a dependent word. Because the fragment expresses an incomplete thought, it leaves the reader expecting something more. The writer must tell *in the same sentence* what happened as a result of the house key being lost. Correct the fragment by connecting it to the sentence that follows it.

- Since I had lost my house **key, I** had to break a window.

Note: Put a comma at the end of a dependent-word group that starts a sentence.

Here is another example to consider:

- School closed early today. Because of a leak in a water main.

Because of a leak in a water main is a fragment that begins with a dependent word. The fragment expresses an incomplete thought and leaves the reader expecting something more. The writer must tell *in the same sentence* what happened because of the leak in a water main. In the sentence below, the fragment was corrected by connecting it to the sentence that comes before it.

- School closed early **today because** of a leak in a water main.

You will often correct a fragment by connecting it to the sentence that comes before it.

➤ *Practice 2*

Underline the dependent-word fragment in each of the following items. Then correct it in the space provided.

1. After he bought a cup of coffee. Eric hurried to the office.

   _____

2. The batter argued with the umpire. While the crowd booed.

   _____

3. All the food will spoil. Unless the refrigerator is fixed soon.

   _____

4. Because the movie was so poor. Many people left the theater.

   _____

5. Everything was peaceful. Before Martha stormed into the room.

   _____

   _____

6. When two guests began to argue. The hostess moved the party outside.

   _____

   _____

7. Although the car accident was a bad one. The passengers were unharmed.

   _____

   _____

8. Since we forgot to buy a battery. Our son can't play with his new toy today.

   _____

   _____

9. Our leaves blew into the neighbor's yard. Before I found time to rake them.

   _____

   _____

10. The police believed the witness. Until he picked the wrong person out of a lineup.

    _____

    _____

More on Dependent-Word Fragments

Some dependent-word fragments begin with the word *who*, *that*, *whose*, or *which*. Here are examples:

- Janice had to clean up the mess. That the kids left in the kitchen.
- I passed the math course. Which I had half-expected to fail.
- Yesterday my wife ran into a fellow. Who was her best friend in high school.

This type of fragment is often best corrected by attaching it to the sentence that comes before it:

- Janice had to clean up the **mess that** the kids left in the kitchen.
- I passed the math **course which** I had half-expected to fail.
- Yesterday my wife ran into a **fellow who** was her best friend in high school.

➤ *Practice 3*

Underline the dependent-word fragment in each of the following items. Then correct it in the space provided.

1. I bought an expensive coat. Which was made of soft leather.

   _____

   _____

2. The police visited the high school. That has a big drug problem.

   _____

   _____

3. The dog growled at the toddler. Who was screaming loudly.

   _____

   _____

4. The pilot refused to fly the jet. That had ice on its wings.

   _____

   _____

5. My neighbor is a quiet man. Whose working day begins at midnight.

   _____

   _____

2   -ING AND TO FRAGMENTS

When -*ing* or *to* appears at or near the beginning of a word group, a fragment may result. Here is an example of an -*ing* fragment:

- Hoping to furnish their new home cheaply. The newlyweds often go to garage sales.

The second statement is a complete sentence. But the first word group lacks both a subject and a verb, so it is a fragment.

Here is an example of a *to* fragment:

- Randy jogged through the park. To clear his mind before the midterm.

The first statement is a complete sentence. But the second word group lacks both a subject and a verb, so it is a fragment.

There are two ways to correct -*ing* and *to* fragments:

1   Connect the fragment to the sentence it explains.

- Hoping to furnish their new home **cheaply, the** newlyweds often go to garage sales.
- Randy jogged through the **park to** clear his mind before the midterm.

Note: Put a comma after an -*ing* or a *to* word group that starts a sentence.

2   Create a complete sentence by adding a subject and a verb to the fragment. To do so, revise the material as necessary.

- The newlyweds often go to garage sales. **They hope** to furnish their new home cheaply.
- Randy jogged through the park. **He wanted** to clear his mind before the midterm.

➤ *Practice 4*

Underline the -*ing* or *to* fragment in each of the following items. Then correct it in the space provided, using one of the two methods given above.

1. The owner has opened a take-out window. To attract more customers to the diner.

   _____

   _____

2. Rising high into the sky. The blue hot-air balloon could be seen for miles.

   _____

   _____

3. To get off the horse. The circus rider did a forward flip.

   _____

   _____

4. Eating the spinach. I felt bits of sand in my mouth.

   _____

   _____

5. The dog sat quietly near the baby's high chair. Waiting for crumbs to fall.

   _____

   _____

6. The hikers broke branches. To mark the trail for their return trip.

   _____

   _____

7. The family saves plastic bags and bottles. To take to the recycling center.

   _____

   _____

8. The man jumped into the firefighters' net. Praying loudly all the while.

   _____

   _____

9. Glancing out the window. Rudy spotted someone taking tomatoes from his garden.

   _____

   _____

10. To enter the contest. My sister wrote a jingle for her favorite potato chips.

   _____

   _____

3   ADDED-DETAIL FRAGMENTS

Another common kind of fragment often begins with one of the following: *like, including, such as, for example, for instance, except, without, especially,* and *also.* These words introduce an additional point or example to what has already been stated.

- The former friends walked past one another. Without speaking a word.
- For a main dish, I often serve beans and grains. For example, lentils with brown rice.

In each of the above examples, the second word group lacks both a subject and a verb. Note that each of those fragments begins with an added-detail word or phrase: *without* and *for example*.

There are two ways to correct an added-detail fragment:

1   Add the fragment to the sentence it explains.

- The former friends walked past one **another without** speaking a word.

2   Create a new sentence by adding a subject and verb to the fragment. To do so, revise the material as necessary.

- For a main dish, I often serve beans and grains. For example, **I mix** lentils and brown rice.

➤ *Practice 5*

Underline the added-detail fragment in each of the following items. Then correct it in the space provided, using one of the two methods given above.

1. Everybody enjoyed Thanksgiving dinner. Except the turkey.

   _____

2. Citrus fruits are full of nutrients. Especially vitamin C.

   _____

3. We had to read several novels for class. Including *Lord of the Flies*.

   _____

   _____

4. Gary is a rude person at times. For instance, interrupting an instructor during a lecture.

   _____

   _____

5. With braces I cannot eat certain foods. Such as popcorn and apples.

_____

_____

6. Andy had to work all summer in a stuffy warehouse. Without air conditioning.

_____

_____

7. Don't touch anything in the science lab. Especially the bubbling tubes on the table.

_____

_____

8. The dentist said the procedure wouldn't hurt. Except for the shot to numb my gums and teeth.

_____

_____

9. There are healthier ways to prepare chicken than frying. For example, broiling.

_____

_____

10. The detective searched the room for clues. Such as old letters, receipts, and ticket stubs.

_____

_____

4 MISSING-SUBJECT FRAGMENTS

Some word groups are fragments because, while they do have a verb, they lack a subject. Here are examples:

- The politician held a smiling baby. Then posed for the photographers.
- The woman paid all of her bills. But then had little money left over for food.

In each of the above examples, the first statement is a complete sentence, and the second word group is a fragment. Note that each fragment is missing a subject. The first fragment omits the subject of the verb _posed_. The second fragment omits the subject of the verb _had_.

There are two ways to correct a missing-subject fragment:

1   Connect the missing-subject fragment to the sentence that comes before it. Add a joining word if needed for a smooth connection, as in the first example below.

   • The politician held a smiling **baby and then** posed for the photographers.
   • The woman paid all of her **bills but had** little money left over for food.

2   Create a new sentence by adding a subject to the fragment. Normally, you will add a pronoun that stands for the subject of the previous sentence.

   • The politician held a smiling baby. Then **he** posed for the photographers.
   • The woman paid all of her **bills. But she had** little money left over for food.

In the first example above, *he* stands for *the politician*. In the second example, *she* stands for *the woman*.

➤ Practice 6

Underline the missing-subject fragment in each of the following items. Then correct it the space provided, using one of the two methods given above.

1. The landlord unclogged the drain. And found a dishcloth stuck in the pipe.

   _____

   _____

2. The dealer shuffled the cards. And asked the man to choose one.

   _____

   _____

3. The cries for help grew more and more faint. Then stopped completely.

   _____

   _____

4. The wallet has room for paper money and credit cards. But has no pocket for coins.

   _____

   _____

5. The dog lifted its head to bark at the mailman. And then went back to sleep.

_____

_____

6. The movie had a catchy soundtrack and popular actors. Yet made little money at the box office.

_____

_____

7. Each morning, the secretary checks the answering machine for messages. Then opens the mail.

_____

_____

8. The wide receiver made a terrific run down the field. But then fumbled the football.

_____

_____

9. Roz skipped her afternoon classes. And worked on a paper due the next morning.

_____

_____

10. Someone stole a rare bird from the zoo. But soon returned it with a note of apology.

_____

_____

CHAPTER REVIEW

Answer each question by filling in the correct word or words in the space provided.

1. To be a sentence, a group of words must contain a subject and a

   _____, and it must express _____

   _____.

2. Words such as *because, until,* and *while* are known as

   _____ words because word groups that begin with

   them depend on another statement to complete the thought.

3. Fragments that begin with words such as *like, especially,* and *for*

   example are known as _____ fragments.

4. One way to correct an added-detail fragment is to create a new

   _____ by adding a subject and a _____

   to the fragment.

5. One way to correct a missing-subject fragment is to add a

   _____ to the fragment.

➤ *Sentence Fragments: Test 1*

Underline the sentence fragment in each item that follows. Then correct the fragment, using one of the methods described in the chapter.

Note: Hints are given for half of the items.

1. Because we have smoke detectors. We survived the fire.
   The first word group begins with the dependent word *because*. Correct the fragment by connecting it to the complete thought that follows it. (And remember that when a dependent-word fragment begins a sentence, it must be followed by a comma.)

   _____

2. Since the movie was on after midnight. We taped it to watch the next day.

   _____

3. The dentist is advertising for an assistant. To work evenings.
   The second word groups lacks a subject and verb. Connect it to the sentence that comes before it.

   _____

4. Monkeys can be trained. To help paralyzed people.

   _____

5. Students can wear anything to our school. Except very short skirts.
   The second word group lacks a subject and a verb. Connect it to the complete statement that comes before it.

   _____

6. Brian loves hot chocolate. Especially topped with whipped cream.

   _____

7. My neighbor loses her temper with her young children. But is trying to become more patient with them.
   Add a subject to the second word group to make a complete thought.

   _____

8. Diane sat down with her boyfriend. And then gently said, "I can't marry you."

   _____

Name_____ Section _____ Date _____

Score: (Number right) _____ x 12.5 = _____%

➤ *Sentence Fragments: Test 2*

Underline the sentence fragment in each item that follows. Then correct the fragment, using one of the methods described in the chapter.

1. My son loves science-fiction shows. Especially all the *Star Trek* reruns.

   _____

2. Rolling slowly backwards. The car in the alley had no driver.

   _____

3. I was very nervous. Because I had not studied for the exam.

   _____

4. Everyone in my family gets New Year's Day off. Except me.

   _____

5. To get himself to be on time. James set all the clocks in his apartment ten minutes ahead.

   _____

   _____

6. Dana becomes happy over little things. Such as her glow-in-the-dark toothbrush.

   _____

   _____

7. Before people in town can burn leaves. They have to get a permit from the police.

   _____

   _____

8. When Connie had saved up enough money for a vacation. Her old car broke down and needed expensive repairs.

   _____

   _____

Name_____ Section _____ Date _____

Score: (Number right) _____ x 12.5 = _____%

➤ *Sentence Fragments: Test 3*

Underline the **two** sentence fragments in each short passage that follows. Then correct each fragment, using one of the methods described in the chapter.

Note: Hints are given for half of the passages.

1. When people are scared. The hair on their bodies really can "stand on end." Each hair is attached to a tiny muscle. Which can pull the hair straight up. The muscles react together in response to a great fright.

   The word groups beginning with *when* and *which* are dependent-word fragments, so each needs to be added to the sentence that comes before or after it.

   _____

   _____

   _____

2. Christmas comes earlier each year. Because merchants like to stretch out the buying season. Right after Halloween this year, store owners hung colored lights. And filled their windows with Christmas decorations.

   _____

   _____

   _____

3. Lasting almost two years. An elephant's pregnancy is the longest of all mammals. Mother elephants devote much of their time to child care. And nurse their babies up to eight years.

   The word group beginning with *Lasting* has no subject or verb. It needs to be added to the sentence that follows it. The missing-subject fragment beginning with *And* can be added to the sentence that comes before it.

   _____

   _____

   _____

4. Karen hates hospitals. Even though she's a nurse. She says they are full of germs and doctors. Waiting to do horrible things to you.

   _____

   _____

   _____

➤ *Sentence Fragments: Test 4*

Underline the **two** sentence fragments in each short passage that follows. Then correct each fragment, using one of the methods described in the chapter.

1. Snakes have the reputation of being slimy. But don't deserve their bad image. Being cool and dry. Snakes actually are quite pleasant to touch.

   _____

   _____

   _____

2. Moving up the mountain at a fast pace. The young hikers were soon exhausted. They were not used to hiking at altitudes. Where the air was thinner.

   _____

   _____

   _____

3. Honey varies quite a bit in taste. Depending on its flower source. In many supermarkets you can find several types of honey. Such as clover and wildflower honey.

   _____

   _____

   _____

4. Jodie likes to pamper herself. After she's had a hard day at work. She loves to relax in an extra-hot bubble bath. When she gets out, her skin is wrinkled. Like a prune.

   _____

   _____

   _____

Run-Ons and Comma Splices

Seeing What You Know

For each of the three groups below, check the item that you think is punctuated correctly. Then read the explanations below.

1. ____ a. The sea is calm today it looks like a blue mirror.
   ____ b. The sea is calm today, it looks like a blue mirror.
   ____ c. The sea is calm today. It looks like a blue mirror.

2. ____ a. The driver saw a dog in his headlights he slammed on the brakes.
   ____ b. The driver saw a dog in his headlights, he slammed on the brakes.
   ____ c. The driver saw a dog in his headlights, so he slammed on the brakes.

3. ____ a. The nurse rubbed alcohol on the cut the child howled in pain.
   ____ b. The nurse rubbed alcohol on the cut, the child howled in pain.
   ____ c. When the nurse rubbed alcohol on the cut, the child howled in pain.

Understanding the Answers

1. **Item *c* is punctuated correctly.**

   In item *c*, two complete thoughts (*the sea is calm today* and *it looks like a blue mirror*) are separated by a period.

   Item *a* is a run-on—the two complete thoughts incorrectly run together with nothing between them. Item *b* is a comma splice—the two complete thoughts are incorrectly joined together by only a comma. A comma alone is not enough to join two complete thoughts.

2. **Item *c* is punctuated correctly.**

   In item *c*, two complete thoughts (*the driver saw a dog in his headlights* and *he slammed on the brakes*) are correctly connected in one sentence by a comma and a joining word (*so*). Item *a*, however, is a run-on sentence, and item *b* is a comma splice.

3. **Item *c* is punctuated correctly.**

   A complete thought (*the child howled in pain*) and a dependent thought (*when the nurse rubbed alcohol on the cut*) can be joined together in one sentence. Item *a*, however, is a run-on sentence, and item *b* is a comma splice.

Run-ons and comma splices are two common, serious writing errors. This chapter will show you how to recognize and how to correct them.

RECOGNIZING RUN-ONS AND COMMA SPLICES

A **run-on** is made up of two complete thoughts that are incorrectly run together without a clear connection between them. Here is an example of a run-on:

• Dolphins have killed sharks they never attack humans.

The complete thoughts are *dolphins have killed sharks* and *they never attack humans.*

A **comma splice** is made up of two complete thoughts that are incorrectly joined (or spliced) together with only a comma. *A comma alone is not enough to connect two complete thoughts.* Here's an example of a comma splice:

• Dolphins have killed sharks, they never attack humans.

➤ *Practice 1*

In each space, write RO if a sentence is a run-on. Write CS if it is a comma splice. Then mark the spot between the two complete thoughts with a slash (/). Look at the examples.

Examples   <u>RO</u>   The garage is locked / no one has a key.

            <u>CS</u>   The house was covered with ivy, / a stone path led to the front door.

_____ 1. Don likes to knit his wife taught him how.

_____ 2. The bell rang, the boxers returned to their corners.

_____ 3. The bicycle is in the basement, it has two flat tires.

_____ 4. Excited fans filled the gym the big game finally began.

_____ 5. The patient sat down with his doctor he brought a list of questions to ask.

_____ 6. Lisa is lucky she can eat anything without gaining weight.

_____ 7. It rained during our entire vacation, we played cards and told stories.

_____ 8. The waiters served soft drinks to the children they offered wine to the adults.

_____ 9. My sister just got married, she and her husband will live with his parents for a while.

_____10. The bee stung the girl on the toe she should not have taken off her shoes.

CORRECTING RUN-ONS AND COMMA SPLICES

There are three methods of correcting run-ons and comma splices.

1 Use a period and a capital letter to create separate sentences.

- Dolphins have killed sharks**. T**hey never attack humans.

2 Use a comma plus a joining word (such as *and, but,* or *so*) to connect the complete thoughts in one sentence.

- Dolphins have killed sharks**, but** they never attack humans.

3 Use a dependent word (such as *because, when, although, if,* or *while*) to make one of the complete thoughts dependent on the other one.

- **Although** dolphins have killed sharks, they never attack humans.

More About Method 1: Using a Period and a Capital Letter

Run-ons and comma splices may be corrected by dividing the complete thoughts into separate sentences.

Run-on: The computer hummed loudly the sound was very irritating.

Comma splice: The computer hummed loudly, the sound was very irritating.

Corrected: The computer hummed loudly**. T**he sound was very irritating.

➢ *Practice 2*

Draw a slash (/) between the two complete thoughts in each run-on or comma splice that follows. Then rewrite the item, using a period and capital letter to divide it into two sentences. Note the example below.

> ***Example***   Our neighbor must hate to mow grass / he filled his yard with green stones.
>
> *Our neighbor must hate to mow grass. He filled his yard with green stones.*

1. Hamsters are small, they are also very cute.

   _____

2. Grape juice spilled on the carpet it made permanent stains.

   _____

3. Kareem's brownies are great, he adds nuts and chocolate chips.

   _____

4. My sister is raising triplets all three of them have red hair.

   _____

5. "Weeds" can be attractive some are even good to eat.

   _____

6. The police officer was puzzled by the crime he found no fingerprints.

   _____

   _____

7. There was an accident on the bridge this morning, traffic was stopped for an hour.

   _____

   _____

8. Coupons help shoppers save money they also help stores to sell products.

   _____

9. The television show was canceled after six episodes, it was not very funny.

   _____

   _____

10. Chipmunks have dug many holes in our yard now it looks like a miniature golf course.

    _____

    _____

More About Method 2: Using a Comma and a Joining Word

Another way of correcting a run-on or a comma splice is to use a comma plus a joining word to connect the two complete thoughts. Common joining words include *and, but,* and *so*. Other joining words are *for, or, nor,* and *yet*. Look at the examples:

Run-on:	Jan had a bad headache she had a fever as well.
Comma splice:	Jan had a bad headache, she had a fever as well.
Corrected:	Jan had a bad headache**, and** she had a fever as well.

Note that the joining word *and* means *in addition:* Jan had a bad headache. *In addition*, she had a fever as well.

Run-on:	Thousands of actors go to Hollywood few ever become stars.
Comma splice:	Thousands of actors to go Hollywood, few ever become stars.
Corrected:	Thousands of actors go to Hollywood**, but** few ever become stars.

Note that the joining word *but* means *however:* Thousands of actors go to Hollywood. *However*, few ever become stars.

Run-on:	Mules are very sure-footed they're useful on steep mountain trails.
Comma splice:	Mules are very sure-footed, they're useful on step mountain trails.
Corrected:	Mules are very sure-footed, **so** they're useful on steep mountain trails.

Note that the joining word *so* means *as a result:* Mules are very sure-footed. *As a result,* they're useful on steep mountain trails.

➤ Practice 3

In each run-on or comma splice below, add a comma and a logical joining word to connect the two complete thoughts. Choose from the following joining words:

and (which means *in addition*)

but (which means *however*)

so (which means *as a result*)

Note the example.

Example The cookies are underdone ____, but____ they still taste good.

1. My parents love jazz _____ I prefer rap music.

2. First I peel the grapefruit _____ then I separate the sections.

3. It was hot and muggy _____ we turned on the air conditioner.

4. Spiders eat many pests _____ their webs are beautiful.

5. Mozart was a genius _____ he died poor and forgotten.

6. I didn't understand the assignment _____ I asked the teacher to explain it.

7. The librarian searched the shelves _____ he did not find the missing book.

8. The beach is littered with garbage _____ there are no lifeguards.

9. The setting sun was almost blinding me _____ I had to keep driving westward.

10. Writing skills are important in college _____ freshmen are required to take a composition course.

➣ *Practice 4*

Draw a slash (/) between the two complete thoughts in each of the run-ons or comma splices that follow. Then rewrite each sentence, using a comma and a logical joining word to connect the two complete thoughts. Choose from the following joining words:

and (which means *in addition*)

but (which means *however*)

so (which means *as a result*)

Note the example.

Example   The applesauce was tart, / the cook added some sugar.

The applesauce was tart, so the cook added some sugar.

1. The garden is overgrown the fence is falling down.

   _____

2. I called Robin three times last night she never answered.

   _____

3. The motorcycle wouldn't start, the man called a taxi.

   _____

4. The alarm clock fell on the floor then it started to ring.

   _____

5. I was out of jelly and butter I spread yogurt on my toast.

   _____

6. The flowers in that yard look wonderful, the grass needs cutting.

   _____

7. Gina is allergic to animals she can't have a pet.

   _____

8. A window was broken, the jewels had been taken.

   _____

9. Mr. Dobbs is friendly with his customers he is rude to his workers.

   _____

10. My back itched in a hard-to-reach place I scratched it on the doorpost.

   _____

   _____

More About Method 3: Using a Dependent Word

A third method of correcting a run-on or comma splice is to add a dependent word to one of the complete thoughts. The sentence will then have one thought that depends upon the remaining complete thought for its full meaning. Here are some common dependent words:

Dependent Words

after	even if	unless	where
although	even though	until	wherever
as	if	when	whether
because	since	whenever	while
before	though		

Look at the following example:

Run-on: The roads are covered with ice school has been cancelled.

Comma splice: The roads are covered with ice, school has been cancelled.

Corrected: **Because** the roads are covered with ice, school has been cancelled.

In the corrected version, one thought is independent. It can stand by itself as a sentence:

School has been cancelled.

However, the thought that begins with a dependent word (*Because the roads are covered with ice*) cannot stand alone. It depends on the rest of the sentence for its full meaning:

Because the roads are covered with ice, school has been cancelled.

Here are two more examples:

Run-on: A large spider crawled out of the drain I was in the shower.

Comma splice: A large spider crawled out of the drain, I was in the shower.

Corrected: A large spider crawled out of the drain **when** I was in the shower.

Run-on: The bus was late I still got to class on time.

Comma splice: The bus was late, I still got to class on time.

Corrected: **Although** the bus was late, I still got to class on time.

Note: When a dependent thought begins a sentence, it is followed by a comma.

➤ *Practice 5*

Draw a slash (/) between the two complete thoughts in each of the run-ons or comma splices that follow. Then rewrite each sentence by adding a dependent word to one of the complete thoughts. Choose from these words: *because, after, since, although, while, if.*

Remember that if the dependent thought comes at the beginning of the sentence, it must be followed with a comma.

Examples

The couple finished their meal / they asked to see the dessert menu.

After the couple finished their meal, they asked to see the dessert menu.

I pulled off the road / my eyes would not stay open.

I pulled off the road because my eyes would not stay open.

1. I care for my elderly parents, I have very little free time.

   _____

2. The water began to boil, I added the ears of corn.

   _____

3. Our neighbor is watering his lawn the forecast is for heavy rain.

   _____

   _____

4. We will have to leave in exactly ten minutes we want to see the kickoff.

   _____

   _____

5. The children swam in the bay, their parents sunned on the beach.

   _____

   _____

6. I finished my written report I spent the rest of the night studying.

   _____

   _____

7. The movie was filmed in black and white, it is being shown on TV tonight in color.

   _____

   _____

8. Lauren is going to Spain next summer she is studying Spanish this year.

_____

_____

9. I take the train to my downtown job finding a space to park can be very difficult.

_____

_____

10. James ordered two scoops of vanilla ice cream there were thirty-two flavors available.

_____

_____

➤ _Practice 6_

The passage below contains two comma splices and one run-on. Correct the first mistake by using a period and a capital letter. Correct the second mistake by adding a comma and the joining word _so_. Correct the third mistake by adding the dependent word _Although_ and a comma.

As you proceed, cross out words and add other words and punctuation marks as needed.

My Human Behavior final exam is next week, I am very worried about passing it. Because I was sick a lot at the start of the semester, I never read many of the chapters in the text. For the past month I've been working full-time, it's hard to find time to study. I will ask the teacher for extra help it may be too late. I am determined never to fall so far behind in class again.

CHAPTER REVIEW

Fill in the missing word in each space.

1. A _____ is made up of two complete thoughts that are incorrectly joined together with nothing between them.

2. A _____ is made up of two complete thoughts that are incorrectly joined together with only a comma between them.

3. One way to correct run-ons and comma splices is to add a _____ and a capital letter.

4. Two complete thoughts can be joined together in a sentence by a comma and a _____ word such as *and, but,* or *so.*

5. Two complete thoughts can be joined together in one sentence by adding a _____ word such as *when* or *because.*

Note: Because run-ons and comma splices are such common errors, two additional tests are provided for practice on the following pages.

Name_____ Section _____ Date _____

Score: (Number right) _____ x 12.5 = _____%

➤ *Run-Ons and Comma Splices: Test 1*

Draw a slash (*/*) between the two complete thoughts in each run-on or comma splice. Then rewrite each sentence using the method stated.

Note: Hints are given for half of the sentences.

A. Use a period and a capital letter to divide the two thoughts into two sentences.

1. The cat slept on the windowsill she was wrapped in warm sunlight.
   The cat slept on the windowsill is the first complete thought.

   _____

   _____

2. Larry is not a good babysitter he treats his little brother like an insect.

   _____

3. There are 125 kinds of goldenrod, they are a common cause of hay fever.
   They are a common cause of hay fever is the second complete thought.

   _____

4. My daughter is easily pleased, she loves hot dogs and other quick meals.

   _____

   _____

B. Use a comma and a logical joining word (*and, but,* or *so*) to connect the two thoughts.

5. Rick is colorblind his wife lays out his clothes every morning.
   Follow the first complete thought (*Rick is colorblind*) with a comma and the joining word *so.*

   _____

6. The wind knocked over a ladder the ladder then broke a window.

   _____

7. The store sells fruits and vegetables it also sells lottery tickets.
   Use a comma and the joining word *and* after the first complete thought.

   _____

8. Doreen did not feel very well she forced herself to go to work.

   _____

Name_____   Section _____   Date _____

Score: (Number right) _____ x 12.5 = _____%

➤ *Run-Ons and Comma Splices: Test 2*

Draw a slash (/) between the two complete thoughts in each run-on or comma splice. Then rewrite each sentence using the method stated.

A. Use a period and a capital letter to divide the two thoughts into two sentences.

1. The hammer and saw began to rust, they had been left out in the rain.

   _____

   _____

2. Pets are more popular today than ever one reason is people's fear of loneliness.

   _____

   _____

3. The fish was served with its head still on, Fred quickly lost his appetite.

   _____

   _____

4. Never leave medicine within reach of a child always return it to a safe place.

   _____

   _____

B. Use a comma and a logical joining word (*and, but,* or *so*) to connect the two thoughts.

5. Alan's new apartment is small it is very comfortable.

   _____

   _____

6. Jill couldn't afford to pay her rent she advertised in the paper for a roommate.

   _____

   _____

7. First you should mop the floor then you should vacuum the carpets.

   _____

   _____

8. The storm flooded the town almost every business closed down for the day.

   _____

   _____

Name_____ Section _____ Date _____

Score: (Number right) _____ x 12.5 = _____ %

➤ *Run-Ons and Comma Splices: Test 3*

Draw a slash (/) between the two complete thoughts in each run-on or comma splice. Then rewrite each sentence using the method stated.

Note: Hints are given for half of the sentences.

A. Use a comma and a logical joining word (*and, but,* or *so*) to connect the two thoughts.

1. The line to the movie was very long we decided to go bowling instead.
   Follow the first complete thought with a comma and the joining word *so.*

   _____

2. Thunder rumbled through the valley, lightning flashed across the sky.

   _____

3. The weatherman predicted a sunny day it is cold and cloudy.
   Follow the first complete thought with a comma and the joining word *but.*

   _____

4. The painter ran out of masking tape he went to the hardware store.

   _____

B. Use a dependent word (*after, although, because,* or *when*) to connect the two thoughts.

5. These raisin cookies are delicious, I can't eat another one.
   This comma splice contains two complete thoughts: *These raisin cookies are delicious* and *I can't eat another one.* Correct the sentence by adding *although* before the first complete thought.

   _____

6. The engine has cooled, you can add more water to the radiator.

   _____

7. We left the restaurant the food was overpriced.
   To correct this run-on, use the dependent word *because* after the first complete thought.

   _____

8. A rumor spread about the bank closing people began withdrawing their money.

   _____

   _____

Name_____ Section _____ Date _____

Score: (Number right) _____ x 12.5 = _____%

➤ *Run-Ons and Comma Splices: Test 4*

Draw a slash (/) between the two complete thoughts in each run-on or comma splice. Then rewrite each sentence using the method stated.

A. Use a comma and a logical joining word (*and, but,* or *so*) to connect the two thoughts.

1. A plane flew noisily overhead, the subway rattled loudly below me.

   _____

   _____

2. I called the police emergency number I received a busy signal.

   _____

   _____

3. My computer crashed I pulled out my old manual typewriter.

   _____

   _____

4. The tree on our city street has a skinny trunk it has only a few thin branches.

   _____

   _____

B. Use a dependent word (*after, although, because,* or *when*) to connect the two thoughts.

5. The children may watch the animals they shouldn't feed them.

   _____

   _____

6. The party ended, we had three hours of cleaning up to do.

   _____

   _____

7. An accident stopped traffic a long line of cars built up on the highway.

   _____

   _____

8. I am more alert in the morning, early classes are better for me.

   _____

   _____

Name_____   Section _____ Date _____

➤ *Run-Ons and Comma Splices: Test 5*

There are **two** run-ons or comma splices in each passage, or one of each. Correct them by using one of the following:

1   A period and a capital letter
2   A comma and one of these joining words: *and, but,* or *so*
3   One of these dependent words: *although, because,* or *when*

Note: Hints are given for two of the passages.

1. Garlic may smell bad it tastes delicious. It has other good qualities as well. Garlic can help lower cholesterol it is also supposed to keep vampires away.

    In the first run-on, add a comma and the joining word *but* between the two complete thoughts. For the second run-on, add a comma and the joining word *and.*

    _____

    _____

    _____

2. The dog raced into the house it was happy to be among people. Its owner bent down to pet it he drew back in disgust. The dog had rolled in something with a horrible smell.

    _____

    _____

    _____

3. Small feet were admired in ancient China, some female infants had their feet tightly bound. The feet then grew into a tiny deformed shape. The women could barely walk their feet were crippled for life.

    Correct the comma splice in the first sentence by adding the dependent word *because* at the beginning. Correct the second run-on by giving each complete thought its own sentence.

    _____

    _____

    _____

4. Steve had never gone skiing before he was rather nervous. He looked at the beginners' slope. It looked like a mountain to him a patient instructor helped him to get over his fears.

    _____

    _____

    _____

Name_____ Section _____ Date _____

Score: (Number right) _____ x 12.5 = _____%

➤ *Run-Ons and Comma Splices: Test 6*

There are **two** run-ons or comma splices in each passage, or one of each. Correct them by using one of the following:

1   A period and a capital letter
2   A comma and one of these joining words: *and, but,* or *so*
3   One of these dependent words: *although, because,* or *when*

1. Davie insisted on dressing himself for nursery school. It was a cold winter day, he put on shorts and a tank top. He also put on cowboy boots over his bare feet. He liked his image in the mirror his mother made him change.

    _____

    _____

    _____

2. The four college friends were losing touch with one another they decided to start a "circle" letter. Each woman receives the letter, she adds a page and then sends it on to the next friend. Each person has to write only one letter to keep the other three informed.

    _____

    _____

    _____

3. Ireland's official language is English some people still speak the old Irish language. Road signs and other public signs are printed in both Irish and English. The Irish did not want their language to die out, children are now taught to speak Irish in school.

    _____

    _____

    _____

4. The night was dark and spooky a cold wind howled. The babysitter was reading the latest scary Stephen King novel. She finished the book she tried to go to sleep on the couch. However, she soon got up and turned on the TV and most of the lights in the house.

    _____

    _____

    _____

Pronouns

Seeing What You Know

In each pair of sentences below, one sentence is correct and the other contains a pronoun mistake. Put a check (✓) in front of each sentence that you think is correct.

1. ____ a. Some companies give its part-time workers benefits.

   ____ b. Some companies give their part-time workers benefits.

2. ____ a. Each of our daughters plans to go to college after she graduates from high school.

   ____ b. Each of our daughters plans to go to college after they graduate from high school.

3. ____ a. Students often complain that you get poor service in the bookstore.

   ____ b. Students often complain that they get poor service in the bookstore.

4. ____ a. I wanted to go to the game, but there was no way you could get a ticket.

   ____ b. I wanted to go to the game, but there was no way I could get a ticket.

Understanding the Answers

1. The correct sentence in pair 1 is *b*.

   A pronoun and the word it refers to must agree in number. The plural noun *companies* needs the plural pronoun *their* to refer to it.

2. Sentence *a* in pair 2 is correct.

   Each is singular and needs the singular pronoun *she* to refer to it.

3. Sentence *b* in pair 3 is correct.

   Students requires the third person pronoun *they*. (The "third person" is a reference to someone or something other than the speaker or the person spoken to.) Sentences that begin in the third person should not shift to the second person, *you*, without a reason.

4. Sentence *b* in pair 4 is correct.

   I is a first person pronoun. Sentences that begin in the first person should not shift to the second person, *you*, without a reason.

A **pronoun** is a word that can be used in place of a noun.

- Mel scrubbed the potatoes. Then he peeled some carrots.

In the second sentence above, the word *he* is a pronoun that is used in place of the word *Mel.*

We often use pronouns to replace nouns. Without pronouns, we would need to repeat the same nouns over and over. We would then get sentences like the following:

- Ray asked Ray's mother if Ray could borrow Ray's mother's car.

Pronouns make our sentences shorter and clearer:

- Ray asked his mother if he could borrow her car.

This chapter deals with two areas in which pronoun mistakes are often made: shifts in number and shifts in person. (More general information about pronouns appears in "Parts of Speech" on pages 67–68 and in "Pronoun Types" on pages 280–285.)

PRONOUN SHIFTS IN NUMBER

One group of pronouns is called **personal pronouns**. They are used to refer to the person speaking, the person spoken to, or the person or thing spoken about.

Here are the singular and plural personal pronouns.

Personal Pronouns

Singular				
I	you	he	she	it
me	your	him	her	its
my	yours	his	hers	
mine				

Plural		
we	you	they
us	your	them
our	yours	their
ours		theirs

A pronoun must agree in number with the word it refers to, which is also called the pronoun's **antecedent**. Singular words require singular pronouns; plural words require plural pronouns.

In the following sentences, pronouns are printed in **boldface type**; the antecedents are printed in *italic type.*

- The dying *tree* lost all **its** leaves.

  (The antecedent *tree* is singular, so the pronoun must be singular: **its**.)

  - When *Vic* was in the Army, **his** little brother wrote to **him** almost every day.

    (The antecedent *Vic* is singular, so the pronouns must be singular: **his** and **him**.)

    - Do the *neighbors* know that **their** dog is loose?

      (The antecedent *neighbors* is plural, so the pronoun must be plural: **their**.)

      - *Linda and Ted* act like newlyweds, but **they** have been married for years.

        (The antecedent *Linda and Ted* is plural, so the pronoun must be plural: **they**.)

➤ *Practice 1*

In each blank space, write the word or words that the given pronoun refers to.

> *Example* The ridges on our fingertips have a function. They help fingers to grasp things.
>
> *They* refers to _____ *ridges* _____.

1. The photographer realized she had run out of film.

   She refers to _____.

2. The cat hid its kittens in the hayloft.

   Its refers to _____.

3. Kate and Barry don't get along with their stepfather.

   Their refers to _____.

4. Martin never drinks coffee in the evening. It keeps him awake all night.

   It refers to _____. *Him* refers to _____.

5. Nora is a year older than her brother, but they are both in sixth grade.

   Her refers to _____. *They* refers to _____

   _____.

➤ *Practice 2*

In the spaces provided for each sentence, write (1) the pronoun used and (2) the word or words that the pronoun refers to.

1. The movie started late, and it was badly out of focus.

   The pronoun _____ refers to _____.

2. Marlene buys most of her clothing at thrift shops.

   The pronoun _____ refers to _____.

3. As the horse neared the finish line, his energy ran out.

   The pronoun _____ refers to _____.

4. A man was at the door a minute ago, but now he is gone.

   The pronoun _____ refers to _____.

5. Carla and Vicki are twins, but they don't look alike.

   The pronoun _____ refers to _____.

Indefinite Pronouns

As stated above, personal pronouns refer to one or more particular persons or things. But another category of pronouns, the **indefinite pronouns**, does not refer to particular persons or things. Indefinite pronouns include the following:

Singular Indefinite Pronouns

each	anyone	anybody	anything
either	everyone	everybody	everything
neither	someone	somebody	something
one	no one	nobody	nothing

The indefinite pronouns in the box are always singular.

- **Something** has left *its* muddy footprints on the hood of the car.
- **One** of my sisters has lost *her* job.
- **Everybody** is entitled to change *his or her* mind.

The indefinite pronouns *something, one,* and *everybody* are singular. The personal pronouns that refer to them must also be singular: *its, her, his or her.*

Note: Choose a pronoun that fits the situation. Because *one of my sisters* is clearly feminine, use *her.* But *everybody* includes males and females, so use *his or her.*

➤ *Practice 3*

In the spaces provided for each sentence, write (1) the pronoun needed and (2) the word that the pronoun refers to. For sentence 5, include the missing verb as well.

Example   Neither of the boys has had *(his, their)* measles shot yet.

   The pronoun needed is __*his*__. The word it refers to is __*neither*__.

1. Everything in the office has *(its, their)* own place.

   The pronoun needed is _____. The word it refers to is _____.

2. Neither of my uncles has ever smoked in *(his, their)* life.

The pronoun needed is _____. The word it refers to is _____.

3. Don't eat anything out of the garden until you've washed (*them, it*).

The pronoun needed is _____. The word it refers to is _____.

4. Each of the girls invited (*her, their*) mother to the mother-daughter luncheon.

The pronoun needed is _____. The word it refers to is _____.

5. Nobody can join that club unless (*they are, he or she is*) invited.

The pronoun(s) and verb needed are _____. The word

the pronoun or pronouns refer to is _____.

PRONOUN SHIFTS IN PERSON

A pronoun that refers to the person who is speaking is called a **first person pronoun**. Examples of first person pronouns are *I, me,* and *our*. A pronoun that refers to someone being spoken to, such as *you,* is a **second person pronoun**. And a pronoun that refers to another person or thing, such as *he, she,* or *it,* is a **third person pronoun**.

Here are the the personal pronouns in first, second, and third person groupings:

Personal Pronouns

	First person	*Second person*	*Third person*
Singular	I, me, my, mine	you, your, yours	he, him, his; she, her, hers; it, its
Plural	we, us, our, ours	you, your, yours	they, them, their, theirs

When a writer makes unnecessary shifts in person, the writing may become less clear. The sentences below, for example, show some needless shifts in person. (The words that show the shifts are boldfaced.)

- The worst thing about **my** not writing letters is that **you** never get any back.

  (The writer begins with the first person pronoun *my,* but then shifts to the second person pronoun *you.*)

- Though **we** like most of **our** neighbors, there are a few **you** can't get along with.

  (The writer begins with the first person pronouns *we* and *our,* but then shifts to the second person pronoun *you.*)

These sentences can be improved by eliminating the shifts in person:

- The worst thing about **my** not writing letters is that **I** never get any back.

- Though **we** like most of **our** neighbors, there are a few **we** can't get along with.

> *Practice 4*

Write the correct pronoun in each space provided.

they, we   1. Whenever students are under a great deal of stress, _____ often stop studying.

one, you   2. If you want to do well in this course, _____ should plan on attending every day.

you, me   3. When I first began to work as a waitress, I was surprised at how rude some customers were to _____.

we, you   4. It's hard for us to pay for health insurance, but _____ don't dare go without it.

you, I   5. When _____ drive on the highway, I get disgusted at the amount of trash I see.

I, you   6. Although I like visiting my Aunt Rita, _____ always feel like my visit has disrupted her life.

we, you   7. When we answer the telephone at work, _____ are supposed to say the company name.

I, one   8. I would like to go to a school where _____ can meet many people who are different from me.

you, they   9. Dog owners should put tags on their dogs in case _____ lose their pets.

we, they   10. People often take a first-aid course so that _____ can learn how to help choking and heart attack victims.

CHAPTER REVIEW

Answer each question by filling in the correct word or words in the space provided.

1. Words such as *each, everyone,* and *something* are _____ _____ pronouns.

2. Words such as *I, you,* and *they* are _____ pronouns.

3. A _____ person pronoun is one that refers to the person being spoken to.

4. *True or false?* _____ A pronoun may be singular even if its antecedent is plural.

5. *True or false?* _____ A writer should not needlessly change from the first person to the second person.

Name_____ Section _____ Date _____

Score: (Number right) _____ x 12.5 = _____ %

➤ *Pronouns: Test 1*

Note: Hints are given for half of the sentences.

A. In each blank space, write the pronoun that agrees in number with the word or words it refers to.

he, they   1. When Ben jogs, _____ takes his dog along.
                              The pronoun you fill in must refer to *Ben*, which is singular.

her, their   2. My mother and her sister often share _____ clothing and jewelry.

his or her, their 3. No one in the class remembered _____ textbook.
                              The indefinite pronoun *no one* is singular. The pronoun you fill in must also be singular.

her, their   4. Neither of my nieces wants to share _____ toys.

B. For each sentence, cross out the pronoun that makes a shift in person. Then, in the space provided, write a pronoun that corrects the shift in person.

_____   5. We work at a store where the owners don't provide you with any health insurance.
                              The sentence begins in the first person *(we)*, and then it shifts unnecessarily to the second person *(you)*.

_____   6. What I liked best about my grandmother was that she always took time to listen to you.

_____   7. Members of the gang said they feel the gang is like your family.
                              The sentence begins with the third person *(they)*, but then it shifts to the second person.

_____   8. I wanted to see the movie star, but one couldn't get past his security guards.

Name_____ Section _____ Date _____

Score: (Number right) _____ x 12.5 = _____ %

➤ *Pronouns: Test 2*

A. In each blank space, write the pronoun that agrees in number with the word or words it refers to.

his, their   1. Each of my brothers has _____ own television.

its, their   2. Some schools have a day-care center for the children of _____ employees and students.

her, their   3. One of the hens has laid _____ egg on an old blanket in the shed.

his or her, their 4. Everybody in our apartment building was told to lock _____ door in the evening.

B. For each sentence, cross out the pronoun that makes a shift in person. Then, in the space provided, write a pronoun that corrects the shift in person.

_____ 5. The constant ringing of my telephone often drives one crazy.

_____ 6. If people want something from the kitchen, you have to go and get it.

_____ 7. Whenever we visit the zoo, you are delighted by the pandas and the monkeys.

_____ 8. The newspaper carrier didn't realize that you would have to deliver papers at 5 a.m.

Name_____ Section _____ Date _____

Score: (Number right) _____ x 12.5 = _____%

➤ *Pronouns: Test 3*

Each of the following passages contains **two** pronoun mistakes. Find these two mistakes and cross them out. Then write the corrections in the spaces provided.

Note: Hints are given for half of the items.

1. First-year students at our school are required to take a math course. You must also pass a computer class. Help is available at a study-skills center. Anyone who brings in their homework receives assistance.

   a. _____

      The passage begins in the third person *(first-year students)*, but then switches to the second person *(you)*.

   b. _____

2. Each of the sisters is a successful artist in their own field. Anna does oil paintings that she sells at several galleries. Clarita makes quilts which one sells by herself from her home.

   a. _____

      The indefinite pronoun *each* is singular; *their* is plural.

   b. _____

3. Richard hated his vacation at the campground. First, the food hall was closed for repairs. Because no one was willing to share their food, Richard ate peanut-butter sandwiches all weekend. Also, it rained the entire weekend, so you couldn't enjoy the outdoors.

   a. _____

      The indefinite pronoun *no one* is singular. The pronoun that refers to it must also be singular.

   b. _____

4. My roommate and I are looking for jobs. We didn't realize that you could look for jobs in places other than the newspaper. One of our friends has visited her college's career center. Two other friends have joined a job agency where you will learn about jobs in the nearby area.

   a. _____

      The second sentence shifts from the first person *(we)* to the second person *(you)*.

   b. _____

Name_____ Section _____ Date _____

Score: (Number right) _____ x 12.5 = _____%

➤ *Pronouns: Test 4*

Each of the following passages contains **two** pronoun mistakes. Find these two mistakes and cross them out. Then write the corrections in the spaces provided.

1. Zena makes wedding cakes. Although she has made dozens of them, you can never be sure that a cake will turn out as planned. Once she had to repair a hole in a cake by filling it in with icing. Fortunately, no one complained that they didn't like the cake.

   a. _____

   b. _____

2. You can make one's own grape juice in a few simple steps. First buy some fresh, ripe grapes. Then put them in a thin cloth and squeeze tightly until all the juice has been drained into a container. We can also add sugar, but you may find that the juice is already sweet enough.

   a. _____

   b. _____

3. Lew and Mandy usually do the crossword puzzle in the Sunday newspaper. There are always a few clues you have to look up in a dictionary. Whenever one of them figures out a clue, they will yell out the answer.

   a. _____

   b. _____

4. Anybody who plays Bingo at our church women's club knows they must cry "bingo" in order to win. The word comes from an early version of the game in which players had to ring a bell when you had won. The sound of the bell— "bing"—gave the game its name.

   a. _____

   b. _____

Capital Letters

Seeing What You Know

Add a capital letter to each word that needs one in the following sentences. Then check your answers by reading the explanations below.

1. the pilot announced, "please wear your seat belts until the seat-belt sign is turned off."

2. Since 1915, mother's day has been a national holiday, celebrated on the second sunday in may.

3. My idea of a four-course meal is a swanson frozen dinner, a can of coca-cola, and two hostess cupcakes.

4. dr. feldmann, who has never traveled outside the united states, teaches a course called european history 201.

Understanding the Answers

1. **T**he pilot announced, "**P**lease wear your seat belts until the seat-belt sign is turned off."

   The first word of a sentence is always capitalized. Also, the first word of a quoted sentence is capitalized.

2. Since 1915, **M**other's **D**ay has been a national holiday, celebrated on the second **S**unday in **M**ay.

   The names of holidays, days of the week, and months are always capitalized.

3. My idea of a four-course meal is a **S**wanson frozen dinner, a can of **C**oca-**C**ola, and two **H**ostess cupcakes.

   Brand names of products are capitalized. General words like *dinner* and *cupcakes* are not capitalized.

4. **D**r. **F**eldmann, who has never traveled outside the **U**nited **S**tates, teaches a course called **E**uropean **H**istory 201.

   People's names, names of countries, and names of specific courses are capitalized.

Certain types of words must be capitalized. The most common are listed in this chapter.

THE FIRST WORD IN A SENTENCE OR DIRECT QUOTATION

Sentences begin with capital letters. The first word of a quoted sentence is also capitalized.

- The ice cream man said, "**T**ry one of the frozen banana bars. **T**hey're delicious."
- "**I**'m sure they are," Leo replied, "but they're too hard for my dentures."

In the last sentence, the word *but* is not capitalized because it does not start a sentence. It is part of the sentence that begins with the words *I'm sure they are*.

THE WORD "I" AND PEOPLE'S NAMES

- Because **I** was the first caller in the radio contest, **I** won a backstage pass to the **B**ruce **S**pringsteen concert.
- Although **I**'m fond of **C**armen, **I** don't care for her husband.

Note: A title that comes before someone's name is treated as part of the name.

- Uncle **D**onald spoke to **O**fficer **J**enkins after the burglary.

NAMES OF SPECIFIC PLACES AND LANGUAGES

In general, if a place is on a map (including a street map), capitalize it.

- Janice, who is the president of a large corporation in **B**oston, grew up on a farm near **K**okomo, **I**ndiana.

Note 1: Places that are not specifically named do not require capital letters.

- Janice, who is the president of a large corporation in a big city, grew up on a farm near a small city.

Note 2: The names of languages come from place names, so languages are also capitalized.

- The signs in the airport terminal were written in **S**panish, **E**nglish, and **J**apanese.

NAMES OF SPECIFIC GROUPS (RACES, RELIGIONS, NATIONALITIES, COMPANIES, CLUBS, AND OTHER ORGANIZATIONS)

- Edward, who is **P**olish-**A**merican, sometimes cooks **C**hinese dishes for his **N**orthside **C**hess **C**lub meetings.
- Arlene, who serves as the local president of **M**others **A**gainst **D**runk **D**riving, works part-time as a real estate agent for **C**entury 21.

➤ *Practice 1*

Underline the words that need capitals. Then write those words with capitals in the spaces provided. The number of spaces shows how many capitals are missing in each sentence.

1. my roommate is so lazy that she once refused to get up for a fire drill.

   _____

2. the instructor said, "no one knows for sure why dinosaurs became extinct."

   _____   _____

3. While she was in college, anna missed her family in puerto rico.

   _____   _____   _____

4. if i'm not back by midnight, call detective harrison.

   _____   _____   _____   _____

5. My neighbor, mrs. Fraser, is a driver for domino's pizza.

   _____   _____   _____

6. The ice skating rink at rockefeller center is a popular manhattan attraction.

   _____   _____   _____

7. Several asian languages can be heard at a chinese market on fifth avenue.

   _____   _____   _____   _____

8. Marco's mother is mexican and a baptist, while his father is an italian catholic.

   _____   _____   _____   _____

9. My doctor, dr. findley, drove an old convertible to the medical convention.

   _____   _____

10. But he flew to the american medical association meeting in hawaii.

    _____   _____   _____   _____

CALENDAR ITEMS

Names of days of the week, months, and holidays should be capitalized. The names of the seasons (*spring, summer, fall, winter*) are not capitalized.

- At first, **T**hanksgiving was celebrated on the last **T**hursday in **N**ovember, but it was changed to the fourth **T**hursday of the month.
- My cousin wants a government job so that he'll get **V**eterans' **D**ay and **P**residents' **D**ay off.
- The children love fall and winter because their favorite holidays occur then.

BRAND NAMES

Capitalize the brand name of a product, but not the kind of product it is.

- Every morning Tony has **M**inute **M**aid orange juice and **F**ruit **L**oops cereal with milk.

- My niece will only eat two kinds of meat: **P**erdue chicken and **O**scar **M**ayer hot dogs.

TITLES

The titles of books, TV or stage shows, songs, magazines, movies, articles, poems, stories, papers, etc. are capitalized.

- As he sat in the waiting room, Dennis nervously paged through issues of *Life* and *People* magazines.

- Gwen wrote a paper titled "**A** **V**iew of **A**frican-**A**merican **W**omen" which was based on the book and movie *The Color Purple*.

Note: The words *the, of, a, an, and*, and other little, unstressed words are not capitalized when they appear in the middle of a title. That is why *of* is not capitalized in the title "A View of African-American Women."

FAMILY WORDS THAT SUBSTITUTE FOR NAMES

- My biggest fan at the dirt bike competitions was **M**om.
- Go help **G**randfather carry those heavy bags.

Note: Capitalize a word such as *mom* or *grandfather* only if it is being used as a substitute for that person's name. Do not capitalize words showing family relationships when they come after possessive words such as *my, her*, or *our.*

- My grandfather and grandmother live next door to my parents.

SPECIFIC SCHOOL COURSES

Capitalize the names of specific courses, including those with a number.

- This semester, Jody has **D**ance 101, **G**eneral **P**sychology, and **E**conomics 235.

But the names of general subject areas are not capitalized.

- This semester, Jody has a gym class, a psychology course, and an economics course.

➤ *Practice 2*

Underline the words that need capitals. Then write those words with capitals in the spaces provided. The number of spaces shows how many capitals are missing in each sentence.

1. Kara likes to eat cherry ices on hot summer days in august.

   _____

2. Julius munched loudly on fritos in his history class.

   _____

3. Rodrigo has introduction to biology at the same time his brother has a literature class.

   _____   _____

4. Every weekend, my little niece watches her videotape of *beauty and the beast.*

   _____   _____

5. Byron heated up some log cabin syrup to pour over his eggo waffles.

   _____   _____   _____

6. Paul's essay titled "an embarrassing moment" appeared in the humor section of the student literary magazine.

   _____   _____   _____

7. On new year's day, we always watch the football games with dad.

   _____   _____   _____   _____

8. The story of Dracula has inspired many movies, including *love at first bite.*

   _____   _____   _____

9. During the summer, I had time to read *newsweek*, the sunday editions of my local newspaper, and a novel titled *watchers.*

   _____   _____   _____

10. Although grandpa eats several snickers candy bars while watching *wheel of fortune*, he never gains any weight.

    _____   _____   _____   _____

CHAPTER REVIEW

Answer each of the following questions by writing **T** (for "true") or **F** (for "false") in the blank space.

1. *True or false?* _____ Sentences begin with a capital letter. The first word of a quoted sentence is also capitalized.

2. *True or false?* _____ The names of the seasons should be capitalized.

3. *True or false?* _____ Capitalize the brand name of a product, but not the kind of product it is.

4. *True or false?* _____ Names of languages, such as *english* and *spanish,* should not be capitalized.

5. *True or false?* _____ A title that comes before a person's name (as in *Dr. Barnes* or *Uncle Russ*) is capitalized.

Name_____ Section _____ Date _____

➤ *Capital Letters: Test 1*

Underline the words that need capitalizing. Then write those words correctly in the spaces provided. The number of spaces shows how many capitals are missing in each sentence.

Note: Hints are given for half of the sentences.

1. Keith, who hates feeling crowded, moved to a small town in alaska.

   a. _____
   Names of specific places are capitalized.

2. We love the chicken curry served at the indian restaurant down the street.

   b. _____

3. One of the best-known protest songs of the 1960s is "blowin' in the wind."

   c. _____   d. _____
   Song titles are capitalized. Little unstressed words in the middle of a title are not capitalized.

4. Although Jessica lives on hollywood boulevard, she claims she has never run into a movie star.

   e. _____   f. _____

5. Last summer, mom and i visited my aunt in New Orleans.

   g. _____   h. _____
   Family words that substitute for names and the word *I* are capitalized. If a family word comes after a possessive word, however, it is not capitalized.

6. The teacher asked everyone in the class to write a paper titled "the dangers of television."

   i. _____   j. _____   k. _____

7. The loud explosion this morning took place in the chemistry 101 class.

   l. _____
   Names of specific school courses are capitalized.

8. Pedro is a member of the hispanic student council at his community college.

   m. _____   n. _____   o. _____

9. For dinner, Ellen bought a roast beef sandwich at arby's, a salad at wendy's, and a bottle of soda at the supermarket.

   p. _____   q. _____
   Names of specific companies are capitalized.

10. Tamara looked through the latest issue of *sports illustrated* to see if there were any articles about her favorite baseball team, the Philadelphia phillies.

    r. _____   s. _____   t. _____

Name _____ Section _____ Date _____

Score: (Number right) _____ x 5 = _____%

➤ *Capital Letters: Test 2*

Underline the words that need capitalizing. Then write those words correctly in the spaces provided. The number of spaces shows how many capitals are missing in each sentence.

1. Vic adds kellogg's corn flakes to his yogurt to make it crunchy.

   a. _____

2. Before moving into her new house, Lynn scrubbed the floors with lysol and washed the windows with vinegar and water.

   b. _____

3. Brian foolishly complained to the police officer, "but sir, I *never* stop at that stop sign."

   c. _____

4. my friend Keshia enjoys her algebra 101 course but hates having to take a gym class.

   d. _____   e. _____

5. A belly dancer is the entertainment at the moroccan restaurant in chicago.

   f. _____   g. _____

6. bridget wondered why her eleven-month-old niece needed tiny reebok high-tops.

   h. _____   i. _____

7. For our religion course, we visited moslem and jewish houses of worship.

   j. _____   k. _____

8. Miguel teaches geology 300 at a community college in brooklyn.

   l. _____   m. _____

9. After the divorce, my mother and i went to live with uncle gary in Houston.

   n. _____   o. _____   p. _____

10. Kwanza is an african-american holiday celebrated from december 26 to january 1.

    q. _____   r. _____   s. _____   t. _____

Name_____   Section _____   Date _____

➤ *Capital Letters: Test 3*

Underline the **two** words that require capital letters in each short passage below. Then write those words (with capital letters) in the spaces provided.

Note: Hints are given for the first item in each passage.

1. Last may, my grandmother visited Mexico City. She bought a beautiful mexican shawl there, and she claims she has never been cold since.

   a. _____

   Names of months are capitalized.

   b. _____

2. Because uncle Paul has an evening class on thursdays, he often stays on campus for dinner. He usually packs a sandwich to eat in the student union.

   a. _____

   Titles that are part of people's names are capitalized.

   b. _____

3. Roald Dahl, a british author, wrote some marvelous children's books in which adults get punished for their evil ways. *James and the giant Peach* is one of his best.

   a. _____

   Names of specific groups, such as nationalities, are capitalized.

   b. _____

4. No one can stop the world from changing, but teachers might wish they could. After the former soviet Union collapsed, some instructors had to turn to magazines such as *newsweek* because textbooks were no longer accurate.

   a. _____

   Names of specific places are capitalized.

   b. _____

5. During the sociology 102 class break, I asked Doris why she was moving out of her apartment. She replied, "my neighbors in the apartment above me are as quiet as mice—mice in combat boots, that is."

   a. _____

   Names of specific school courses are capitalized.

   b. _____

Name_____   Section _____   Date _____

Score: (Number right) _____ x 10 = _____%

➤ *Capital Letters: Test 4*

Underline the **two** words that require capital letters in each short passage below. Then write those words (with capital letters) in the spaces provided.

1. Nora is taking education courses at Rider college. She plans to become a high school english teacher.

   a. _____

   b. _____

2. A sleek black sports car with tinted windows came to a sudden stop on Spruce street. A woman and her german shepherd then came out of a pet store and hopped into the back seat.

   a. _____

   b. _____

3. Jeremy liked his new red Nike sneakers. He told his mom, "no one in the world can catch me when I wear these, except maybe for you and dad."

   a. _____

   b. _____

4. Michael Jackson was eleven when the first jackson 5 recording was released in november of 1969. It was for the song "I Want You Back," which sold two million copies in its first six weeks.

   a. _____

   b. _____

5. Sally and Rose have very different tastes in movies. While Rose enjoys action movies such as *cliffhanger,* Sally likes quieter ones such as *Howard's End.* They even differ in what they eat while they watch the movie. Rose loves to bring little red boxes of sunkist raisins, but Sally prefers popcorn.

   a. _____

   b. _____

Commas

Seeing What You Know

Insert commas where needed in the following sentences. Then read the explanations below.

1. The infant's mother won't leave home without a bottle extra diapers two blankets and a rattle.

2. Although she is seventy my grandmother can do thirty pushups.

3. The box of crackers if I remember correctly is on the nightstand.

4. The menu was six pages long but my fussy son still could not find anything to order.

5. The beautician said "It may take you a while to get used to this haircut."

Understanding the Answers

1. The infant's mother won't leave home without a bottle**,** extra diapers**,** two blankets**,** and a rattle.

   Commas are needed to separate the items in a series.

2. Although she is seventy**,** my grandmother can do thirty pushups.

   The comma separates the introductory phrase from the rest of the sentence.

3. The box of crackers**,** if I remember correctly**,** is on the nightstand.

   The words *if I remember correctly* interrupt the flow of the rest of the sentence, so they are set off by commas.

4. The menu was six pages long**,** but my fussy son still could not find anything to order.

   The comma separates two complete thoughts connected by the joining word *but*.

5. The beautician said**,** "It may take you a while to get used to this haircut."

   The comma separates a direct quotation from the rest of the sentence.

This chapter explains five main uses of the comma:

1   Between items in a series
2   After introductory material
3   Around words that interrupt the flow of a sentence
4   Between complete thoughts connected by a joining word
5   With direct quotations

A comma often marks a slight pause, or break, in a sentence. These pauses or breaks occur at the point where one of the five main comma rules applies. When you read a sentence aloud, you can often hear the points where slight pauses occur.

In general, use a comma only when a comma rule applies or when a comma is otherwise needed to help a sentence read clearly. When in doubt about whether or not to use a comma, it is often best to leave it out.

1   BETWEEN ITEMS IN A SERIES

The comma is used to separate three or more items in a series.

- The school cafeteria has learned not to serve broccoli, spinach, or brussels sprouts.
- The letters k, j, x, z, and q are the least frequently used letters of the alphabet.
- Our tasks for the party are blowing up balloons, setting the table, and planning the music.

Note: Do not use a comma when the series contains only two items.

- Our tasks for the party are blowing up balloons and planning the music.

➤ *Practice 1*

In the following sentences, insert commas between items in a series.

1. President Thomas Jefferson was also an architect inventor and scientist.

2. Mark's summer jobs have included being a waiter a dog walker and a birthday party clown.

3. The student driver went through a stop sign steered off the side of the road and ended up in a ditch.

4. Creating booby traps reading other people's mail and annoying people are my brother's hobbies.

5. The zookeeper stuffed vitamins into raw meat for the lions put fresh hay in the stables for the horses and planned a lecture for a visiting student group.

➤ *Practice 2*

Complete the following three sentences with a series of three or more items.

1. The little boy's pockets contained _____

   _____

2. Three people I have had trouble relating to are my _____

   _____

3. _____ and

   _____ are three of my favorite activities.

2   AFTER INTRODUCTORY MATERIAL

A comma is used to separate introductory material from the rest of the sentence. (If you were reading the sentence aloud, you would probably pause slightly at the end of the introductory material, where the comma belongs.)

- After taking a hot shower, Ed fell asleep on the sofa.
- When covered with chocolate syrup, low-fat frozen yogurt is no diet food.
- As the movie credits rolled, we stretched and headed toward the exits.

Read each of the above sentences aloud. You will probably pause slightly at the end of the introductory material, where the comma belongs.

➤ *Practice 3*

Insert commas after the introductory material in each of the following sentences.

1. By the end of the day our math teacher is usually covered in chalk dust.
2. Throughout the horserace the announcer's voice kept getting louder and higher.
3. Decorated in green flowers the Girl Scout float won first prize.
4. When I put down the fascinating book I realized that three hours had passed.
5. Stacked in the middle of the room the toy blocks formed a mountain of colorful shapes.

➤ *Practice 4*

Complete the following three sentences. Remember to include a comma after the introductory material in each sentence.

1. Because Jeff was tired of studying _____

   _____

2. Looking under the bed _____

   _____

3. When the alarm sounded _____

   _____

3   AROUND WORDS THAT INTERRUPT THE FLOW OF A SENTENCE

Sentences sometimes contain material that interrupts the flow of thought. Such words and word groups should be set off from the rest of the sentence by commas. For example:

- Our station wagon, which has stickers from every state we've visited, seems like part of the family.

If you read this sentence out loud, you can hear that the words *which has stickers from every state we've visited* interrupt the flow of thought.

Here are some other examples of sentences with interrupters:

- Liza, **who was wearing a new dress,** yelled at the waiter who spilled wine on her.
- The waiter, **however,** was not very apologetic.
- The restaurant manager, **afraid that Liza might cause a scene,** rushed to help.

➤ *Practice 5*

Insert commas around the interrupting words in each of the following sentences.

1. Penguins' wings which are short and thick are not designed for flight.

2. King Arthur according to legend will return some day to rule Britain.

3. My boss it is rumored is about to be fired.

4. Betsy Ross despite popular belief did not design the American flag.

5. Grandfather likes to joke that his hometown which has only one traffic light and two gas stations could be missed if a traveler blinked.

➤ *Practice 6*

Write three sentences using the suggested interrupters. Add words both before and after the interrupting words. Then add the necessary commas.

1. Use the words *who is my best friend* in the middle of a sentence.

    _____

    _____

2. Use the words *which is my favorite snack* in the middle of a sentence.

    _____

    _____

3. Use the words *wearing an all-white outfit* in the middle of a sentence.

    _____

4   BETWEEN COMPLETE THOUGHTS CONNECTED BY A JOINING WORD

When two complete thoughts are combined into one sentence by a joining word like *and*, *but*, or *so*, a comma is used before the joining word.

*   Gabe eats like a horse**, but** he is pencil-thin.

Each part of the sentence is a complete thought: *Gabe eats like a horse. He is pencil-thin.* The two complete thoughts are combined into one sentence by the joining word *but*.

Here are more sentences in which two complete thoughts are connected by a joining word:

*   The student didn't want to dissect a frog**, so** he took chemistry instead of biology.
*   I studied for the exam all night**, and** then I slept through it this morning.

A Note About Joining Words

Don't add a comma just because a sentence contains the word *and*, *but*, or *so*. Use a comma only when the joining word comes between two complete thoughts. Each of those thoughts must have its own subject and verb.

*   *Comma:* My neighbor's dog dislikes children**, and it hates** the mailman.

    (Each complete thought has a subject and a verb: *dog dislikes* and *it hates*.)

*   *No comma:* My neighbor's dog dislikes children **and hates** the mailman.

    (The second thought is not complete because it doesn't have its own subject.)

➤ *Practice 7*

Insert a comma between the two complete thoughts (and before the joining word) in each of the following sentences.

1. The smoke detector was buzzing and we could smell something burning.

2. The roast should have been ready but the cook forgot to turn on the oven.

3. A severe storm was forecast so many people bought candles and flashlights.

4. I needed some cough medicine badly but the drug store had already closed.

5. Members of the marching band sold oranges to raise funds for their trip to Florida and they sold mittens for their trip to Alaska.

➤ *Practice 8*

1. Write a sentence with two complete thoughts that are joined with a comma and the word *but*. _____

   _____

2. Write a sentence with two complete thoughts that are joined with a comma and the word *so*. _____

   _____

3. Write a sentence with two complete thoughts that are joined with a comma and the word *and*. _____

   _____

5 WITH DIRECT QUOTATIONS

Commas are used to separate directly quoted material from the rest of the sentence.

- The exercise instructor chanted, "Move that body!"
- "My body wasn't made for this kind of abuse," grumbled a woman in a red leotard.
- "After this workout," a man in a sweat suit whispered to his friend, "let's get ice cream."

A Note About Punctuation

When the comma comes at the end of directly quoted words, it is included within the quotation marks. Look at the second and third examples above.

➤ *Practice 9*

Insert commas to set off direct quotations in the following sentences.

1. "Check out our specials in aisle eight" said a cheerful voice on the store loudspeaker.

2. "That shirt" complained the woman to her husband "is three dollars cheaper at the other store."

3. "I don't care" growled the tired man. "I'm not driving back to that store now."

4. The cashier said "I'll have to find out if we take travelers' checks."

5. "Every time I line up to pay" moaned the impatient man "a customer in front of me has a problem."

➤ *Practice 10*

1. Write a sentence that begins with the words *Larry said.* _____

   _____

   _____

2. Write a sentence that begins with the words *Carla replied.* _____

   _____

   _____

3. Write a sentence that has the words *I said* in the middle. _____

   _____

   _____

CHAPTER REVIEW

Answer each of the following questions by writing **T** (for "true") or **F** (for "false") in the blank space.

1. *True or false?* _____ When reading out loud, you often hear a pause where a comma is written.

2. *True or false?* _____ When two items are listed in a sentence, you should separate them with a comma.

3. *True or false?* _____ When a comma separates two complete thoughts, it comes after the joining word.

4. *True or false?* _____ When a comma comes before directly quoted material, it should be written before the quotation mark.

5. *True or false?* _____ When a comma comes at the end of directly quoted material, it should be placed after the quotation mark.

Name_____ Section _____ Date _____

Score: (Number right) _____ x 10 = _____%

➤ *Commas: Test 1*

On the lines provided, write the word or words in each sentence that need to be followed by a comma. Include each missing comma as well.

Note: Hints are given for five of the sentences.

1. Peering through the bars of its cage the canary watched the cat closely.

   _____   Use a comma after introductory material.

2. Five years after the hurricane most of the damaged houses had been repaired.

   _____

3. Annie has an older brother so all her hand-me-down baby clothes were blue.

   _____   A comma is needed before the word that joins two complete thoughts.

4. Most Eskimos live in modern housing but igloos can still be found in some places.

   _____

5. The sick child a blanket draped over his shoulders slumped in his chair.

   _____   Place commas around words that interrupt the flow of a sentence.

6. India ink despite its name comes from China or Egypt.

   _____

7. Herbert Hoover is supposed to have said "Blessed are the young, for they shall inherit the national debt."

   _____   The comma separates a direct quotation from the rest of the sentence.

8. "To be perfectly honest" the student confessed "I haven't read the assignment."

   _____

9. Some of the dinner guests brought a houseplant a bunch of flowers or a bottle of wine to the hostess.

   _____   Commas separate items in a series.

10. False names that students have used when substitute teachers were in class include Sandy Beech Frank Furter and Ben Dover.

    _____

➤ *Commas: Test 2*

In each space, write the letter of the one comma rule that applies to the sentence. Then insert one or more commas where they belong in the sentence.

> a Between items in a series
> b After introductory material
> c Around interrupting words
> d Before a word that joins two complete thoughts
> e With direct quotations

_____ 1. Glaring around the room the professor demanded silence.

_____ 2. I heard a siren so I glanced up at my rearview mirror.

_____ 3. The campers unused to the silence of the forest found it hard to sleep.

_____ 4. A fully grown porcupine has around thirty thousand quills on its head back sides and tail.

_____ 5. "You must never repeat what I'm about to say" whispered the mysterious caller.

_____ 6. At any given moment there are about 1,800 thunderstorms taking place on Earth.

_____ 7. My sister won't leave the house without her makeup her charge card and her boyfriend.

_____ 8. An English essayist once wrote "Reading is to the mind what exercise is to the body."

_____ 9. I hopped out of the tub and ran to the phone but the caller had hung up.

_____ 10. It was during the movie's most suspenseful part of course that my little brother demanded to be taken to the bathroom.

Name_____ Section _____ Date _____

➤ *Commas: Test 3*

On the lines provided, write out the parts of each passage that need commas. Include each missing comma as well.

Note: Hints are given for half of the items.

1. Watching the passing circus parade the children shrieked with excitement. One small boy told his father "I want to be an elephant when I grow up."

   a. _____

   A comma belongs after the introductory words.

   b. _____

2. Mammals have red blood and insects have yellow blood. The blood of lobsters believe it or not is blue.

   a. _____

   A comma belongs before the word that joins two complete thoughts.

   b. _____

3. Tony Jane and Kareem studied for the biology final together. Each of them however got a different grade on the test.

   a. _____

   b. _____

   Commas must be placed around the word that interrupts the flow of the sentence.

4. I was pleased with the election results but my husband felt different. "It's the end of the world" he groaned.

   a. _____

   b. _____

   A comma is needed to separate the quoted words from the rest of the sentence.

5. After working for many months on a project Jesse finally got a vacation. He has spent his time listening to the rain trying to read and wondering what's going on at the office.

   a. _____

   b. _____

   Commas are needed to separate the items in a series.

➤ *Commas: Test 4*

On the lines provided, write out the parts of each passage that need commas. Include each missing comma as well.

1. Tess heard a scratching sound at the window. She checked the locks turned on all the lights and called her best friend. Her friend replied sleepily "You've seen too many scary movies."

   a. _____

   b. _____

2. The two brothers are close friends but they disagree about nearly everything. They have entirely different views on politics religion money and women.

   a. _____

   b. _____

3. Emily Dickinson one of America's greatest poets had only seven poems published during her lifetime. After her death in 1886 over a thousand of her poems were found in a bureau.

   a. _____

   b. _____

4. It was late Sunday evening and Stanley began to feel depressed. "I really hate my job" he told his wife. "I think I'd better start looking for a new one."

   a. _____

   b. _____

5. A study of two hundred of the Grimm brothers' fairy tales reveals an unequal treatment of the sexes. The stories for example include twenty-three evil female witches. In contrast only two wicked male witches are mentioned.

   a. _____

   b. _____

Apostrophes

Seeing What You Know

Underline the word in each sentence that needs an apostrophe. Then write the word, with the apostrophe, in the space provided.

_____ 1. The football referee didnt see the illegal tackle.

_____ 2. The new cereal doesnt absorb milk, so it stays crunchy for hours.

_____ 3. My uncles garage is almost as big as his house.

_____ 4. The old dictionarys pages were creased and bent.

Understanding the Answers

1. The football referee **didn't** see the illegal tackle.

   Didn't is the contraction of the words *did not*. The apostrophe takes the place of the letter *o*, which has been left out.

2. This new cereal **doesn't** absorb milk, so it stays crunchy for hours.

   Doesn't is the contraction of the words *does not*. The apostrophe takes the place of the letter *o* in the word *not*.

3. My **uncle's** garage is almost as big as his house.

   The apostrophe plus *s* shows that the garage belongs to the uncle. The apostrophe goes after the last letter of *uncle*.

4. The old **dictionary's** pages were creased and bent.

   The apostrophe plus *s* shows that the pages belong to the dictionary. *Pages* does not need an apostrophe before the *s* because it is simply a plural word meaning "more than one page."

The apostrophe is a punctuation mark with two main purposes.

    1   It is used in a contraction to show that one or more letters have been left out of a word.

    2   It is used to show possession—that is, to show that something belongs to someone or something.

Each use of the apostrophe is explained on the following pages.

THE APOSTROPHE IN CONTRACTIONS

A contraction is formed when two words are combined to make a new word. The apostrophe takes the place of the letter or letters omitted in forming the contraction. It goes where the missing letters used to be.

Here are a few common contractions:

I + am = **I'm** (the letter *a* in *am* has been left out)
it + is = **it's** (the *i* in *is* has been left out)
does + not = **doesn't** (the *o* in *not* has been left out)
do + not = **don't** (the *o* in *not* has been left out)
she + will = **she'll** (the *wi* in *will* has been left out)
you + would = **you'd** (the *woul* in *would* has been left out)
will + not = **won't** (*o* takes the place of *ill*; the *o* in *not* has been left out)

Contractions are commonly used in everyday speech and writing, as seen in the following passage:

Isn't this lab work going to take longer than we expected? *Shouldn't* we ask the instructor for help? Maybe he *didn't* give us the right instruments, or he *doesn't* realize how long it takes to dissect a frog. Wait, I *don't* think you were supposed to make that cut. Now we definitely *won't* get finished on time.

➤ Practice 1

Combine the following words into contractions.

1. we + are	= _____		6. they + will	= _____
2. you + will	= _____		7. did + not	= _____
3. could + not	= _____		8. you + are	= _____
4. what + is	= _____		9. can + not	= _____
5. I + would	= _____		10. who + is	= _____

➤ *Practice 2*

In the spaces provided, write the contractions of the words in parentheses.

1. The thief *(was not)* _____ considered dangerous, so the judge *(did not)* _____ give him a jail sentence.

2. The water at that end of the lake *(is not)* _____ deep, but I *(do not)* _____ think the children should play by themselves.

3. *(He would)* _____ rather take that children's medicine because *(it is)* _____ covered with a fruity coating. The adult version is bitter.

4. I *(would not)* _____ force a child to take music lessons—music *(should not)* _____ be a punishment.

5. *(I would)* _____ like to visit my parents soon, but I *(have not)* _____ got any vacation time left.

➤ *Practice 3*

Write two sentences that include contractions. Use a different contraction in each sentence.

1. _____

_____

2. _____

_____

THE APOSTROPHE TO SHOW POSSESSION

To show that something belongs to someone, we could say, for example, *the stereo owned by Rita*. But it's much simpler to say:

• *Rita's stereo*

To make a word possessive, add an apostrophe plus an *s*. To help you decide what to make possessive, ask yourself the following:

1. What is owned?
2. Who is the owner?

Then put the apostrophe plus an *s* after the name of the owner. For example:

What is owned? *The stereo*

Who is the owner? *Rita*

When an apostrophe plus an *s* is added to the name of the owner, the result is *Rita's stereo*.

Here is another example:

- *the beak belonging to the pigeon*

Again, ask yourself, "What is owned?" The answer is *beak*. Then ask, "Who is the owner?" The answer is *the pigeon*. So add an apostrophe plus *s* after the name of the owner: *the pigeon's beak*. The apostrophe plus *s* shows that the beak belongs to the pigeon.

Here is a third example:

- *the glow of the lightbulb*

Again, ask yourself, "What is owned?" The answer is *glow*. Then ask, "What is the owner?" The answer is *the lightbulb*. So add an apostrophe plus *s* after the name of the owner: *the lightbulb's glow*. The apostrophe plus *s* shows that the glow belongs to the lightbulb.

➤ Practice 4

Rewrite the items below into possessives with an apostrophe plus *s*. First write the name of the owner. Then write in the possessive form. One is done for you as an example.

	Who is the owner?	*Possessive form*
1. the bike belonging to Randy	*Randy*	*Randy's bike*
2. the purr of the cat		
3. the hobby of my father		
4. the temper of our neighbor		
5. the sunglasses belonging to Cindy		
6. the ending of the story		
7. the stinger belonging to the bee		
8. the news of the day		
9. the mummy belonging to the museum		
10. the best song of Michael Jackson		

➤ *Practice 5*

Underline the word in each sentence that needs an apostrophe plus *s*. That word is the owner. Then write the word correctly, along with what is owned, in the space provided. The first one is done for you as an example.

1. <u>Gary</u> new neighbor is from China.   *Gary's new neighbor*

2. I tracked mud on my mother white rug.   _____

3. The athlete knee was bothering him.   _____

4. Vietnam climate is hot and damp.   _____

5. A wallet was left at Gail house.   _____

6. A gorilla diet is mainly vegetarian.   _____

7. Diane nickname is Smiley.   _____

8. People have searched for Noah ark.   _____

9. The photographer camera was stolen.   _____

10. The bride wedding dress was knee-high.   _____

Notes:

1 An apostrophe plus *s* is used to show possession, even with a singular word that already ends in *s*:

- Gus**'s** computer (the computer belonging to Gus)
- Bess**'s** radio (the radio belonging to Bess)

2 But an apostrophe alone is used to show possession with a plural word that ends in *s*:

- the contestants**'** answers (the answers of a number of contestants)
- the three lawyers**'** office (the office belonging to three lawyers)

When Not to Use an Apostrophe: In Plurals

People sometimes confuse possessive and plural forms of words. Remember that a plural is formed simply by adding an *s* to a word; no apostrophe is used. Look at the sentence below to see which words are plural and which is possessive:

- Lola's necklace has pearls and diamond chips.

The words *pearls* and *chips* are plurals—there is more than one pearl, and there is more than one diamond chip. But *Lola's*, the word with the apostrophe plus *s*, is possessive. Lola owns the necklace.

➤ *Practice 6*

In the spaces provided under each sentence, add the one apostrophe needed. Also, explain why the other word or words ending in *s* do not get apostrophes.

Example The patients eyelids opened slowly after surgery.

patients: *patient's, meaning "belonging to the patient"*

eyelids: *plural, meaning "more than one eyelid"*

1. In a new version of the fairy tale, the princes wife rescues him from fire-breathing dragons.

   princes: _____

   dragons: _____

2. That countrys flag has blue stripes and a yellow star on a field of green.

   countrys: _____

   stripes: _____

3. Hunters value a seals beautiful fur.

   hunters: _____

   seals: _____

4. The doodles in Jacks notebook show just how much he pays attention in class.

   doodles: _____

   Jacks: _____

5. The grasshoppers powerful hind legs allow the insect to jump many times its own height.

   grasshoppers: _____

   legs: _____

   times: _____

6. The chocolates in the silver box were a gift from my mothers best friend.

   chocolates: _____

   mothers: _____

7. It takes eight minutes for the suns light to reach Earth.

   minutes: _____

   suns: _____

8. The trains cars were filled with tons of coal and lumber.

   trains: _____

   cars: _____

   tons: _____

9. Sheer white curtains and fresh lilacs added to the rooms simple charm.

   curtains: _____

   lilacs: _____

   rooms: _____

10. The hypnotists only tools are a soothing voice and a watch that makes very loud ticks.

    hypnotists: _____

    tools: _____

    ticks: _____

➤ Practice 7

Write three sentences that include words ending in apostrophe plus *s*.

1. _____

   _____

2. _____

   _____

3. _____

   _____

CHAPTER REVIEW

Circle the letter of each correct answer.

1. A contraction is two words combined into
    a. one word.
    b. a possessive.
    c. a plural.

2. In the contraction *she'd*, the apostrophe
    a. shows that *she* possesses something.
    b. takes the place of *woul*.
    c. indicates a plural.

3. To make a possessive, an apostrophe plus an *s* is usually added to
    a. the name of the owner.
    b. whatever is owned.

4. An apostrophe is not needed in
    a. a contraction.
    b. a plural.

Name_____ Section _____ Date _____

➤ *Apostrophes: Test 1*

Each of the sentences below contains one word that needs an apostrophe. Write each word, with its apostrophe, in the space provided.

Note: Hints are given for half of the sentences.

1. Susans eyes were glassy with fatigue.

   _____   The eyes belong to Susan. *Eyes* is a plural.

2. Fixing drippy faucets is the landlords job.

   _____

3. There is no bread, so well have crackers with our soup.

   _____   *Well* is a contraction of *we will*, with the *wi* left out. *Crackers* is a plural.

4. I havent ever gone on a roller coaster, and I never will.

   _____

5. Four tiny packages arrived in Saturdays mail.

   _____   The mail belongs to Saturday. *Packages* is a plural.

6. Many presents have been delivered to the brides home.

   _____

7. Leo knows his girlfriend is angry at him, but hes not sure why.

   _____   An apostrophe should take the place of the missing *i* in the contraction of *he is*.

8. You can tell by looking at me that I wasnt expecting company.

   _____

9. The keyboards plastic cover protects the keys from crumbs and dust.

   _____   The plastic cover belongs to the keyboard. *Keys* and *crumbs* are plurals.

10. There are about 100,000 hairs on the average persons head.

    _____

➤ *Apostrophes: Test 2*

Each of the sentences below contains one word that needs an apostrophe. Write each word, with its apostrophe, in the space provided.

1. My neighbor will water my plants while Im in the hospital.

   _____

2. Both of Janes husbands were named Andrew.

   _____

3. Half-finished paintings filled the artists studio.

   _____

4. Why wouldnt the bank cash your check?

   _____

5. Floridas neighbors are Alabama and Georgia.

   _____

6. We didnt recognize our teacher without his beard.

   _____

7. The snowflakes glittered in the flashlights glare.

   _____

8. The farmers may lose their entire wheat crop if it doesnt rain soon.

   _____

9. Someday Ill tell you the story of Uncle Harry and the mad bull.

   _____

10. The film reviewers were careful not to give away the movies surprise ending.

    _____

Name_____ Section _____ Date _____

➤ *Apostrophes: Test 3*

Each sentence in the short passages below contains a word that needs an apostrophe. Underline the words that need apostrophes. Then write each word, with its apostrophe, in the space provided.

Note: A hint is given for the first sentence in each passage.

1. The towns main stoplight is broken. Theres a police officer directing traffic at that corner.

    a. _____   The main stoplight belongs to the town.

    b. _____

2. Tri Lee and his wife didnt date at first. She was originally his sisters friend.

    The contraction of *did not*
    a. _____   needs an apostrophe.

    b. _____

3. One mans hiccups lasted for sixty-five years. Thats the longest hiccup attack known.

    a. _____   The hiccups belonged to the man.

    b. _____

4. Most of us cant imagine how difficult being homeless can be. A homeless persons life is filled with frustration and danger.

    The contraction of *can not*
    a. _____   needs an apostrophe.

    b. _____

5. Yesterday was my weeks high point. I got an A on a term paper, and a girl I really like said shed go out with me.

    a. _____   The high point belongs to the week.

    b. _____

Name_____ Section _____ Date _____

Score: (Number right) _____ x 10 = _____%

➤ *Apostrophes: Test 4*

Each sentence in the short passages below contains a word that needs an apostrophe. Underline the words that need apostrophes. Then write each word, with its apostrophe, in the space provided.

1. My friends father is the mayor of a small town. Hes also the animal control officer.

   a. _____

   b. _____

2. "You shouldnt take my grades so seriously," said Ned to his father. "Grades are no measure of a persons true worth."

   a. _____

   b. _____

3. Wouldnt you know it! The cat has been visiting the fish markets garbage cans again.

   a. _____

   b. _____

4. The family was sleeping and hadnt realized their house was burning. A neighbors phone call woke them up.

   a. _____

   b. _____

5. The mountain towns roads are often closed by snow. Residents sometimes cant travel by car for weeks at a time.

   a. _____

   b. _____

Quotation Marks

Seeing What You Know

Insert quotation marks where needed in the following sentences. One sentence does not need quotation marks. Then read the explanations below.

1. The lifeguard warned, No diving at that end of the pool.

2. Is your wife home? asked a voice on the phone.

3. We're out of lobster and steak, said the waitress, but we've got plenty of hamburgers and hot dogs.

4. Before her surprise party, the girl complained that everyone had forgotten her birthday.

Understanding the Answers

1. The lifeguard warned, "No diving at that end of the pool."

   The words *No diving at that end of the pool* need quotation marks around them. They are the lifeguard's exact words. *No* is the first word of a quoted sentence, so it is capitalized.

2. "Is your wife home?" asked a voice on the phone.

   The words *Is your wife home* need quotation marks around them. They are the exact words spoken. The question mark should be included within the quotation marks, too.

3. "We're out of lobster and steak," said the waitress, "but we've got plenty of hamburgers and hot dogs."

   The waitress's exact words are given in two word groups, so each group needs a set of quotation marks.

4. Before her surprise party, the girl complained that everyone had forgotten her birthday.

   The words *that everyone had forgotten her birthday* are not the speaker's exact words. (Her exact words would have been, "Everyone forgot my birthday.") No quotation marks are used for indirect quotations.

This chapter will show you how and when to use quotation marks. Also, it will tell you when *not* to use quotation marks.

DIRECT QUOTATIONS

A **direct quotation** is the exact words of a speaker or writer. Use quotation marks to set off all direct quotations.

- I raised my hand during the exam and said, "My pen is out of ink."

  (The student's exact words are enclosed in quotation marks.)

- "Your car is in big trouble," the mechanic muttered to Fred.

  (The mechanic's exact words are enclosed in quotation marks.)

- "What keeps us from floating off the earth?" the teacher asked the class.

  (The exact words of the teacher's question are enclosed in quotation marks.)

- "We cannot solve a problem by hoping that someone else will solve it for us," writes psychiatrist M. Scott Peck.

  (The exact words that Peck wrote are enclosed in quotation marks.)

How to Punctuate Quotations

By looking at the above examples, you should be able to complete the following statements that explain how a direct quotation is punctuated:

1. (*Capitalize* or *Do not capitalize?*) _____
   the first word of the direct quotation.

2. Put quotation marks (*before* or *after?*) _____ the speaker's first

   word and (*before* or *after?*) _____ the speaker's last word.

3. Put the comma or period or question mark that comes at the end of a quotation

   (*inside* or *outside?*) _____ the quotation marks.

4. Use a (*period* or *comma?*) _____ to set off the direct quotation
   from the rest of the sentence.

Your answers should be (1) *Capitalize;* (2) *before . . . after;* (3) *inside;* (4) *comma.*

➤ *Practice 1*

Insert quotation marks where needed in the following sentences. Look at the example below.

Example The kids shouted, "Let's go to the pool!"

1. That movie is full of nonstop violence, my friend warned.

2. The operator stated, Please deposit another quarter to continue this call.

3. Do not discuss the trial during your break, the judge reminded the jury.

4. The children's voices sang, Row, row, row your boat, gently down the stream.

5. With a happy grin on his face, the exterminator announced, I'm afraid you've got carpenter ants in your walls.

➤ *Practice 2*

Write each sentence requested. Use a comma and quotation marks to set off a speaker's exact words. One is done for you as an example.

1. Write a sentence that begins with the words *Rosa said.*

   Rosa said, "I'm going to take a nap for an hour."

2. Write a sentence that begins with the words *Fred asked.*

   _____

3. Write a sentence that begins with the words *My boss said.*

   _____

4. Write a sentence that ends with the words *Mother yelled.*

   _____

5. Write a sentence that ends with the words *mumbled the little boy.*

   _____

More About Punctuating Quotations

Quotations with Split Sentences

In a direct quotation, one sentence may be split into two parts:

• "After inserting the disk," said the instructor, "turn on the computer."

Note that the instructor's exact words are set off by two sets of quotation marks. The words *said the instructor* are not included in the quotation marks since they were not spoken by the instructor.

Note also that *turn on the computer* begins with a small letter because it is a continuation of a sentence, not a new sentence. (The full sentence spoken by the instructor is "After inserting the disk, turn on the computer.")

Finally, note that commas are used to set off the quoted parts from the rest of the sentence:

• "After inserting the disk," said the instructor, "turn on the computer."

Quotations of More Than One Sentence

At times, a direct quotation will have more than one sentence:

- Our minister always says, "It's every citizen's responsibility to vote. If you don't vote, you shouldn't complain."

Note that only one pair of quotation marks is used. Do not use quotation marks for each new sentence as long as one person continues to speak.

➤ *Practice 3*

Insert quotation marks where needed in the following sentences.

1. It wasn't nice, said the little girl's mother, to fill up the sugar bowl with salt.

2. I don't mind if you borrow my new sweater, said my roommate, but I don't expect to find it rolled up in a ball under your bed.

3. The newspaper editor said to the new reporter, I'm sorry to have to tell you this. I can't use the article that you spent two weeks writing.

4. Our math teacher is unfair, complained James. He assigns four hours of homework for each class. Does he think we have nothing else to do?

5. Why don't you go to the video store, suggested Sara, and pick up a movie for us to watch tonight.

INDIRECT QUOTATIONS

Often we express someone's spoken or written thoughts without repeating the exact words used. We quote indirectly by putting the message into our own words. **Indirect quotations** do not require quotation marks.

The following example shows how the same material could be handled as either a direct or an indirect quotation.

Direct Quotation

- The baker said, **"I forgot** to put yeast in the dough."

(These are the baker's exact words, so they are put in quotation marks.)

Indirect Quotation

- The baker said **that he had forgotten** to put yeast in the dough.

(These are not the baker's exact words. No quotation marks are used. The word *that* often signals an indirect quotation.)

➤ *Practice 4*

Rewrite each of the following indirect quotations as a direct quotation. The direct quotation will include the words that *someone actually spoke*.

Note that you will have to change some of the words as well as add capital letters, quotation marks, and any other punctuation needed. The first one is done for you as an example.

1. The child asked if the Milky Way candy bar was really full of milk.

   The child asked, "Is the Milky Way candy bar really full of milk?"

2. My sister said that she would help me with my math homework if she could wear my new blouse.

   _____

   _____

3. The bookstore manager grumbled that she couldn't accept books that had writing in them.

   _____

   _____

4. Our gym teacher announced that we would have to run one lap for each minute we were late to class.

   _____

   _____

5. The artist joked that he began painting landscapes when the local art supply store had a sale on green paint.

   _____

   _____

CHAPTER REVIEW

Fill in each blank space with one of the choices in parentheses.

1. The exact words of *(a speaker, a writer,* or *a speaker or writer?)*

   _____ must be set off with
   quotation marks.

2. Use a *(comma* or *period?)* _____ to set off a direct
   quotation from the rest of a sentence.

3. A split quotation requires *(one* or *two?)* _____ set(s) of
   quotation marks.

4. *True or false?* _____ Indirect quotations are not set off
   with quotation marks.

Name_____   Section _____   Date _____

Score: (Number right) _____ x 12.5 = _____%

➤ *Quotation Marks: Test 1*

On the lines provided, rewrite the following sentences, adding quotation marks as needed. Two of the sentences do not need quotation marks.

Note: Hints are given for half of the sentences.

1. Somebody has stuck gum all over my typewriter keys, Ted said angrily.

_____

Ted's words and the comma at the end of the direct quotation should be enclosed within quotation marks.

2. One lucky caller wins a trip to Disneyland, the radio announcer promised.

_____

3. I bought a truck, Julie stated, because I sit higher and feel safer.

_____

Each of the two parts of Julie's statement requires a set of quotation marks. *Julie stated* should not be within the quotation marks because the words are not part of what was said.

4. When you see me next, laughed the brunette, I'll be a blonde.

_____

5. The race car driver said he wanted a quart of milk waiting for him at the finish line.

_____

The race car driver's request is expressed indirectly.

6. My father said that when he goes to garage sales, he feels like a treasure hunter.

_____

7. I'm starving. What's for dinner? Rudy asked an hour after lunch.

_____

The two sentences spoken by Rudy are uninterrupted. They (and the question mark) should be included within one set of quotation marks.

8. Go to the control panel. Then press the red button, shouted the engineer.

_____

Name_____ Section _____ Date _____

➤ *Quotation Marks: Test 2*

On the lines provided, rewrite the following sentences, adding quotation marks as needed. One of the sentences does not need quotation marks.

1. Thanks for the lollipop, shouted the little girl to her dentist.

   _____

2. The camp adviser said, Watch out for ticks.

   _____

3. I need to move back home, said Rick to his parents.

   _____

4. Watching golf, complained Ann, is as exciting as watching grass grow.

   _____

   _____

5. The movie, said the reviewer, will scare everyone in the family.

   _____

   _____

6. Jen announced that she could open the locked door with a bent hanger.

   _____

   _____

7. Someone help me, the factory worker gasped. My hand is caught.

   _____

   _____

8. The boss advised, Don't be late again. Or I'll have to fine you.

   _____

   _____

Name _____ Section _____ Date _____

Score: (Number right) _____ x 10 = _____%

➤ *Quotation Marks: Test 3*

Place quotation marks where needed in the short passages that follow. Each passage needs **two** sets of quotation marks.

Note: Hints are given for one set of quotation marks in each passage.

1. Hospitals have odd ways, explained the patient. Where else do they wake you up at 4 a.m. to make sure you're all right?

   The patient's first remark about hospitals and the comma at the end should be enclosed in quotation marks. The words *explained the patient* should not be within quotation marks because the words are not part of what was said.

2. After serving the couple expensive lobster dinners, the waitress was upset to find that they had left her only fifty cents for a tip. Wait, mister, she called after the man, you can use this more than I can.

   Wait, mister are the waitress's exact words, so they should be placed in quotation marks.

3. The interviewer poked her head out of the office door and called out, Please come in, Mr. Taylor. She asked him a few questions about his experience. Then she said, We've had twenty-five applicants for this position. Tell me why you deserve to be hired rather than any of those others.

   The interviewer's invitation to Mr. Taylor to come in should be included in quotation marks.

4. Scott was amazed when his friends surprised him with a birthday party. After the presents were opened, one of his friends asked him to give a speech. I've truthfully never been so surprised, he told the gathering. I'm probably even more surprised than you can imagine because, you see, it isn't my birthday.

   I've truthfully never been so surprised are Scott's exact words, so they need quotation marks. The comma should also be within the quotation marks.

5. How do you like it? Cindy asked, showing off her new purple fake-fur jacket.

   Her mother thought for a moment and then replied that it certainly was a cheerful color.

   Her brother was less tactful. You look like a giant purple marshmallow, he said.

   Cindy's question and the question mark after it should be put in quotation marks.

➤ *Quotation Marks: Test 4*

Place quotation marks where needed in the short passages that follow. Each passage needs **two** sets of quotation marks.

1. Pointing to the newspaper at the supermarket counter, the boy exclaimed, Look at this story about the space aliens who landed in Minnesota.

    You'd have to be from space to believe those newspapers, stated his mother.

2. My uncle and aunt have different ways of dealing with guests who stay too long. My aunt will hint politely, Well, it sure has been nice visiting with you. My uncle is much more direct. He says, Let's go to bed, Norma, and let these nice people go home.

3. This vacation was lots of fun, said the woman, but after all of this sightseeing and shopping, I'm going to need a vacation from my vacation.

4. As the space shuttle launched into orbit, one astronaut stated, I'm really going to miss my five-year-old son.

    To make him feel more comfortable, his partner asked in a whining voice, Are we there yet?

5. The Hollywood tourist asked the handsome man in the coffee shop for his autograph. He graciously signed her menu. When she read the signature, she sputtered, Sheldon Levine? You're nobody famous!

    The man shrugged. I didn't say I was. You're the one who asked for my autograph.

Homonyms

Seeing What You Know

In the following sentences, underline the correct word in each pair of parentheses. Then read the explanations below.

1. The chicken pot pie was inexpensive, but (there, their, they're) was only one (piece, peace) of meat in the entire dish.

2. If (your, you're) expecting that course to be easy, you don't (know, no) anything about the teacher.

3. (Its, It's) too late to call a cab, so why don't you sleep (here, hear) tonight?

4. Jan couldn't decide (whether, weather) to have a brownie or (two, too, to) scoops of ice cream, so she had both.

5. We all (new, knew) when my little brother (passed, past) an exam because he would tape it on the refrigerator door.

Understanding the Answers

1. The chicken pot pie was inexpensive, but **there** was only one **piece** of meat in the entire dish.

   There is used with a form of the verb *to be*. *Piece* means "a portion of something."

2. If **you're** expecting that course to be easy, you don't **know** anything about the teacher.

   You're is the contraction of *you are*. *Know* means "understand."

3. **It's** too late to call a cab, so why don't you sleep **here** tonight?

   It's is the contraction of *it is*. *Here* means "in this place."

4. Jan couldn't decide **whether** to have a brownie or **two** scoops of ice cream, so she had both.

   The word *whether* is used to introduce alternatives. *Two* is the spelling of the number 2.

5. We all **knew** when my little brother **passed** an exam because he would tape it on the refrigerator door.

   Knew means "were aware of." *Passed* means "completed successfully."

This chapter looks at a number of words that are mistaken for one another. These commonly confused words, known as **homonyms**, are pronounced the same (or almost the same), but are spelled differently and are different in meaning.

THE BIG FOUR

The following four groups of words cause writers the most trouble.

its   *belonging to it*

it's   contraction of *it is*

- **It's** a shame that the shiny car lost **its** muffler and now roars like an old truck.

  (*It is* a shame that the shiny car lost the muffler *belonging to it* and now roars like an old truck.)

  Spelling Hint: In *it's*, the apostrophe takes the place of the *i* in the word *is*.

their   *belonging to them*

there   (1) *in or to that place*; (2) used with *is, are, was, were,* and other forms of the verb *to be*

they're   contraction of *they are*

- Our neighbors are health-food addicts. When we attend parties at **their** home, they serve pizza with broccoli florets on the top. **They're** also fond of serving carrot juice. I hope they won't be offended when we don't go **there** very often.

  (Our neighbors are health-food addicts. When we attend parties at the home *belonging to them*, they serve pizza with broccoli florets on the top. *They are* also fond of serving carrot juice. I hope they won't be offended when we don't go *to that place* very often.)

  Spelling Hints: Here, there, and *where,* which all end in *-ere,* all describe places.

  In *they're,* the apostrophe takes the place of the *a* in *are.*

to   (1) used before a verb, as in "to serve"; (2) *so as to reach*

too   (1) *overly* or *extremely*; (2) *also*

two   *the number 2*

- I'll take these **two** letters **to** the post office for you, but you'll need **to** put more postage on one of them. It is **too** heavy for only one stamp.

(I'll take these *2* letters *so as to reach* the post office for you, but you'll need *to put* more postage on one of them. It is *overly* heavy for only one stamp.)

Spelling Hint: *Too* has one *o*, and it **also** has another one.

your   *belonging to you*

you're   contraction of *you are*

• **You're** going to need a first-aid kit and high boots for **your** camping trip.

(*You are* going to need a first-aid kit and high boots for the camping trip *belonging to you.*)

Spelling Hint: In *you're*, the apostrophe takes the place of the *a* in *are*.

➤ Practice 1

In each blank space, write one of the words in the margin. Use each word in the margin once.

it's, its   1. _____ natural for an animal to protect _____ young.

you're, your   2. Remember, _____ a role model for _____ younger brothers and sisters.

there, their, they're 3. _____ go those rabbits, leisurely eating _____ lunch in our garden. _____ getting more and more bold.

to, too, two   4. If you take Kim _____ the fair, you must take her _____ best friends _____.

➤ Practice 2

On each line, write a short sentence using the word shown.

1. *its* _____

2. *you're* _____

3. *too* _____

4. *their* _____

OTHER COMMONLY CONFUSED WORDS

brake   (1) *to slow* or *to stop*; (2) *the part of a vehicle used to slow or stop it*

break   (1) *to cause to come apart*; (2) *a temporary stop or rest*

> • If you get a **break** from your work, could you check the **brake** on my bike?

> *Spelling Hint:* That bird can br**eak** a nut with its b**eak**.

➤ Fill in each blank with either *brake* or *break*.

1. No child will be able to _____ this toy.

2. I took my lunch _____ at 2 p.m.

3. The driver didn't _____ until he heard a police siren.

4. Poor _____s have caused numerous car accidents.

5. I had to _____ the coconut with a hammer.

hear   (1) *to take in by ear;* (2) *to be informed*

here   *in or to this place*

> • There is so much noise in **here** that I can't **hear** the announcer's voice.

> *Spelling Hint:* You h**ear** sounds with your **ear**.

➤ Fill in each blank with either *hear* or *here*.

1. When I asked Sal where he had been, he replied, "_____ and there."

2. I can _____ a cricket chirping somewhere in this house.

3. Stay _____ while I get the police!

4. I _____ that there's a new Greek restaurant in town.

5. The teacher yelled, "Bring that note right _____."

hole   *an empty or hollow spot*

whole   *complete* or *entire*

> • The joking boy told his mother that he hadn't eaten the **whole** doughnut; he had left the doughnut **hole**.

> *Spelling Hint:* A m**ole** lives in a h**ole** in the ground.

➤ Fill in each blank with either *hole* or *whole*.

1. My father insisted that he wanted to hear the _____ story.

2. There's a huge _____ in our yard where a pool will be built.

3. Slices of the pie sell for seventy-five cents each, but a _____ pie is only three dollars.

4. Mary put the _____ egg in the batter even though the recipe said to use only the yolk.

5. A tunnel in California is actually a long _____ in a huge tree.

knew   (the past tense of *know*) (1) *understood*; (2) *was or were aware of*

new   (1) *the opposite of old*; (2) *having arrived recently*; (3) *unfamiliar*

- The **new** girl in our class **knew** only two people here on her first day of school.

   Spelling Hint: If you **kn**ew something, you had **kn**owledge.

➤ Fill in each blank with either *knew* or *new.*

1. The bride insisted on all _____ furniture in her house.

2. We followed Jen, who _____ the way to the picnic grounds.

3. The _____ fad in men's jeans is baggy and big.

4. Tanya _____ only two people at the party, and she didn't like either of them.

5. Although the woman insisted we had gone to high school together, her face was _____ to me.

know   (1) *to understand;* (2) *to be aware of*

no   (1) *not any;* (2) *the opposite of yes*

- Puffing away on a cigar, the man claimed he didn't **know** there was a **no**-smoking sign above his head.

   Spelling Hint: If you **kn**ow something, you have **kn**owledge.

➤ Fill in each blank with either *know* or *no.*

1. I _____ how to handle rude callers—I hang up.

2. There are _____ muffins left in the basket.

3. Glenn claims he doesn't _____ how to wash dishes.

4. "_____," replied the five-year-old's mother, "you cannot have a slingshot."

5. Since you _____ Alison better than I do, you should tell her about the dent in her car.

passed (the past tense of *pass*) (1) *handed to*; (2) *went by*; (3) *completed successfully*

past (1) *the time before the present*; (2) *by*

- In the **past**, I have **passed** all my courses, but I may not pass them all this semester.

   Spelling Hint: If you need a verb, use *passed.* The *-ed* at its end shows it is the past tense of the verb *to pass*.

➤ Fill in each blank with either *passed* or *past*.

1. Only five minutes have _____ since I last looked at the clock.

2. A bumblebee just flew _____ my head.

3. Mick _____ his driver's test on the third try.

4. Unfortunately, one of the cars that Marylou _____ on the highway was a police car.

5. Life was not always as carefree in the _____ as some people would like to believe.

peace (1) *the absence of war*; (2) *calmness or quiet*

piece *a separate part or portion of something*

- Danny would not give the babysitter any **peace** until she gave him a **piece** of candy.

   Spelling Hints: Have a **piece** of **pie**.

   We all want **peace** on **earth**.

➤ Fill in each blank with either *peace* or *piece*.

1. One _____ of the torn love letter was missing.

2. A white dove is often used as a symbol of _____.

3. An open-faced sandwich is made with only one _____ of bread.

4. Broken _____s of antique glass were found by construction workers.

5. The leaders of the city gangs finally agreed to get along with each other in

   _____.

right (1) *correct*; (2) *the opposite of left*

write *to form letters and words*

- I had to **write** my name on the upper **right**-hand corner of each page of the test.

Spelling Hint: When you write, you use words.

➤ Fill in each blank with either *right* or *write*.

1. Please _____ to me while you're away at college.

2. I always forget the _____ way to fold a diaper.

3. After you pass a big shopping mall, take a _____ turn.

4. Before starting my paper, I tried to _____ down all the ideas that were in my head.

5. My father used to say, "There's a _____ way and a wrong way to do anything."

than   a word used in comparisons

then   *at that time; next*

   • First Dad proved he was a better wrestler **than** I am; **then** he helped me improve.

Spelling Hint: Then is the time wh**en** something happened.

➤ Fill in each blank with either *than* or *then*.

1. I scrubbed the potatoes, and _____ I poked holes in them.

2. Crossword puzzles are more difficult _____ word searches.

3. My parents were born in the 1930s. There were no TV sets or computers _____.

4. You should learn about the candidates and _____ go and vote.

5. The tiny family-owned shop is always more crowded _____ the huge supermarket.

threw   (the past tense of *throw*) *tossed*

through   (1) *into and out of;* (2) *finished*

   • As the inconsiderate couple drove **through** the tunnel, they **threw** paper cups out of their car.

Spelling Hint: You may have a **rough** time getting th**rough** the reading.

➤ Fill in each blank with either *threw* or *through*.

1. My boss _____ a pile of work on my desk at 6 p.m.

2. Please hand in your tests when you are _____ with them.

3. I walked _____ the shoe store quickly; all the sneakers cost over fifty dollars.

4. When it began to rain, we quickly _____ a plastic cloth over our picnic table.

5. As we drove _____ the state, we were disappointed by all the ugly billboards.

wear   *to have on* (as with clothing)

where   *in what place* or *to what place*

• Susan planned to **wear** her new sweater, but she couldn't remember **where** it was.

Spelling Hint: You w**ear** a fancy earring on your **ear**.

➤ Fill in each blank with either *wear* or *where*.

1. _____ is the Hillside Hotel?

2. Bruce likes to _____ his baseball jersey to school.

3. Each year, I forget _____ I stored my Christmas decorations.

4. Vanessa likes to _____ soft pinks, blues, and greens—she looks best in those colors.

5. Before he left on his trip, Earl told us _____ to store his mail and newspapers.

weather   *outside conditions* (rain, wind, temperature, etc.)

whether   *if;* used to introduce alternatives

• **Whether** or not the picnic is a success depends a great deal on the **weather**.

Spelling Hint: W**eather** occurs on **earth**.

➤ Fill in each blank with either *weather* or *whether*.

1. Carmen hasn't decided _____ to go to the football game or to study tonight.

2. The _____ in England is rainy much of the time.

3. I wondered _____ I should take biology or chemistry as my science course.

4. Uncle Karl likes rainy, dark _____; it matches his personality.

5. I didn't know _____ I should call the teacher Mrs. Murray or Ms. Murray.

whose   *belonging to whom*

who's   contraction of *who is* or *who has*

> • When the call came into the police station, the officer asked, "**Who's** willing to help a woman **whose** pet snake just escaped?"

> ***Spelling Hint:*** Remember that the apostrophe in *who's* takes the place of the *i* in *is* (for *who is*) or the *ha* in *has* (for *who has*).

➤ Fill in each blank with either *whose* or *who's*.

1. _____ already seen the new Tom Hanks movie?

2. _____ driving to the football game?

3. _____ car is parked behind mine?

4. The chef _____ going to make the food for the party is famous for his tarts.

5. The butcher _____ shop burned down has decided to go back to college.

CHAPTER REVIEW

Answer each of the following questions by writing **T** (for "true") or **F** (for "false") in the blank space.

1. *True or false?* _____ *It's* means "belonging to it."

2. *True or false?* _____ *Their* means "belonging to them."

3. *True or false?* _____ *Too* represents the number 2.

4. *True or false?* _____ *Your* means "belonging to you."

5. *True or false?* _____ *Past* describes an action.

6. *True or false?* _____ *Than* is a word used to compare.

7. *True or false?* _____ *Threw* is the past tense of *throw*.

8. *True or false?* _____ *Where* means "to have on."

9. *True or false?* _____ *Piece* refers to a part of something.

10. *True or false?* _____ *Whose* means "belonging to whom."

Name_____   Section _____   Date _____

Score: (Number right) _____ x 5 = _____%

➤ *Homonyms: Test 1*

In each space, write the word in the margin that fits the sentence.

Note: Hints are given for half of the sentences.

Your, You're
its, it's

1. _____ dog has lost _____ flea collar.

   The dog belonging to you has lost the flea collar belonging to it.

Its, It's
brake, break

2. _____ always a good idea to take a _____ after an hour of studying.

their, there, they're
to, too, two

3. The Turners feel that _____ son is working _____ many hours each week.

   The Turners feel that the son belonging to them is working overly many hours each week.

Your, You're
to, too, two

4. _____ not going _____ believe whom Ricki is dating!

hear, here
than, then

5. Hawks can _____ very well, but their eyesight is even sharper _____ their hearing.

   Hawks can take in by ear very well, but their eyesight is even sharper in comparison to their hearing.

Who's, Whose
know, no

6. _____ going to tell Paul that there are _____ more tickets to the concert?

Weather, whether
passed, past

7. _____ you _____ the test or failed it, you will still pass the course.

   You may have done either of these alternatives: 1) successfully completed the test or 2) failed it, but you will still pass the course.

peace, piece
hear, here

8. "Can we have some _____ and quiet _____?" yelled the father of six children.

to, too, two
threw, through

9. My grandparents are going to spend _____ months driving in a motor home _____ parts of the country.

   My grandparents are going to spend 2 months driving in a motor home into and out of parts of the country.

Their, There, They're
passed, past

10. _____ planning to drive right _____ Disney World and go to the Everglades instead.

➤ *Homonyms: Test 2*

In each space, write the word in the margin that fits the sentence.

know, no
right, write

1. I _____ Sally is the _____ woman for the job.

Its, It's
new, knew

2. _____ clear that the Raders didn't want us to have their _____ address.

Whose, who's
hole, whole

3. _____ baseball has made this large _____ in my garage window?

than, then
to, too, two

4. Not having enough water to drink is more dangerous _____ having _____ little food.

wear, where
peace, piece

5. Angela couldn't remember _____ she had put the _____ of paper with Cory's phone number.

knew, new
threw, through

6. We _____ it would be difficult getting _____ the holidays the year after Dad died.

weather, whether
wear, where

7. When I see what the _____ will be tomorrow, I'll decide what to _____ to work.

Than, Then
threw, through

8. Some teens began a fight in the restaurant. _____ the manager came and _____ them out.

right, write
peace, piece

9. It is not easy to _____ a treaty that will bring a lasting _____ between the warring countries.

hole, whole
to, too, two

10. The _____ community is working together _____ raise the money needed for the repair of the town's water tower.

Name_____ Section _____ Date _____

Score: (Number right) _____ x 10 = _____%

➤ *Homonyms: Test 3*

Each passage below contains **two** errors in commonly confused words. Find these errors and cross them out. Then write the correct words in the spaces provided.

Note: Hints are given for half of the sentences.

1. Your knew skirt is very pretty, but their is a small hole in the fabric.

   a. _____
      Your *opposite-of-old* skirt is very pretty, . . .

   b. _____

2. "Who are you too order me around?" asked the angry waiter. "Your only the bartender!"

   a. _____
      Order is a verb.

   b. _____

3. My journalism teacher says that know one has the write to tell lies about a person in the newspaper.

   a. _____
      My journalism teacher says that *not anyone* . . .

   b. _____

4. When I visited my friend in Montreal, he said, "Their is more French spoken here then English."

   a. _____
      Is is a form of the verb *to be*.

   b. _____

5. In the passed, I didn't realize that a single peace of cake could have several hundred calories and a great deal of fat. Now I am more careful about my diet.

   a. _____
      In the *time before the present*, . . .

   b. _____

Name_____   Section _____ Date _____

Score: (Number right) _____ x 10 = _____%

➤ *Homonyms: Test 4*

Each passage below contains **two** errors in commonly confused words. Find these errors and cross them out. Then write the correct words in the spaces provided.

1. "Your going to have to speak loudly," said our host at the retirement home. "Many of us can't here very well."

    a. _____

    b. _____

2. As we past the same bank a second time, our two children in the back seat groaned. When we saw the bank again, we new we were lost.

    a. _____

    b. _____

3. If you brake your promises, whose going to believe you in the future?

    a. _____

    b. _____

4. The workman casually tossed a hammer aside. Than he watched in horror as it crashed threw the stained-glass window he had just installed.

    a. _____

    b. _____

5. When you're leg "falls asleep," its because a nerve has been squeezed between a bone and another hard surface.

    a. _____

    b. _____

Proofreading

Seeing What You Know

The following passage has five errors. Proofread the passage by going through it several times, looking in turn for each of the following:

1 missing capital letter   **1 comma splice**   **1 verb error**
1 sentence fragment   **1 missing apostrophe**

Underline each error in the passage. Then correct the errors, crossing out or adding words or punctuation marks as needed.

¹When I was nineteen, I lived in Costa rica for a few months. ²The country is very beautiful, fruits and flowers are growing everywhere. ³The country is also blessed with beautiful rain forests, mountains, and inactive volcanoes. ⁴One of my favorite memories are of a time I was staying overnight on the beach with some friends. ⁵At about midnight, we decided to stand waist-deep in the warm ocean water. ⁶A gentle rain began to fall, and we could see lightning flashing in the clouds many miles away. ⁷Suddenly, we all gasped in amazement. ⁸Lines of flickering green light were dancing across the tops of the waves. ⁹As they rolled toward us. ¹⁰We learned later that the light was caused by tiny glowing animals which live on the oceans surface. ¹¹That night was a magical time for us.

Understanding the Answers

1. The word that needs capitalizing is in sentence 1. Both parts of the country's name need to be capitalized: Costa **R**ica.

2. The comma splice is in sentence 2. A good way to correct it is to create two separate sentences: "The country is very beautiful**.** **F**ruits and flowers are growing everywhere."

3. The verb error is a lack of subject-verb agreement in sentence 4. The subject *one* is singular, but the verb *are* is plural. Correct the mistake by changing the verb to *is*: "One of my favorite memories **is** of a time . . ."

4. The sentence fragment is word group 9. A good way to correct it is to add it to the preceding sentence: "Lines of flickering green light were dancing across the tops of the **waves as** they rolled toward us."

5. An apostrophe is missing in sentence 10, where the surface of the ocean is referred to. The apostrophe is needed to show possession: "ocean**'**s surface."

An important step in becoming a good writer is learning to proofread. When you proofread, you check the final draft of a paper for grammar, punctuation, and other mistakes. Such mistakes are ones you did not find and fix in earlier drafts of a paper because you were working on content.

All too often, students skip the key step of proofreading in their rush to hand in a paper. As a result, their writing may contain careless errors that leave a bad impression and result in a lower grade.

HOW TO PROOFREAD

1   Proofreading is a special kind of reading that should not be rushed. Don't try to proofread a paper minutes before it is due. If you do, you are likely to see what you intended to write, not what is actually on the page. Instead, do one of the following:

- Read your writing out loud.
- Alternatively, do the reading "aloud" in your head, perhaps mouthing it as you read.

In either case, listen for spots that do not read smoothly and clearly. You will probably be able to hear where your sentences should begin and end. You will then be more likely to find any fragments and run-ons that are present. Other rough spots may reveal other grammar or punctuation errors. Look at such spots closely.

2   Go through your paper several times, looking for different types of errors in each reading. Here is a good sequence to follow:

a   Look for sentence fragments, run-ons, and comma splices.

b   Look for verb mistakes.

c   Look for capital letter and punctuation mistakes.

d   Look for missing words or missing -s endings.

e   Look for spelling mistakes, including errors in homonyms.

This chapter will give you practice in proofreading for the above kinds of mistakes.

SENTENCE FRAGMENTS, RUN-ONS, AND COMMA SPLICES

Sentence Fragments

When proofreading for sentence fragments, remember to look for:

- Dependent-word fragments
- *-Ing* and *to* fragments
- -Added-detail fragments
- -Missing-subject fragments

In general, correct a fragment by doing one of the following:

1. Connect the fragment to the sentence that comes before or after it.

2. Create a completely new sentence by adding a subject and/or a verb.

(To further refresh your memory about fragments, turn to pages 147–158.)

Run-On Sentences and Comma Splices

When proofreading for run-on sentences and comma splices, keep the following definitions in mind:

- A *run-on sentence* results when one complete thought is immediately followed by another, with nothing between them.

- A *comma splice* is made up of two complete thoughts that are incorrectly joined by only a comma.

To correct run-on sentences and comma splices, do one of the following:

1. Use a period and a capital letter to create separate sentences.

2. Use a comma plus a joining word (such as *and, but,* or *so*) to connect the two complete thoughts into one compound sentence.

3. Use a dependent word to make one of the complete thoughts dependent upon the other one.

(To further refresh your memory about run-on sentences and comma splices, turn to pages 163–172.)

➤ *Practice 1*

Read each of the following short passages aloud to yourself. Each passage contains a sentence fragment, a run-on, or a comma splice. Find and underline the error. Then correct it in the space provided.

1. That bookcase is too heavy on top it could fall over. Take some of the big books off the highest shelf and put them on the bottom one.

   _____

   _____

2. The detective asked everyone to gather in the library. He announced that he had solved the mystery. And would soon reveal the name of the murderer. Suddenly the lights went out.

   _____

   _____

3. That rocking chair is very old. It belonged to my great-grandfather, he brought it to the United States from Norway. I like to think about all the people who have sat in it over the years.

   _____

   _____

4. Before you leave the house. Please close all the windows in case it rains. I don't want the carpet to get soaked.

_____

_____

5. For vacation this year, we are going to rent a cabin. It is on a lake in the mountains we can swim, fish, and sunbathe there. Everyone in the family is looking forward to that week.

_____

_____

6. My aunt took a trip on a boat off the coast of California. She wanted to see whales. Whales are always sighted there. At a certain time of the year.

_____

_____

7. Hsia is from Taiwan, she uses the English name Shirley, which is easier for her American friends to say. Everyone in her family has both a Chinese and an English name.

_____

_____

8. Rosalie went to the beauty parlor on Friday. Intending to get her long hair trimmed just a little. However, she changed her mind and had it cut very short.

_____

_____

9. The Webbs put a white carpet in their living room. Now they feel that was a foolish choice. Every smudge of dirt or spill of food shows on the white surface. And is nearly impossible to get rid of.

_____

_____

10. That waiter is quick and hard-working, he is not friendly with customers. For that reason he doesn't get very good tips. His boss tells him to smile and be more pleasant, but he doesn't seem to listen.

_____

_____

COMMON VERB MISTAKES

When proofreading, look for the following common verb mistakes:

- Needless shifts of verb tense
- The wrong past or past participle forms of irregular verbs
- Lack of subject-verb agreement

(To further refresh your memory about common verb mistakes, turn to pages 95–106, pages 111–118, and pages 123–128.)

➤ *Practice 2*

Read each of the following sentences aloud to yourself. Each contains a verb mistake. Find and cross out the error. Then correct it in the space provided.

_____ 1. The girls swimmed all the way to the raft.

_____ 2. The rock climbers wears safety ropes in case they fall.

_____ 3. Because my brother studied hard, he does very well on the exam.

_____ 4. When he growed up, Marlin married his babysitter.

_____ 5. Neither of our cars are working right now.

_____ 6. The phone rang twenty times before someone went and answers it.

_____ 7. The public swimming pools in the city is not open yet.

_____ 8. After being out all night, Lee Ann sleeped until noon.

_____ 9. There are poison ivy growing all over that empty lot.

_____ 10. Gerald tells everybody it's his birthday and then claimed he doesn't want presents.

CAPITAL LETTER AND PUNCTUATION MISTAKES

When proofreading, be sure the following begin with **capital letters**:

- The first word in a sentence or direct quotation
- The word *I* and people's names
- Names of specific places and languages
- Names of specific groups
- Days of the week, months and holidays (but not the seasons)
- Brand names
- Titles
- Words that substitute for names
- Specific school courses

When proofreading, look for **commas**:

- Between items in a series
- After introductory material
- Around words that interrupt the flow of a sentence
- Between complete thoughts connected by a joining word
- With direct quotations

When proofreading, be sure **apostrophes** are used:

- In contractions
- In possessives (but not plurals)

When proofreading, look for **quotation marks** around direct quotations. Eliminate any quotation marks around indirect quotations.

(To further refresh your memory, turn to "Capital Letters," pages 189–194; "Commas," pages 199–206; "Apostrophes," pages 211–218; and "Quotation Marks," pages 223–228.)

➤ *Practice 3*

Read each of the following sentences aloud to yourself. Each passage contains a capital letter error, a missing comma, an apostrophe error, or **two** missing quotation marks. Find the mistake, and correct it in the space provided.

_____ 1. I loaded up my low-fat frozen yogurt with fudge sauce peanuts, cherries, and whipped cream.

_____ 2. Bobs uncle is an actor in a soap opera.

_____ 3. The deli clerk yelled "Who's next?"

_____ 4. Our flight to chicago was delayed two hours because of mechanical problems.

_____ 5. Please call me Tom, our business instructor said.

_____ 6. I dread the Summer because I get hay fever so badly.

_____ 7. A person doesnt have to be great at a sport to be a great coach.

_____ 8. Although he's only a cartoon character Mickey Mouse is loved by millions.

_____ 9. The fresh watermelon's in the supermarket look delicious.

_____ 10. "I'd like to ask you a question, Marvin told June. I hope you don't think it's too personal."

MISSING *-S* ENDINGS AND MISSING WORDS

Since you know what you meant when you wrote something, it is easy for you not to notice when a word ending or a word is missing. The following two sections will give you practice in proofreading for such omissions.

Missing *-s* Endings

When you proofread, remember the following about noun and verb endings:

- The plural form of most nouns ends in *s* (for example, two *cups* of coffee).
- Present tense verbs for the singular third-person subjects end with an *s*.

(To further refresh your memory about the present tense, turn to pages 97–98.)

➤ *Practice 4*

Read each of the following sentences aloud to yourself. In each case an *-s* ending is needed on one of the nouns or verbs in the sentence. Find and cross out the error. Then correct it in the space provided, being sure to add the *s* to the word.

_____ 1. All of the pay telephone are being used.

_____ 2. You should check your front left tire, which look a little flat.

_____ 3. My uncle is always telling terrible joke.

_____ 4. Most barn are painted a dark red color.

_____ 5. Ella make new friends quite easily.

_____ 6. Luis got his job because he speak Spanish and English equally well.

_____ 7. The drugstore close at nine o'clock, but the other mall stores stay open till ten.

_____ 8. The grass always grow faster whenever we have a heavy summer rain.

_____ 9. There are two can of soda hidden on the bottom shelf of the refrigerator.

_____ 10. Many red-haired people have freckle on their skin and also get sunburned quickly.

Missing Words

When you proofread, look for places where you may have omitted such short connecting words as *a, of, the,* or *to.*

> ## *Practice 5*

Read each of the following sentences aloud. In each sentence, one of the following little words has been omitted:

a	and	by	of	the	to	with

Add a caret (∧) at the spot where the word is missing. Then write the word in the space provided.

Example ____*the*____ All sections of course that I wanted to take were closed.
∧

_____ 1. Several pieces this puzzle are missing.

_____ 2. When she went to the grocery store, Louise forget buy bread.

_____ 3. Some the programs on TV are too violent for children.

_____ 4. That orange shirt looks great the black pants.

_____ 5. Not a single lottery ticket that I bought last year won prize.

_____ 6. Paul plays both the piano the bass guitar.

_____ 7. Sandra became tired climbing up steep hill.

_____ 8. Everyone was surprised Helen and Stan's divorce.

_____ 9. Do you drink your coffee cream or just sugar?

_____ 10. It's hard pay attention to a boring speaker.

HOMONYM MISTAKES

When proofreading, pay special attention to the spelling of words that are easily confused with other words. (To refresh your memory of the homonyms listed in this book, turn to pages 233–242.)

> ## *Practice 6*

Read each of the following sentences aloud. Each sentence contains a mistake in a commonly confused word. Find and cross out the error. Then correct it in the space provided.

_____ 1. We left the beach early because there were to many flies.

_____ 2. It's you're own fault that you missed the deadline.

_____ 3. No one knows who's sweatshirt this is.

_____ 4. If your hungry, fix yourself something to eat.

_____ 5. I can't get close enough to the stray dog to read the tag on it's collar.

_____ 6. My cousins have promised that their coming here soon for a visit.

_____ 7. I can think of too practical reasons for staying in school: to improve your skills and to prepare for a better job.

_____ 8. These greeting cards have pictures on they're covers, but there's no message inside.

_____ 9. Although its tempting to keep the money, you should return it to the man whose name appears in the wallet.

_____ 10. As we waited in the emergency room to hear whether our sick friend would be okay, time past slowly.

A NOTE ON MAKING CORRECTIONS IN YOUR PAPERS

You can add several corrections to a paper and still hand it in. Just make the corrections neatly. Draw a straight line through any words or punctuation you wish to eliminate or correct. Add new material by inserting a caret (∧) at the point where the addition should be. Then write the new word or words above the line at that point. Add periods and commas right on the line, exactly where they belong. Add an apostrophe within the word it belongs to. Here's an example of a sentence that was corrected during proofreading:

Japan   *in*
• Some Hondas are made in ~~japan,~~ but others are made this country.
                                                         ∧

Retype or recopy a paper if you discover a great many errors.

➣ *Practice 7*

Here are five sentences, each of which contains **two** errors. Correct the errors right on the lines by crossing out or adding words or punctuation marks, as in the example above.

1. Helena is taking two english course in school this semester.

2. I feel sorry for Donnas dog, it lost a leg in a car accident.

3. Rusty cans plastic bags, and scraps of wood washed up on deserted beach.

4. My mother take night classes at college, wear she is learning to use a computer.

5. Because of an anonymous tip. Police were able to raid the drug house they made five arrests.

CHAPTER REVIEW

Answer each question by filling in the correct word or words in the space provided.

1. Proofreading is reading done to find any _____ you missed in previous drafts of a paper.

2. Proofreading is best done (*aloud, quickly,* or *right before the paper is due?*) _____.

3. You can find sentence fragments, run-ons, and comma splices in a paper by hearing where _____ should begin and end.

4. It's best to proofread your paper carefully (*once* or *several times?*)_____.

5. When correcting a paper, insert a caret where you wish to (*add* or *remove?*) _____ material.

Name_____ Section _____ Date _____

Score: (Number right) _____ x 20 = _____%

➤ *Proofreading: Test 1*

Read the following passage aloud to yourself, looking in turn for each of the following mistakes:

---

1 fragment	**1 run-on**	**1 verb mistake**
1 comma mistake	**1 apostrophe mistake**	

Underline all five mistakes in the passage. Then correct the mistakes, crossing out or adding words or punctuation marks as needed.

Note: Here are hints for two of the corrections.

1. Correct the fragment in word group 8 by connecting it to the sentence that comes before it.

2. In the last sentence, the wrong past tense of the irregular verb *spend* is used.

[1]When Emily was in college, she adopted a kitten she named Zooey. [2]By the end of the year, she had grown very fond of the cat. [3]She wanted to take him home with her on the train the railroad didnt allow pets on board. [4]Emily asked her veterinarian for help, and he gave her pills to put Zooey to sleep. [5]Before the trip began, Emily gave Zooey a pill. [6]When he became drowsy, she put him in a cardboard box with plenty of airholes and boarded the train. [7]Everything was fine for several hours, but then Zooey woke up. [8]And began to yowl loudly. [9]The other passengers giggled and looked at Emily. [10]When she took Zooey out of the box he stopped yowling and rested happily on her lap. [11]Emily and Zooey spended the last nine hours of the trip sitting on a couch in the women's restroom.

Name_____   Section _____   Date _____

Score: (Number right) _____ x 20 = _____%

➤ *Proofreading: Test 2*

Read the following passage aloud to yourself, looking in turn for each of the following mistakes:

```
1 comma splice        1 verb mistake        1 capital letter mistake
1 missing -s ending   1 quotation mark mistake
```

Underline all five mistakes in the passage. Then correct the mistakes, crossing out or adding words or punctuation marks as needed.

¹Elaine and Don were on a long drive. ²They stopped at a convenience store to buy something to drink. ³While Elaine picked up cans of pepsi and fruit juice, Don browsed through the snacks. ⁴He decided that it would be fun to try something new and unusual, so he bought pickled hard-boiled eggs, a bag of pork rinds, and a tasty-looking sausage. ⁵Back in the car, Elaine nibbles on a pickled egg. ⁶"Hey, I like this," she said. ⁷What are you going to try first?" ⁸But Don didn't answer, he just made choking sound as he hurriedly opened a can and gulped down some soda. ⁹"Don't eat that sausage!" he finally gasped. ¹⁰Elaine picked up the sausage package and read the label. ¹¹"Fire-Eater's Favorite Chili Sausage," she said. ¹²"Maybe you should have read the label first."

Name_____ Section _____ Date _____

➤ *Proofreading: Test 3*

Read the following passage aloud to yourself, looking in turn for each of the following mistakes:

---

1 fragment	**1 run-on**	**1 missing apostrophe**
1 homonym mistake	**1 missing quotation mark**	

Underline all five mistakes in the passage. Then correct the mistakes, crossing out or adding words or punctuation marks as needed.

Note: Here are hints for two of the corrections.

1. Word group 2 is a run-on. Correct it by adding a comma and the joining word *and* between the two complete thoughts.
2. You'll find the homonym error in the last sentence.

¹Last week, a girl I dated in high school called me. ²She and her new husband had just moved to town she wanted us to meet them for dinner. ³"Sherry is really nice, and I'm sure her husband is also," I told my wife. ⁴We'll have a good time." ⁵Boy, was I wrong. ⁶We met Sherry and Jake at a crowded restaurant. ⁷"Wow, aren't you a babe," was Jakes first remark to my wife. ⁸Next he decided that our waiter was gay. ⁹He kept making loud remarks. ¹⁰About "queers" and "fairies." ¹¹When a black woman and white man sat down nearby, Jake started complaining about "race mixing." ¹²By that time, my wife had had enough. ¹³She stood up and said, "Sorry, Jake. I don't eat with people like you." ¹⁴Than she stormed out of the restaurant.

Name _____   Section _____   Date _____

Score: (Number right) _____ x 20 = _____ %

➤ *Proofreading: Test 4*

Read the following passage aloud to yourself, looking in turn for each of the following mistakes:

1 fragment	**1 comma splice**	**1 verb mistake**
1 comma mistake	**1 missing apostrophe**	

Underline all five mistakes in the passage. Then correct the mistakes, crossing out or adding words or punctuation marks as needed.

¹When a group of rare white lions arrived at the Philadelphia Zoo. ²It was an exciting event. ³The lions were the only ones of their kind in North America, they soon became the zoo's most popular exhibit. ⁴The lions are native to southern Africa. ⁵They are so rare because of a problem caused by their unusual color. ⁶Most lions, with their golden-brown color, can sneak through grass and trees without being detected. ⁷But the moonlight shining on the white lions' coats make it difficult for them to hunt at night. ⁸Its too easy for other animals to see them. ⁹Therefore, most white lions in the wild starve to death. ¹⁰Although all the white lions in Philadelphia are female the zoo is hoping to get a white male soon and raise a family of white lion cubs.

Dictionary Use

OWNING A GOOD DICTIONARY

It is a good idea to own two dictionaries. The first dictionary should be a paperback one that you can carry with you. Any of the following would be an excellent choice:

The American Heritage Dictionary, Paperback Edition

The Random House Dictionary, Paperback Edition

Webster's New World Dictionary, Paperback Edition

Your second dictionary should be a full-sized, hardcover edition which should be kept in the room where you study. All the above dictionaries come in hardbound versions, which contain a good deal more information than the paperback editions.

UNDERSTANDING DICTIONARY ENTRIES

Each word listed alphabetically in a dictionary is called an **entry word**. Here are an entry word and its definitions taken from *The American Heritage Dictionary* (abbreviated in the rest of this chapter as the *AHD*)*:

---

thun·der (thŭn′dər) *n.* **1.** The explosive sound emitted as a result of the electrical discharge of lightning. **2.** A rumbling sound similar to thunder. —*v.* **1.** To produce thunder or similar sounds. **2.** To utter loudly.

Spelling and Syllables

The dictionary first gives the correct spelling and syllable breakdown of a word. Dots separate the words into syllables. Each syllable is a separate sound, and each sound includes a vowel. In the entry shown above, *thunder* is divided into two syllables.

The American Heritage Dictionary, Paperback Edition. Copyright © 1983 by Houghton Mifflin Company. *The American Heritage Dictionary*, Second College Edition. Copyright © 1991 by Houghton Mifflin Company. Reprinted by permission.

➤ Use your dictionary to separate the following words into syllables. Put a slash (/) between each syllable and the next. Then write the number of syllables in each word. The first one is done for you as an example.

1. g u a r / a n / t e e   _3_ syllables

2. m o l e c u l e   ____ syllables

3. v o c a b u l a r y   ____ syllables

4. c a u l i f l o w e r   ____ syllables

Pronunciation Symbols and Accent Marks

Most dictionary entry words are followed first by a pronunciation guide in parentheses, as in the entry for *thunder*:

thun·der (thŭn′dər)

The information in parentheses includes two kinds of symbols: pronunciation symbols and accent marks. Here are explanations of each.

Pronunciation Symbols

The pronunciation symbols tell the sounds of consonants and vowels in a word. The sounds of the consonants are probably familiar to you, but you may find it helpful to review the vowel sounds. Vowels are the letters *a, e, i, o, u,* and sometimes *y.* To know how to pronounce the vowel sounds, use the **pronunciation key** in your dictionary. Here is the key found on every other page of the *AHD*:

Pronunciation Key

ă pat	ā pay	â care	ä father	ĕ pet	ē be	ĭ pit
ī tie	î pier	ŏ pot	ō toe	ô paw, for		oi noise
ŏŏ took	ōō boot	ou out	th thin	*th* **th**is		ŭ cut
û **urge**	yōō abuse	zh vision	ə about, item, edible, gallop, circus			

The key tells you, for instance, that the sound of ă (called "short a") is pronounced like the *a* in *pat,* the sound of ā (called "long a") is pronounced like the *ay* in *pay,* and so on. All the vowels with a cup-shaped symbol above them are called short vowels. All the vowels with a horizontal line above them are called long vowels. Note that long vowels have the sound of their own name. For example, long *a* sounds like the name of the letter *a.*

To use the above key, first find the symbol of the sound you wish to pronounce. For example, suppose you want to pronounce the short *i* sound. Locate the short *i* in the key and note how the sound is pronounced in the short word *(pit)* that appears next to the short *i.* This tells you that the short *i* has the sound of the *i* in the word *pit.* The key also tells you, for instance, that the short *e* has the sound of the *e* in the word *pet,* that the short *o* has the sound of the *o* in the word *pot,* and so on.

Finally, note that the last pronunciation symbol in the key looks like an upside-down *e*: ə. This symbol is known as the **schwa**. As you can see by the words that follow it, the schwa has a very short sound that sounds much like "uh" (as in "ab**ou**t," "gall**o**p," and "circ**u**s") or "ih" (as in "it**e**m" and "ed**i**ble").

➤ Refer to the pronunciation key to answer the questions about the following words. Circle the letter of each of your answers.

1. **hic·cup** (hĭk′ŭp)

   The *i* in *hiccup* sounds like the *i* in

   a. *pit.*   b. *tie.*

2. **si·lent** (sī′lənt)

   The *i* in *silent* sounds like the *i* in

   a. *pit.*   b. *tie.*

3. **na·tive** (nā′tĭv)

   The *a* in *native* sounds like the *a* in

   a. *father.*   b. *pay.*

4. **lot·ter·y** (lŏt′ə-rē)

   The *o* in *lottery* sounds like the *o* in

   a. *pot.*   b. *for.*

➤ Use your dictionary to find and write in the pronunciation symbols for the following words. Make sure you can pronounce each word. The first word has been done for you as an example.

1. reluctant   _____*rĭ-lŭk′tənt*_____

2. solitary   _____

3. extravagant   _____

4. unanimous   _____

Accent Marks

Notice the mark in the pronunciation guide for *thunder*. The mark is similar to an apostrophe:

thun·der (thŭn′dər)

The dark mark (′) is a bold accent mark, and it shows which syllable has the stronger stress. That means the syllable it follows is pronounced a little louder than the others. Syllables without an accent mark are unstressed. Some syllables are in between, and they are marked with a lighter accent mark (′).

The word *recognize*, for example, is accented like this:

rec·og·nize (rĕk′əg-nīz′)

Say *recognize* to yourself. Can you hear that the strongest accent is on *rec*, the first syllable? Can you hear that the last syllable, *nize*, is also accented but not as strongly? If not, say the word to yourself again until you hear the differences in accent sounds.

➤ Answer the questions following each of the words below.

1. **pep·per·mint** (pĕp′ər-mĭnt′)

    a. How many syllables are in *peppermint*? _____

    b. Which syllable is most strongly accented? _____

2. **in·ter·me·di·ate** (ĭn′tər-mē′dē-ĭt)

    a. How many syllables are in *intermediate*? _____

    b. Which syllable is most strongly accented? _____

3. **in·her·it** (ĭn-hĕr′ĭt)

    a. How many syllables are in *inherit*? _____

    b. Which syllable is accented? _____

4. **con·tra·dic·tion** (kŏn′trə-dĭk′shən)

    a. How many syllables are in *contradiction*? _____

    b. Which syllable is most strongly accented? _____

Parts of Speech

Every word in the dictionary is either a noun, a verb, an adjective, or another part of speech. In dictionary entries, the parts of speech are shown by abbreviations in italics. In the entry for *thunder*, for example, the abbreviations *n.* and *v.* tell us that *thunder* can be both a noun and a verb.

When a word is more than one part of speech, the dictionary gives the definitions for each part of speech separately. In the above entry for *thunder*, the abbreviation telling us that *thunder* is a noun comes right after the pronunciation symbols; the two noun definitions follow. When the noun meanings end, the abbreviation *v.* tells us that the verb definitions will follow.

Parts of speech are abbreviated in order to save space. Following are common abbreviations for parts of speech.

n.—noun	*v.*—verb
pron.—pronoun	*conj.*—conjunction
adj.—adjective	*prep.*—preposition
adv.—adverb	*interj.*—interjection

Irregular Verb Forms and Irregular Spellings

After the part of speech, special information is given in entries for irregular verbs, for adjectives with irregularly spelled forms, and for irregularly spelled plurals.

For irregular verbs, the dictionary gives the past tense, the past participle, and the present participle. For example, the entry for *blow* shows that *blew* is the past tense, *blown* is the past participle, and *blowing* is the present participle.

blow (blō) *v.* **blew** (bloo), **blown** (blōn), **blowing**.

For adjectives with irregularly spelled forms, the comparative (used when comparing two things) and the superlative (used when comparing three or more things) are shown after the part of speech. The entry for *skinny*, for instance, shows that the comparative form of that adjective is *skinnier* and the superlative form is *skinniest*.

skin·ny (skĭn′ē) *adj.* **-ni·er, -ni·est.**

Irregular plural spellings are also included in this spot in an entry. For example, after the part of speech, the entry for *party* tells us that the word's plural ends in *-ies*.

par·ty (pär′tē) *n., pl.* **-ties.**

Definitions

Words often have more than one meaning. When they do, their definitions may be numbered in the dictionary. You can tell which definition of a word fits a given sentence by the meaning of the sentence. For example, the following are the three definitions of the verb form of *surprise*:

1. To encounter suddenly or unexpectedly.
2. To attack or capture suddenly or without warning.
3. To astonish by the unexpected.

Which of these definitions best fits the sentence below?

The soldiers *surprised* the enemy troops, who had bedded down for the night.

The answer is definition 2: The soldiers *suddenly attacked* the enemy troops.

➤ *Practice A*

Use your dictionary to answer the questions below. To help you, hints are provided for items 1 and 3.

1. Which syllable in *obstinate* is most strongly accented? _____
   Hint: Look for the bold accent mark.

2. How many syllables are in the word *obstinate*? _____

3. How many *schwa* sounds are in the word *obstinate*? _____

   Hint: Look for the symbol of the *schwa* sound.

4. Does the first syllable in *obstinate* have a long or a short *o* sound?

5. Which definition of *obstinate* applies in the following sentence? (Write out the full definition from your dictionary.)

   Felicia stayed home all week with an *obstinate* case of the flu.

   Definition: _____

   _____

➤ *Practice B*

Use your dictionary to answer the questions below.

1. How many syllables are in the word *solitary*? _____

2. Which syllable in *solitary* is most strongly accented? _____

3. Does the first syllable in *solitary* have a long or a short *o* sound? _____

4. Which definition of *solitary* applies in the following sentence? (Write out the definition from your dictionary.)

   The box of cookies was bought yesterday, and today there's only a *solitary* cookie remaining.

   Definition: _____

   _____

5. Which definition of *solitary* applies in the following sentence? (Write out the definition from your dictionary.)

   Some people like to study in groups, but Serita prefers *solitary* study.

   Definition: _____

   _____

Spelling Hints

FINDING A WORD IN THE DICTIONARY

The single most important way to improve your spelling is to get into the habit of checking words in a dictionary. But you may at times have trouble locating a given word. "If I can't spell a word," you might ask, "how can I find it in the dictionary?" The answer is that you have to guess what the letters might be.

Here are some hints to follow.

Hint 1

If you're not sure about the vowels in a word, you will have to experiment. Vowels often sound the same. So try an *i* in place of an *a*, an *e* in place of an *i*, and so on.

Hint 2

Following are groups of letters or letter combinations that often sound alike. If your word isn't spelled with one of the letters in a pair or group shown below, it might be spelled with another in the same pair or group. For example, if it isn't spelled with a *k*, it may be spelled with a *c*.

c / k	c / s	f / v / ph	sch / sc / sk
ai / ay	ate / ite	au / aw	shun / tion / sion
ou / ow	oo / u		

Hint 3

Consonants are sometimes doubled in a word. If you can't find your word with single consonants, try doubling them.

SPELLING RULES

Even poor spellers can improve by following a few spelling rules. Here is a rule that will help you spell *ie* and *ei* words:

I before E rule: *I* before *E* except after *C*
Or when sounded like *A*, as in *neighbor* and *weigh*.

	I *before* E	*Except after* C	*Or when sounded like* A
• *Examples:*	belief, chief, field	receive, ceiling	vein, eight

• *Exceptions:* either, leisure, foreign, science, society

The following rules tell you how to add endings (such as *-ed* and *-ly*) to words.

Silent E rule: If a word ends in a silent (unpronounced) *e*, drop the *e* before adding an ending that starts with a vowel. Keep the *e* when adding an ending that begins with a consonant.

	Drop the e *with endings that start with a vowel*	*Keep the* e *with endings that start with a consonant*
• *Examples:*	like + **ed** = lik**ed**	love + **ly** = lovely
	confuse + **ing** = confusing	shame + **ful** = shameful
	fame + **ous** = fam**ous**	hope + **less** = hopeless
	guide + **ance** = guid**ance**	manage + **ment** = management

Y rule: Change the final *y* of a word to *i* when:

   a   The last two letters of the word are a consonant plus *y*.

   b   The ending being added begins with a vowel or is *-ful, -ly,* or *-ness*.

      But: Keep a *y* that follows a vowel. Also, keep the *y* if the ending being added is *-ing*.

	Change the y *to* i	*Keep the* y
• *Examples:*	happy + **ness** = happiness	destroy + **s** = destroys
	lucky + **ly** = luckily	display + **ed** = displayed
	beauty + **ful** = beautiful	gray + **ed** = grayed
	try + **ed** = tried	try + **ing** = trying
	carry + **er** = carrier	carry + **ing** = carrying

Doubling rule: Double the final consonant of a word before adding an ending when:

   a   The last three letters of the word are a consonant, a vowel, and a consonant (CVC).

   b   The word is only one syllable (for example, *stop*) or is accented on the last syllable (for example, *begin*).

   c   The ending being added begins with a vowel.

	One-syllable words that end in CVC	*Words accented on the last syllable that end in CVC*
• *Examples:*	stop + **e**d = sto**pp**ed	begin + **i**ng = begi**nn**ing
	flat + **e**r = fla**tt**er	control + **e**r = contro**ll**er
	red + **e**st = re**dd**est	occur + **e**nce = occu**rr**ence

Rules for adding -*es* to form plurals: Most plurals are formed by adding -*s* to the singular noun, but in some cases -*es* is added:

a   Add -*es* to form the plural of nouns that end in *s, sh, ch,* or *x.*

   • *Examples:* ki**ss** + es = ki**sses**   coa**ch** + es = coa**ches**

                wi**sh** + es = wi**shes**   ta**x** + es = ta**xes**

b   Add -*es* to form the plural of nouns that end in a consonant plus *y* (in which the *y* should be changed to *i*).

   • *Examples:* fl**y** + es = fl**ies**   la**dy** + es = la**dies**   canar**y** + es = canar**ies**

Rule for adding -*es* to verbs ending in a consonant and a *y*: Most third person singular verbs end in -*s* (he run**s**, she sing**s**, it grow**s**). But for verbs that end in a consonant plus *y*, form the third person singular by changing the *y* to an *i* and adding -*es*.

   • *Examples:* pit**y** + es = pit**ies**   marr**y** + es = marr**ies**   bull**y** + es = bull**ies**

   Note on* a lot *and* all right*: With amazing frequency, students misspell the words *a lot* and *all right*. In each case they incorrectly combine the words to form one word: *alot* and *alright*. Remember that both *a lot* and *all right* are each two words!

➤ *Practice A*

Use the above rules to write out each new word indicated below. To help you, hints are provided for items 1 and 3.

   1. variety + es = _____

       Hint: The last two letters of *variety* are a consonant plus *y*.

   2. rely + ed = _____

   3. trip + ed = _____

       Hint: Trip ends in CVC. The ending being added begins with a vowel.

Complete each word with either *ie* or *ei*.

   4. dec_____ve

   5. bel_____ve

➤ *Practice B*

Use the above rules to write out each new word indicated below.

1. holy + ness =   _____

2. growl + ed =   _____

3. abuse + ing =   _____

Complete each word with either *ie* or *ei*.

4. br_____f

5. fr_____ght

Nonstandard Verbs

Nonstandard expressions such as *ain't, we has, I be* or *he don't* are often part of successful communication among family members and friends. In both college and the working world, however, standard English is widely accepted as the norm for speaking and writing.

STANDARD AND NONSTANDARD VERB FORMS

The chart below shows both standard and nonstandard forms of the regular verb *like.* Practice using the standard forms in your speech and writing.

	Nonstandard Forms		*Standard Forms*	
Present tense	I likes	we likes	I like	we like
	you likes	you likes	you like	you like
	he, she, it like	they likes	he, she, it likes	they like
Past tense	I like	we like	I liked	we liked
	you like	you like	you liked	you liked
	he, she, it like	they like	he, she, it liked	they liked

Notes:

1 In standard English, always add *-s* or *-es* to a third-person singular verb in the present tense.

   Nonstandard: Mark dislike his new job in Ohio, and he miss his New York friends.

   Standard: Mark dislikes his new job in Ohio, and he misses his New York friends.

2 Always add the ending *-ed* or *-d* to a regular verb to show it is past tense.

   Nonstandard: As a child, Jen enjoy her piano lessons but hate practicing.

   Standard: As a child, Jen enjoyed her piano lessons but hated practicing.

➤ *Practice A*

In each slot below, write the standard form of the verb in parentheses. To help you, hints are provided for sentences 1 and 3.

1. When the skinny boxer saw his huge opponent, he *(decide, decided)*

   _____ he was against violent sports.
   Hint: In standard English, the past tense forms of regular verbs end in *-ed* or *-d*.

2. Before he ate the popcorn, Pat *(add, added)* _____ grated cheese.

3. Every week, Betty *(make, makes)* _____ soup from the leftovers she finds in her refrigerator.
   Hint: In standard English, third-person present tense verbs end in *-s* or *-es*.

4. The movie was so bad that everyone *(laugh, laughed)* _____ at the "scary" parts.

5. Jade *(wish, wishes)* _____ that her parents would get back together.

➤ *Practice B*

In each slot below, write the standard form of the verb in parentheses.

1. Lester *(play, plays)* _____ the saxophone better than anyone I've ever heard.

2. Two nights a week, my mother *(attend, attends)* _____ night classes.

3. Before she left on her vacation, Laura *(water, watered)* _____ her plants, canceled her newspaper, and ate the leftovers in her refrigerator.

4. In bed, my brother always *(pull, pulls)* _____ the covers over his head.

5. At high tide during yesterday's storm, powerful waves *(pound, pounded)*

   _____ the shore.

Misplaced Modifiers

A **modifier** is one or more words that describe another word or word group. To illustrate, the modifier below is boldfaced, and the word it modifies is underlined.

- My cousin has a <u>cat</u> **with all-white fur**.

The modifier *with all-white fur* describes *cat*. Here are a few more examples:

- The <u>woman</u> **behind the cash register** is my boss.
- I have **nearly** <u>a thousand</u> baseball cards.
- He <u>printed</u> his name **neatly**.

A **misplaced modifier** is a modifier that is incorrectly separated from the word or words that it describes. Misplaced modifiers seem to describe words that the author did not intend them to describe. When modifiers are misplaced, the reader may misunderstand the sentence. Generally, the solution is to place the modifier as close as possible to the word or words it describes. Look at the following examples.

Misplaced modifier: Sam bought a used car from a local dealer with a smoky tailpipe.

Corrected version: Sam bought a used car **with a smoky tailpipe** from a local dealer.

In the first sentence above, the modifier *with a smoky tailpipe* is misplaced. Its unintentional meaning is that the local dealer has a smoky tailpipe. To avoid this meaning, place the modifier next to the word that it describes, *car*.

Misplaced modifier: The robin built a nest at the back of our house of grass and string.

Corrected version: The robin built a nest **of grass and string** at the back of our house.

In the first sentence above, the words *of grass and string* are misplaced. Because they are near the word *house*, the reader might think that the house is made of grass and string. To avoid this meaning, place the modifier next to the word that it describes, *nest*.

Misplaced modifier: Christie almost sneezed fifteen times last evening.

Corrected version: Christie sneezed **almost** fifteen times last evening.

Because the word *almost* is misplaced in the first sentence above, readers might think Christie almost sneezed fifteen times, but in fact did not sneeze at all. To prevent this confusion, put *almost* in front of the word it modifies, *fifteen*.

➤ *Practice A*

Underline the misplaced word or words in each sentence. Then rewrite the sentence on the line, placing the modifier where it will make the meaning clear. To help you, hints are provided for sentences 1 and 3.

1. I'm returning the shirt to the store that is too small.
   Hint: Move the words *that is too small* closer to the word they describe, *shirt.*

   _____

2. The customer demanded that the waiter take her order rudely.

   _____

3. We watched as our house burned to the ground with helpless anger.
   Hint: The words *with helpless anger* are meant to modify the word *watched.*

   _____

4. By the end of the war, twenty countries were almost involved in the fighting.

   _____

5. The bracelet on Roberta's arm made of gold links belongs to her mother.

   _____

➤ *Practice B*

Underline the misplaced word or words in each sentence. Then rewrite the sentence on the line, placing the modifier where it will make the meaning clear.

1. The man bought a tie at the department store with yellow and blue stripes.

   _____

2. The plants by the lamp with small purple blossoms are violets.

   _____

3. Carrie nearly has sixty freckles on her face.

   _____

4. The woman in that boat that is waving is trying to tell us something.

   _____

5. The child playing on the jungle gym with fuzzy orange hair is my nephew.

   _____

Dangling Modifiers

A modifier that starts a sentence must be followed by the word it is meant to describe. Otherwise, the modifier is said to be **dangling**, and the sentence often takes on an unintended meaning. Look at the example:

Dangling modifier: Sitting in the dentist's chair, the sound of the drill awakened Larry's old fears.

The modifier *sitting in the dentist's chair* is followed by *the sound of the drill*, giving the impression that the sound of the drill was sitting in the dentist's chair. Clearly, that is not what the author intended. The modifier was intended to describe the word *Larry*.

There are two methods of correcting a dangling modifier:

1 Add a subject and a verb to the opening word group, and revise as necessary. Using this method, we could correct the above dangling modifier as follows:

Corrected version: **As Larry was** sitting in the dentist's chair, the sound of the drill awakened **his** old fears.

2 Place the word or words being described immediately after the opening word group, and revise as necessary. For example, we could correct the above dangling modifier like this:

Corrected version: Sitting in the dentist's chair, **Larry found that** the sound of the drill awakened **his** old fears.

Following is another example of a dangling modifier. How could you correct it, using the two methods above? Write your corrections in the space below.

Dangling modifier: Depressed and disappointed, running away seemed the only thing for me to do.

_____

_____

_____

_____

You could add a subject and verb to the opening word group: **"Since I was** depressed and disappointed, running away seemed the only thing for me to do." Or you could place the word being described right after the opening word group: "Depressed and disappointed, **I felt that** running away **was** the only thing for me to do."

➤ *Practice A*

Underline the dangling modifier in each sentence. Then, on the line provided, rewrite the sentence so that the intended meaning is clear. To help you, hints are provided for sentences 1 and 3.

1. While jogging, a good topic for Anton's English paper occurred to him.
   Hint: A good way to correct this dangling modifier is to put the word being modified (*Anton*) right after its modifier, and then revise as necessary.

   _____

2. Touched by the movie, tears came to my eyes.

   _____

3. Bored by the lecture, Jed's thoughts turned to dinner.
   Hint: It is Jed who was bored, not his thoughts.

   _____

4. After being shampooed, Trish was surprised by the carpet's new look.

   _____

5. Moving around the sun, Earth's speed is more than 66,000 miles per hour.

   _____

➤ *Practice B*

Underline the dangling modifier in each sentence. Then, on the line provided, rewrite the sentence so that the intended meaning is clear.

1. Born on the Fourth of July, Rob's birthday cake was always red, white, and blue.

   _____

2. Out of money, my only choice was to borrow from a friend.

   _____

3. While waiting for an important call, Peg's phone began making weird noises.

   _____

4. Loudly booing and cursing, the fans' disapproval of the call was clear.

   _____

5. After eating one too many corn dogs, Stella's stomach rebelled.

   _____

Parallelism

At times, you will need to present two or more equal ideas in a sentence. You must then be careful to present the ideas in matching form. This matching form is called **parallelism**. Look at the following example.

Not parallel: Dinner consisted of baked potatoes, pork chops that were broiled, and steamed broccoli.

Baked potatoes and *steamed broccoli* are parallel. The descriptive words *(baked* and *steamed)* come before the nouns they describe *(potatoes* and *broccoli)*. But *pork chops that were broiled* is not parallel. To achieve parallelism, give the nonparallel item the same form as the others:

Parallel: Dinner consisted of baked potatoes, **broiled pork chops**, and steamed broccoli.

The unmatched idea has been corrected: the descriptive word *broiled* has been placed before *pork chops*. The sentence now reads clearly and smoothly.

Here are additional examples of faulty parallelism.

Not parallel: On summer weekends, my family spends time hiking, visiting friends, and they go to the movies.

Parallel: On summer weekends, my family spends time hiking, visiting friends, and **going to the movies**.

Hiking and *visiting* both end in *-ing*. To be parallel, *they go to the movies* must be revised to include an *-ing* word.

Not parallel: The children were arguing in the lobby, talked during the movie, and complained on the ride home.

Parallel: The children **argued in the lobby**, talked during the movie, and complained on the ride home.

Both *talked* and *complained* end in *-ed*. To be parallel, *were arguing in the lobby* needs to be revised to include an *-ed* verb.

Not parallel: The speaker had sweaty hands, an upset stomach, and a voice that was nervous.

Parallel: The speaker had sweaty hands, an upset stomach, and **a nervous voice**.

Two of the items in this series (*sweaty hands* and *upset stomach*) have the same word order: a descriptive word followed by a noun. To be parallel, the third item in the series should have the same order.

➤ *Practice A*

The part of each sentence that is not parallel is italicized. On the line, rewrite this part to make it match the other items listed. To help you, hints are provided for sentences 1 and 3.

1. Getting the mail, taking out the trash, and *to feed the dog* are Sam's daily chores.
   Hint: Getting the mail and *taking out the trash* begin with *-ing* words.

   _____

2. On hot days I close the windows, turn on the fans, and *am complaining a lot.*

   _____

3. For lunch we were given limp bologna sandwiches, *peanut-butter crackers that were stale*, and warm sugary punch.
   Hint: The first and third items listed have the same pattern: descriptive words are followed by the nouns they describe.

   _____

4. My neighbors include a carpenter, a salesperson, and *a person who teaches second grade.*

   _____

5. Rachel spent her vacation *with books to read*, working in the garden, and fixing up her house.

   _____

➤ *Practice B*

The part of each sentence that is not parallel is italicized. On the line, rewrite this part to make it match the other items listed.

1. Running through the park, riding a bike, and *to lift hand weights* are Wanda's favorite forms of exercise.

   _____

2. My uncle usually wears loud ties, *shoes that are scuffed*, and wrinkled shirts.

   _____

3. Attending class regularly and *to take notes carefully* are two keys to success in school.

   _____

4. The man bought after-shave from a drug store, socks from a department store, and *thrift shop jeans*.

   _____

5. Roast turkey, baked sweet potatoes, and *pie made from pumpkin* are traditional Thanksgiving foods.

   _____

Pronoun Types

As you learned in the parts of speech chapter, a pronoun is a word used in place of a noun. The different types of pronouns are listed and explained in this chapter.

PERSONAL PRONOUNS

Personal pronouns can act in a sentence as subjects, objects, or possessives, as explained below.

Subject Pronouns

Subject pronouns act as the subjects of verbs. Here are the subject forms of personal pronouns:

	First Person	Second Person	Third Person
Singular:	I	you	he, she, it
Plural:	we	you	they

- **It** is a dreary day. (*It* is the subject of the verb *is*.)
- **She** always remembers her children's birthdays. (*She* is the subject of the verb *remembers*.)

Object Pronouns

Object pronouns act as the objects of verbs or of prepositions. Here is a list of object forms of personal pronouns:

	First Person	Second Person	Third Person
Singular:	me	you	him, her, it
Plural:	us	you	them

- Jeff is addicted to Coca-Cola. He drinks **it** for breakfast. (*It* receives the action of the verb *drinks*.)
- My sister tossed the car keys to **me**. (*Me* is the object of the preposition *to*.)

Possessive Pronouns

Possessive pronouns show that something is owned, or possessed. Here are possessive forms of personal pronouns:

	First Person	Second Person	Third Person
Singular:	my, mine	your, yours	his, her, hers, its
Plural:	our, ours	your, yours	their, theirs

- If Lucille needs a sweater, she can borrow **mine**. (*Mine* means *the sweater belonging to me*.)
- Roger and Emily saw many of **their** friends at the party. (*Their friends* means *the friends belonging to Roger and Emily*.)
- The barn lost most of **its** roof during the tornado. (*Its roof* means *the roof belonging to the barn*.)

Note: Possessive pronouns never contain an apostrophe.

- During the last storm, our apple tree lost all of **its** blossoms (not "*it's* blossoms").

RELATIVE PRONOUNS

Relative pronouns usually refer to someone or something already mentioned in the sentence. They start a word group that gives extra information about that person or thing. Relative pronouns include the following:

who	whose	whom	which	that

- The customer ***who is waiting at the front of the store*** seems very angry. (*Who* refers to the customer. *Who is waiting at the front of the store* tells something about the customer.)
- The potatoes ***that* were boiled** can now be mashed. (*That* refers to the potatoes. *That were boiled* tells something about the potatoes.)
- Please mail the package to my office address, **which is also my home address**. (*Which* refers to the office address. *Which is also my home address* tells something about the office address.)

Here are some rules to remember about relative pronouns:

1   *Whose* is the possessive form of *who*. Don't confuse it with *who's*, which means *who is*.

   - The police found the person **whose** fingerprints are all over the gun.
   - The man **who's** marrying Jean is an inventor.

2   The pronouns *who* and *whom* refer to people. *Whose* usually refers to people, but may also refer to things. *Which* refers to things. *That* can refer to either people or things.

3   *Who* is a subject pronoun; *whom* is an object pronoun.

   - The person **who** owns the expensive car won't let anybody else park it. (*Who* is the subject of the verb *owned*.)
   - The babysitter **whom** they trust cannot work tonight. (*Whom* is the object of the verb *trust*.)

Note: To determine whether to use *who* or *whom*, find the first verb after *who* or *whom*. Decide whether that verb already has a subject. If it doesn't have a subject, use the subject pronoun *who*. If it does have a subject, use the object pronoun *whom*.

See if you can choose the right pronoun in the following sentence.

   - The arrested person is a man *(who, whom)* I once dated.

Look at the verb *dated*. Does it have a subject? Yes, the subject is *I*. Therefore, the object pronoun *whom* is the correct choice:

   - The arrested person is a man **whom** I once dated.

INTERROGATIVE PRONOUNS

Interrogative pronouns are used to ask questions. Here are common interrogative pronouns:

who	whose	whom	which	what

   - **Who** are you?
   - **Which** is the correct answer?
   - **What** did you call about?

Here are two rules to remember about interrogative pronouns:

1   Choose *who* or *whom* in the same manner as you would for relative pronouns.

- **Whom** should I hire?

  (*I* is the subject of the verb *should hire*, so use *whom*.)

- **Who** should go?

  (The verb after *who* is *should go*, which does not have another subject. Therefore use the subject form of the word, *who*.)

2 *Whose* is the possessive form of *who. Who's* means *who is.*

- **Whose** car is parked in front of my driveway?

- **Who's** going to eat the leftover chicken?

DEMONSTRATIVE PRONOUNS

Demonstrative pronouns are used to point out particular persons or things. These are the demonstrative pronouns:

this	that	these	those

This and *these* generally refer to things that are near the speaker; *that* and *those* refer to things farther away.

- **This** cough syrup tastes like lemon and honey.

- **Those** cough drops on the shelf taste like cherries.

Note: Do not use *them* (as in *them shoes*), *this here, that there, these here,* or *those there* to point out.

REFLEXIVE PRONOUNS

Reflexive pronouns are those that end in *-self* or *-selves*. A reflexive pronoun is used in two types of situations:

1 As the object of a verb when it is the same as the subject of that verb

- Cary cut **herself**.

  The subject of this sentence is *Cary*. She is also the one who was cut. (*Herself* is the object of the verb *cut*.)

2 As the object of a preposition when it is the same as the subject of the verb

- Jack sent a birthday card to **himself**.

  The subject of this sentence is *Jack*—he is the person who sent something. He is also the person to whom something was sent. (*Himself* is the object of the preposition *to*.)

Here are the reflexive pronouns:

	First Person	*Second Person*	*Third Person*
Singular:	myself	yourself	himself, herself, itself
Plural:	ourselves	yourselves	themselves

- Terry often praises **himself**.

  (The subject and the object of the verb *praises* are the same person—Terry.)

- The Wallaces bought a used computer for **themselves**.

  (The Wallaces are the ones who did the buying. They are also the people for whom the buying was done.)

INTENSIVE PRONOUNS

Intensive pronouns have exactly the same forms as reflexive pronouns. The difference is in how they are used. Intensive pronouns are used to add emphasis.

- We can put up the tent **ourselves**.

- I **myself** will need to read the contract before I sign it.

INDEFINITE PRONOUNS

Indefinite pronouns do not refer to a particular person or thing. Most indefinite pronouns are singular, including:

each	anyone	anybody	anything
either	everyone	everybody	everything
neither	someone	somebody	something
one	no one	nobody	nothing

- **Each** of the puppies *is* cute in his own way.

(See more on singular indefinite pronouns on pages 128 and 182.)

The following indefinite pronouns are always plural:

both	few	many	others	several

- **Both** of the puppies *are* cute in their own ways.

The following indefinite pronouns are singular or plural, depending on their context:

all	any	more	most	none	some

- **Most** of his outfit *is* white.
- **Most** of the salespeople *are* friendly.

➤ *Practice A*

Choose the correct pronoun from each pair in parentheses. Then write it in the space provided. To help you, hints are provided for sentences 1 and 3.

1. She and *(I, me)* _____ have been friends since we were five.
   Hint: The missing word is one of the subjects of the sentence, so choose the subject form of the pronoun.

2. The brothers blamed *(themself, themselves)* _____ for the failure of their business.

3. Although Josh was very curious, Tina made *(he, him)* _____ wait to open his birthday present.
   Hint: The missing word is the object of the verb *made*, so use the object form of the pronoun.

4. *(Who's, Whose)* _____ jacket is lying on the floor?

5. Are you going to read *(these, these here)* _____ magazines?

➤ *Practice B*

Choose the correct pronoun from each pair in parentheses. Then write it in the space provided.

1. The mechanic *(who, whom)* _____ usually works on my car is on vacation.

2. Since my aunt enjoys basketball more than I do, I gave the tickets to *(her, she)* _____.

3. Please hand me *(that, that there)* _____ screwdriver.

4. I love my old bathrobe, even though *(its, it's)* _____ seams are ripped.

5. *(Them, Those)* _____ teenagers are cleaning up the park.

Word Choice

Not all writing problems involve grammar. A sentence may be grammatically correct, yet fail to communicate effectively because of the words that the writer has chosen. Slang, clichés, and wordiness are three enemies of clear communication.

SLANG

Slang expressions are lively and fun to use. But while slang adds color to our everyday speech, it is generally out of place in formal writing.

> *Slang:* After a bummer of a movie, we pigged out on a pizza.
>
> *Revised:* After a **disappointing** movie, we **ate** a pizza.

CLICHÉS

A cliché is an expression that was once lively and colorful. However, because too many people have used it, it has become dull and boring. Try to use fresh wording in place of predictable expressions. Following are a few of the clichés to avoid in your writing:

avoid like the plague	last but not least	sick and tired
better late than never	light as a feather	sigh of relief
bored to tears	make ends meet	time and time again
easy as pie	pie in the sky	tried and true
in the nick of time	pretty as a picture	under the weather
in this day and age	sad but true	without a doubt

WORDINESS

Some writers think that using a lot of words to express an idea makes their writing sound important. Actually, wordiness just annoys and confuses your reader. Try to edit your writing carefully. Don't use several words when one or two will do. Look at the following sentences.

Wordy: Due to the fact that the printer was out of paper, Renee went to a local store for the purpose of buying some.

Revised: **Because** the printer was out of paper, Renee went to a local store **to buy** some.

In general, work to express your thoughts in the fewest words possible that are still complete and clear. Notice, for example, how easily the following wordy expressions can be replaced by one or two words:

Wordy Expression	*Single Word*
a large number of	many
at an earlier point in time	before
at this point in time	now
due to the fact that	because
during the time that	while
each and every day	daily
few in number	few
green in color	green
in order to	to
in my own opinion	I think
in the event that	if
in the near future	soon
made the decision to	decided
on account of	because
postponed until later	postponed
small in size	small

➤ *Practice A*

Rewrite the italicized words in the space provided, using more effective language. To help you, hints are provided for sentences 1 and 3.

1. *In this day and age* teenagers face many temptations.
   Hint: In this day and age is a cliché. Express the idea in one or more simple, direct words.

   _____

2. *Due to the fact that* Harry won the lottery, he won't be coming to work today.

   _____

3. Tiffany did not *have a clue about* what was being taught in her algebra class.
   Hint: The italicized words are slang. Write the idea in one or more words that everyone is likely to understand.

   _____

4. On the first day of summer vacation, I felt *free as a bird*.

_____

5. My sister *went ahead and made the decision* to take a job in Maryland.

_____

➤ *Practice B*

Rewrite the italicized words in the space provided, using more effective language.

1. *Owing to the fact that* I was depressed, I did not study for my final exams.

_____

2. When my parents see my final grades, I will be *dead meat*.

_____

3. I do not know *at this point in time* if I will return to school next semester.

_____

4. Although the box was *light as a feather*, Jeremy refused to carry it.

_____

5. Everyone was *grossed out* when the cat brought home a dead rat.

_____

Punctuation Marks

Here are the eleven most common marks of punctuation:

Period	**Comma**	**Colon**	**Dash**
Question mark	**Apostrophe**	**Semicolon**	**Parentheses**
Exclamation point	**Quotation marks**	**Hyphen**	

Some of these punctuation marks have been covered in Part One of the book. For the sake of easy reference, they will be briefly described below, along with the other marks of punctuation.

END MARKS

Three of the eleven punctuation marks are end marks, which are explained on pages 56–57. The period, the question mark, and the exclamation point are all placed at the end of a sentence.

Period (.)

Use a period at the end of a statement or an indirect question.

- The election will be held tomorrow.
- I wonder if my parents will notice the pizza stains on the rug.

Question Mark (?)

Use a question mark after a direct question.

- Are you going to vote in the election?
- What's moving inside that paper bag?

Indirect questions end in a period instead of a question mark. Indirect questions tell the reader about a question rather than ask it directly.

- I wonder if it's OK to leave work early since I feel sick.
- The caller asked Cindy what kind of toothpaste she used.

Exclamation Point (!)

1 An exclamation point may be used to show excitement or another strong feeling.

- That car is coming right at us!

2 An exclamation point may be used at the end of a strong command.

- Stop that thief!

OTHER PUNCTUATION MARKS

Comma (,)

There are five main uses of the comma:

1 Use commas between items in a series.

- Trisha bought hair dye, neon lipstick, and false eyelashes before deciding she wanted a "natural" look.

2 Insert a comma after introductory material.

- During the country fair, prizes were awarded for the largest tomato and the reddest apples.

3 Put commas around words that interrupt the flow of a sentence.

- My uncle, who is a plumber, sometimes gets emergency calls in the middle of the night.

4 Use commas between complete thoughts connected by a joining word.

- Smoke poured out of the oven, and then the smoke detector began to sound.

5 Use commas with direct quotations.

- Reggie asked, "Aren't you going to recycle those glass bottles?"

The above five uses of the comma are explained in more detail on pages 200–206. Following is information about other uses of the comma:

6 Use a comma to set off the name of a person spoken to.

- You can't have candy bars and soda for dinner, Robert.
- Shannon, will you help us out at the car wash?
- All right, Fred, we won't ask you to give a speech.

7 Use a comma in dates to separate the day from the year and the year from any following text.

- Craig began taking a sewing class on September 8, 1993.
- He finished a small blanket on December 13, 1993, for his infant son.

8   Use commas in addresses as follows:

- My sister moved to Greenlands Housing Center, 816 Pine Street, Battle Creek, Michigan 49017.

Note that no comma is used before the zip code.

9   Use a comma after the opening of an informal letter and the closing of any letter.

- Dear Dad,   • Sincerely,
- Dear Janet,   • With warm regards,

For formal letters, follow the opening with a colon.

- Dear Ms. Graham: • Dear Sir or Madam:

10   Use commas in numbers four or more digits long.

- The tallest building in the United States is the Sears Tower, which is 1,454 feet and 110 stories tall.
- There are 154 national forests in the United States covering over 343,000 square miles.

Apostrophe (')

1   Use an apostrophe to show possession.

- I dropped Terry's VCR.
- Bess's father fixed it.

2   Use an apostrophe in contractions. (**Contractions** are words formed by joining two or more words into one, omitting one or more letters.)

- Phil won't go out with a woman who's taller than he is.
- Since he's six feet tall, that isn't much of a problem.

The above uses of apostrophes are explained in more detail on pages 212–218. Following is additional information about the apostrophe:

3   Use the apostrophe in certain plurals.

a   Of letters:

- How many *s*'s are in the word *possessive*?

b   Of numbers:

- There should be four 8's in that item number.

c   Of words used as words:

- We counted twenty *like*'s in Karen's speech.

Quotation Marks (" ")

1   Use quotation marks to set off the exact words of a speaker or writer.

- "If I fail the test," said Ralph, "I'll have to repeat the course."
- "Knowledge is of two kinds," writes Samuel Johnson. "We know a subject ourselves, or we know where we can find information about it."

   Note: Quoted material is usually set off from the rest of the sentence by a comma. When the comma comes at the end of the quoted material, it is included *inside* the quotation marks. The same is true for a period, exclamation point, or question mark that ends quoted material. (The above use of quotation marks is explained in more detail on pages 224–228.)

2   Use quotation marks to set off the titles of short works, such as the titles of magazine or newspaper articles, stories, songs, poems, individual TV shows, and book chapters.

- The test will be on the chapter titled "Group Influence" in the textbook <u>Social Psychology</u>.

   Note: The titles of longer works, such as books, newspapers, and magazines, should be underlined when written. (When longer works are mentioned in printed material, their titles are usually set in *italic type*.)

Colon (:)

The colon directs attention to what follows. It has three main uses:

1   Use a colon to introduce a list.

- On her first day of vacation, Carrie did three things: she read a funny novel, took a long nap, and ate at her favorite restaurant.

2   Use a colon to introduce a long or a formal quotation.

- The autobiography of Arthur Ashe begins with the following Biblical quotation: "Since we are surrounded by so great a cloud of witnesses, let us lay aside every weight, and the sin which so easily ensnares us, and let us run with endurance the race that is set before us."

3   Use a colon to introduce an explanation.

- Bert suddenly cancelled his evening plans for a simple reason: his car was out of gas.

Semicolon (;)

Semicolons indicate that the reader should pause. Following are the main uses of the semicolon:

1   Use semicolons to join two complete thoughts not connected by a joining word (such as *and, but,* or *so*).

- Our cat spilled a can of Coca-Cola; the soda foamed over the white carpet.

2 Use semicolons to join two complete thoughts with a transitional word or word group (such as *however, therefore,* and *on the other hand).* Follow the transitional word or word group with a comma.

- LeQuita began school without knowing any English; nevertheless, she will graduate at the top of her class.

   Note: Transitional words and word groups differ from joining words such as *and* and *but*: They need a semicolon (not a comma) to connect two complete thoughts. Other common transitional words and word groups are *furthermore, meanwhile, as a result, by the way, in addition.*

3 Use semicolons to separate items in a series when the items themselves contain commas.

- Driving down Sunset Strip, we passed La Boutique, which sells women's clothing; The Friendly Cafe, which serves twenty different kinds of coffee; and Pet Palace, which sells snakes, parrots, and spiders.

Hyphen (-)

Following are the main uses of hyphens:

1 Use a hyphen to join two or more words that act together to describe a noun that follows them.

- The sportscar swerved around the slow-moving truck.

2 Use a hyphen to divide a word at the end of a line of writing.

- The lawyer put on her jacket, shoved a thick bundle of papers into her brief-case, and hurried to court.

   Note: Divide words only between syllables, and never divide a word which has only one syllable. Consult your dictionary if you are unsure about a word's syllable divisions.

3 Put a hyphen between the two parts of a fraction: one-fourth, two-thirds.

4 Put a hyphen between words when spelling out any number from twenty-one to ninety-nine.

Dash (—)

A dash may be used to set off and emphasize interrupting material. Use it when you wish to give special attention to words that interrupt the flow of the sentence.

- My wallet—minus the cash—was found in a trash can.
- Floyd was promised a new car for his junior-high graduation—a toy Matchbox car.

Parentheses ( )

Here are two common uses of parentheses:

1 Use parentheses to set off material that interrupts the flow of a sentence. In general, use parentheses for material you do not wish to emphasize.

   • Aunt Fern (who arrived two hours late) brought the biggest gift.

2 Place parentheses around numbers that introduce items in a list within a sentence.

   • Ron's work for the evening is as follows: (1) finish a history term paper, (2) read a chapter in the psychology text, and (3) wash a load of laundry.

➤ *Practice A*

Add the punctuation mark needed in each of the following sentences. Use each of the following once.

Period	**Exclamation point**	**Apostrophe**
Question mark	**Comma**	

To help you, hints are provided for sentences 1 and 3.

1. I asked Nick how he managed to lose his socks
   Hint: This sentence is about a question. It doesn't directly ask one.

2. How did you manage to lose your socks

3. That golf ball is heading right for us
   Hint: Use an end mark that shows the speaker's strong emotion.

4. The mail carrier was fired because he wouldnt deliver mail during the heavy rain.

5. The police searched the woods where the boy was last seen but all they found was his torn sneaker.

➤ *Practice B*

Add the punctuation mark needed in each of the following sentences. Use each of the following once.

Colon	Hyphen	Parentheses (a pair)
Semicolon	Dash	Quotation marks (a pair)

1. My goals this semester are 1 to pass all my courses and (2) to spend more time with my children.

2. Although Trudy turned thirty last month, she tells everyone she's twenty eight.

3. Only four people attended our tenth-year class reunion: Nelson, an auto mechanic; Will, a nurse Holly, a lawyer; and Rob, a medical technician.

4. Craig recently learned he has a brother a twin from whom he has been separated since birth.

5. The police officer wrote down the following stolen items a watch, diamond earrings, a color TV, and a stereo.

6. We received a letter in the mail that read, You can be the next winner of our grand prize of ten million dollars.

Adjectives and Adverbs

As you already learned in the parts of speech chapter, the two kinds of descriptive words are **adjectives** and **adverbs**.

ADJECTIVES

Identifying Adjectives

An **adjective** describes a noun. An adjective may come before the noun it describes or after a linking verb.

- The **weary** hikers walked slowly down the **dusty** road.

    (The adjective *weary* describes the noun *hikers*. The adjective *dusty* describes the noun *road*.)

- That dog's skin is **wrinkled** and **dry**.

    (The adjectives *wrinkled* and *dry* describe the noun *skin*. The adjectives follow the linking verb *is*.)

Adjectives in Comparisons

Adjectives are used in comparisons. To make comparisons, add *-er* or *-est* to adjectives of one syllable and some adjectives with two syllables. Use *-er* when comparing two things. Use *-est* to compare three or more things.

- Grilling food is **faster** than roasting.
- Grilling food is **faster** than roasting, but microwaving is **fastest** of all.

For adjectives of three or more syllables and many of two syllables, do not add *-er* or *-est*. Instead, add the word *more* when comparing two things and *most* when comparing three or more things.

- My dog is **more intelligent** than my cat.
- My dog is **more intelligent** than my cat, but my parrot is the **most intelligent** pet I have ever had.

Note 1: Do not use both an *-er* ending and *more*, or an *-est* ending and *most*.

> *Incorrect:* My uncle's hair is more curlier than my aunt's.

> *Correct:* My uncle's hair is **curlier** than my aunt's.

Note 2: Certain short adjectives have irregular forms:

	Comparing two	*Comparing three or more*
bad	worse	worst
good, well	better	.best
little	less	least
much, many	more	most

- The grape cough syrup tastes **better** than the orange syrup, but the lemon cough drops taste the **best**.

ADVERBS

Identifying Adverbs

An **adverb** is a word that describes a verb, an adjective, or another adverb. Most adverbs end in *-ly*.

- The chef **carefully** spread raspberry frosting over the cake.

  (The adverb *carefully* describes the verb *spread*.)

- Ann was **extremely** embarrassed when her father showed her baby pictures.

  (The adverb *extremely* describes the adjective *embarrassed*.)

- That lamp shines **very** brightly.

  (The adverb *very* describes the adverb *brightly*.)

Using Adverbs

Be careful to use an adverb—not an adjective—after an action verb. Compare the following:

Incorrect	*Correct*
The boss snored loud at his desk. (*Loud* is an adjective.)	The boss snored **loudly** at his desk.
Speak slow during your lecture. (*Slow* is an adjective.)	Speak **slowly** during your lecture.
The batter swung wild at all the pitches. (*Wild* is an adjective.)	The batter swung **wildly** at all the pitches.

A TROUBLESOME PAIR: *GOOD* AND *WELL*

Good is an adjective that often means "enjoyable," "talented," or "positive."

- I had a **good** day.
- Sue is a **good** skier.
- Think **good** thoughts.

As an adverb, *well* often means "skillfully" or "successfully."

- Sue skis **well**.
- The schedule worked **well**.
- José works **well** with others.

As an adjective, *well* means "healthy."

- The patient feels **well** once again.

➤ *Practice A*

Cross out the incorrect adjective or adverb in each of the following sentences. Then write the correction on the line provided. To help you, hints are provided for sentences 1 and 3.

_____ 1. This bag of potato chips is more full than that one.
   Hint: To make a comparison using one-syllable adjectives (such as *full*), choose *-er* (not *more*).

_____ 2. Sandra read the book very slow.

_____ 3. The most importantest thing in Julia's life is clothes.
   Hint: Never use *most* and *-est* together. For words of three or more syllables such as *important*, choose *most*.

_____ 4. That was the baddest accident I've ever seen.

_____ 5. Al hums really good.

➤ *Practice B*

Cross out the incorrect adjective or adverb in each of the following sentences. Then write the correction on the line provided.

_____ 1. Come quick if you want to see a beautiful rainbow.

_____ 2. The frog hid quiet alongside the pond.

_____ 3. Of the twenty students in my class, Juan is the more artistic.

_____ 4. The macaroni salad tastes badder than the potato salad.

_____ 5. Because of his cold, Mr. Turner didn't sing very good today.

Numbers and Abbreviations

Here are guidelines to follow when using numbers or abbreviations.

NUMBERS

1 Spell out any number that can be written in one or two words. Otherwise, use numerals.

- When my grandmother turned **sixty-nine**, she went on a **fifteen**-day trip across **nine** states.
- The mail carrier delivered **512** pieces of mail today.

   Note: When written out, numbers twenty-one through ninety-nine are hyphenated.

2 Spell out any number that begins a sentence.

- **Eight hundred and seventy-one** dollars were found in the briefcase.

To avoid writing out a long number, you can rewrite the sentence:

- The briefcase contained **$871**.

3 If one or more numbers in a series need to be written as numerals, write *all* the numbers as numerals.

- The movie theater sold **137** tickets to a horror movie, **64** to a comedy, and **17** to a romance.

4 Use numerals to write the following.

a Dates:

- My grandfather was born on July **4, 1909**.

b Times:

- The last guest left at **1:45** a.m.

   (But when the word *o'clock* is used, the time is spelled out: I got home at **six o'clock**. Also spell out the numbers when describing amounts of time: I worked **fifty** hours last week.)

c   Addresses:

- The bookstore is located at **1216** North **48th** Street.

d   Percentages:

- Nearly **70** percent of my class donated blood.

e   Parts of a book:

- Jeff read pages **40–97** of the novel, which includes chapters **2** and **3**.

f   Exact amounts of money that include change:

- My restaurant bill came to **$8.49**.

ABBREVIATIONS

Abbreviations can save you time when taking notes. However, you should avoid abbreviations in papers you write for classes. The following are among the few that are acceptable in formal writing.

1   Titles that are used with proper nouns:

- **Ms.** Glenda Oaks   **Dr.** Huang   Keith Rodham, **Sr.**

2   Initials in a person's name:

- Daphne **A.** Miller   **T.** Martin Sawyer

3   Time and date references:

- The exam ended at 4:45 **p.m.**
- Cleopatra lived from about 69 to 30 **B.C.**

4   Organizations, agencies, technical words, or corporations known by their initials. They are usually written in all capital letters and without periods:

- **NAACP**   **NBA**   **YMCA**   **FBI**   **AIDS**   **NBC**

➤ *Practice A*

Cross out the **one** number or abbreviation mistake in each of the following sentences. Then write the correction on the line provided. To help you, hints are provided for sentences 1 and 3.

_____ 1. 102 patients visited Dr. Jamison's clinic today.
Hint: Never begin a sentence with a numeral.

_____ 2. I wrote 3 protest letters to CBS when my favorite show was cancelled.

_____ 3. That univ. has 143 professors and 894 students.
Hint: Abbreviations of general words are not used in formal writing.

_____ 4. Only thirteen percent of the customers preferred the new brand of cereal.

_____ 5. The hosp. has treated eighteen patients with AIDS.

➤ *Practice B*

Cross out the **one** number or abbreviation mistake in each of the following sentences. Then write the correction on the line provided.

_____ 1. Ms. Bradley begins her day at 5 o'clock.

_____ 2. The twenty-seven students in Mrs. Greene's class are learning about South Amer.

_____ 3. Shelly watched a program on PBS for 30 minutes before going to work.

_____ 4. I listed Dr. Keenan as a ref. on my résumé.

_____ 5. The vendors sold eighty soft pretzels, 145 soft drinks, and 106 hot dogs.

Part Three

Readings for Writing

Introduction to the Readings

This part of the book will help you become a better reader as well as a stronger writer. Reading and writing are closely connected skills—so that practicing one skill helps develop the other. Included here are six high-interest reading selections that provide ideas for a wide range of paragraph writing assignments.

THE FORMAT OF EACH SELECTION

To help you read and write about the selections effectively, the book provides the following:

1 A short preview introducing you to each selection.

2 A list of difficult words in each selection with their paragraph numbers and meanings within the reading. You may find it helpful to read through these "Words to Watch" to remind yourself of meanings or to learn new ones.

3 A series of questions that will give you practice in four reading skills widely recognized as important to good comprehension:

a **Understanding vocabulary in context.** The context of a word is the meaning of the words that surround it. We learn many words by guessing their meaning from context. For example, look at the sentence below. Can you figure out the meaning of the boldfaced word? After reading the sentence, try to answer the question that follows.

> Using sign language, chimpanzees can **convey** messages such as "Candy sweet" and "Gimme hug."

> The word *convey* in the sentence above means
> a. write down.
> b. communicate.
> c. believe.
> d. ignore.

We know that chimpanzees do not use sign language to write, so answer *a* is incorrect. Also, we can guess that the author of the above sentence is not referring to what chimps believe or ignore (the examples of messages have nothing to do with believing or ignoring). So answers *c* and *d* are also incorrect. If you chose answer *b*, you're right—the chimps can communicate messages with sign language. You have figured out a meaning of *convey* based on its context. Developing this skill is very useful since we frequently meet new words in our reading. By paying attention to their context, we may not need a dictionary to figure out what they mean.

b **Determining main ideas.** You've already learned that a paragraph is about a point, or main idea, which is often expressed in a topic sentence. In a reading made up of many paragraphs, there is also an overall main idea, often called the **central idea**. Sometimes the author states it directly; sometimes the reader must figure it out. In either case, to know what an author is really saying, readers must determine the central idea of a reading.

c **Recognizing key supporting details.** Supporting details are the reasons, examples, and other kinds of information that help to explain or clarify main ideas and the central idea. Recognizing key supporting details is an important part of understanding an author's message.

d **Making inferences.** Often an author does not state a point directly. Instead, he or she may only suggest an idea, and a good reader must **infer** it—in other words, figure it out. We make such inferences every day, based on our understanding and experience. For example, suppose you have been up all night studying for a final. A friend may say to you, "You certainly look bright and energetic this morning." You conclude from the circumstances that your friend is not saying directly what she means. What she really means is the opposite of what she has said. Or consider the statement below. What can you infer from it? Circle the letter of the most logical inference.

The dog we just got from the humane society cringes when someone tries to pet him.

The sentence suggests that the dog
a. is very large.
b. is small.
c. was expensive.
d. has previously been mishandled.

Nothing in the sentence suggests the size of the dog, so answers *a* and *b* are incorrect. Since the dog came from the pound, we can infer that it was not expensive, so answer *c* is also incorrect. From our understanding of behavior, we can infer that previous mishandling may be the reason the dog cringes when a hand reaches toward him. Thus answer *d* is correct. Making such inferences is often necessary to a full understanding of an author's points.

4 Technique questions that point to methods which writers have used to present their material effectively. In particular, the questions make you aware of a directly stated central idea; of methods used to organize ideas; and of vivid details that help the writer's experiences become alive and real for the reader. The focus on such techniques should make you more ready to use them in your own writing.

5 Writing assignments based on each selection. Many assignments provide guidelines on how to proceed, including suggestions about prewriting, possible topic sentences, and methods of development.

SOME HINTS FOR EFFECTIVE READING

Effective reading, like effective writing, does not happen all at once. Rather, it is a process. Often you begin with a general impression of what something means, and then, by rereading, you move to a deeper level of understanding of the material.

Here are some hints for becoming a better reader.

1 **Read in the right place.** Ideally, you should get settled in a quiet spot that encourages concentration. If you can focus your attention while lying on a bed or curled up in a chair, that's fine. But if you find that being very comfortable leads to daydreaming or dozing off rather than reading, then avoid getting too relaxed. You might find that sitting in an upright chair promotes concentration and keeps your mind alert.

2 **Preview the selection.** Begin by reading the overview that precedes the selection. Then think for a few moments about the title. A good title often hints at a selection's main idea, giving you insight into the piece even before you read it. For example, the title of Scott Peck's essay, "Responsibility," suggests that Peck will focus on what it takes to be a responsible person.

3 **Read the selection right through for pleasure.** Allow yourself to be drawn into the world that the author has created. Don't slow down or turn back. Instead, just read to understand as much as you can the first time through. After this reading, sit back for a moment and think about what you enjoyed in the piece.

4 **Deepen your sense of the selection.** Go back and reread it, or at least reread passages that may not have been clear the first time through. Look up any words that you cannot figure out from context and write their meanings in the margin.

Now ask yourself the following questions:

- What is the central idea of the piece?
- What support is provided for the central idea?
- What seem to be other important ideas in the selection?

Reread carefully the parts of the selection that seem most relevant to answering the above questions. By asking yourself the questions and by rereading, you will gradually deepen your understanding of the material.

Reading and writing about the selections will have many rewards. Chances are you will improve your vocabulary, spelling, and reading comprehension, as well as your grammar and writing skills. You will learn to develop the command of language necessary for success in today's job world. In addition, the readings by the six authors are likely to inspire and motivate you in your own active quest for self-improvement and for learning.

Responsibility
M. Scott Peck

Preview

M. Scott Peck is the author of the best-selling book *The Road Less Traveled.* The book begins with the sentence "Life is difficult." It then encourages readers to meet those difficulties head-on, rather than go through life trying to avoid pain. In this excerpt from his book, Dr. Peck describes a basic first step in dealing with life's problems.

Words to Watch

self-evident (1): not requiring any explanation
ludicrous (2): laughable because of being obviously ridiculous
clarified (19): made clear
whining (29): childish complaining
glared (37): stared angrily

We cannot solve life's problems except by solving them. This statement may seem idiotically self-evident°, yet it is seemingly beyond the comprehension of much of the human race. This is because we must accept responsibility for a problem before we can solve it. We cannot solve a problem by saying "It's not my problem." We cannot solve a problem by hoping that someone else will solve it for us. I can solve a problem only when I say, "This is my problem and it's up to me to solve it." But many, so many, seek to avoid the pain of their problems by saying to themselves: "This problem was caused by other people, or by social circumstances beyond my control, and therefore it is up to other people or society to solve this problem for me. It is not really my personal problem." 1

The extent to which people will go psychologically to avoid assuming responsibility for personal problems, while always sad, is sometimes almost ludicrous°. A career sergeant in the army, stationed in Okinawa and in serious trouble because of his excessive drinking, was referred for psychiatric evaluation 2 and, if possible, assistance. He denied that he was an alcoholic, or even that his use of alcohol was a personal problem, saying, "There's nothing else to do in the evenings in Okinawa except drink."

"Do you like to read?" I asked. 3

"Oh yes, I like to read, sure." 4

"Then why don't you read in the evening instead of drinking?" 5

"It's too noisy to read in the barracks." 6

"Well, then, why don't you go to the library?" 7

"The library is too far away." 8

"Is the library farther away than the bar you go to?" 9

"Well, I'm not much of a reader. That's not where my interests lie." 10

"Do you like to fish?" I then inquired. 11

"Sure, I love to fish."

"Why not go fishing instead of drinking?"

"Because I have to work all day long."

"Can't you go fishing at night?"

"No, there isn't any night fishing in Okinawa."

> *"We cannot solve a problem by hoping that someone else will solve it for us. I can solve a problem only when I say, 'This is my problem and it's up to me to solve it.'"*

"But there is," I said. "I know several organizations that fish at night here. Would you like me to put you in touch with them?"

"Well, I really don't like to fish."

"What I hear you saying," I clarified°, "is that there are other things to do in Okinawa except drink, but the thing you like to do most in Okinawa is drink." 19

"Yeah, I guess so." 20

"But your drinking is getting you in trouble, so you're faced with a real problem, aren't you?" 21

"This damn island would drive anyone to drink." 22

I kept trying for a while, but the sergeant was not the least bit interested in seeing his drinking as a personal problem which he could solve either with or without help, and I regretfully told his commander that he was not amenable to assistance. His drinking continued, and he was separated from the service in mid-career. 23

A young wife, also in Okinawa, cut her wrist lightly with a razor blade and was brought to the emergency room, where I saw her. I asked her why she had done this to herself. 24

"To kill myself, of course." 25

"Why do you want to kill yourself?" 26

"Because I can't stand it on this dumb island. You have to send me back to the States. I'm going to kill myself if I have to stay here any longer." 27

"What is it about living on Okinawa that's so painful for you?" I asked. 28

She began to cry in a whining° sort of way. "I don't have any friends here, and I'm alone all the time." 29

"That's too bad. How come you haven't been able to make any friends?" 30

"Because I have to live in a stupid Okinawan housing area, and none of my neighbors speak English." 31

"Why don't you drive over to the American housing area or to the wives' club during the day so you can make some friends?" 32

"Because my husband has to drive the car to work." 33

"Can't you drive him to work, since you're alone and bored all day?" I asked.   34

"No. It's a stick-shift car, and I don't know how to drive a stick-shift car, only   35
an automatic."

"Why don't you learn how to drive a stick-shift car?"   36

She glared° at me. "On these roads? You must be crazy."   37

Reading Comprehension Questions

1. The word *inquired* in "'Do you like to fish?' I then inquired" (paragraph 11)
   means
   a. joked.
   b. stuttered.
   c. thought.
   d. asked.

2. The word *amenable* in "but the sergeant was not the least bit interested in
   seeing his drinking as a personal problem which he could solve either with or
   without help, and I regretfully told his commander that he was not amenable to
   assistance" (paragraph 23) means
   a. opposed.
   b. lost.
   c. agreeable.
   d. transported.

3. Which sentence best expresses the central idea of the selection?
   a. People in the military have trouble solving their personal problems.
   b. Americans in Okinawa had many problems.
   c. A young army wife who refused to help make her life on Okinawa better
      wanted someone else to solve her problem.
   d. Before a problem can be solved, a person must take responsibility for it,
      which many refuse to do.

4. A main idea may cover more than one paragraph. Which sentence best
   expresses the main idea of paragraphs 2–23?
   a. An army sergeant had a serious drinking problem.
   b. An army sergeant was referred for evaluation because of his drinking.
   c. An army sergeant refused to accept responsibility for his drinking, even
      though it was causing him serious career problems.
   d. An army sergeant said he drank excessively because there was nothing else
      to do in the evenings in Okinawa.

5. Which sentence best expresses the main idea of paragraphs 24–37?
   a. A young American woman refused to consider any possible solutions to her
      unhappiness.
   b. A young American woman was unhappy living in Okinawa, where she was
      surrounded by neighbors who did not speak English.
   c. One reason the young American woman was so unhappy in Okinawa was
      she was unable to drive her husband's car.
   d. A young American woman thought that learning to drive a stick-shift car on
      the Okinawan roads would be very difficult.

6. According to the author, many people see their problems as being
   a. beyond their control.
   b. easy to solve.
   c. caused by drinking.
   d. caused by loneliness.

7. The young wife
   a. couldn't speak English.
   b. couldn't drive a car.
   c. was lonely.
   d. lived in the American housing area.

8. We can infer that the author believed the young woman
   a. should return to the United States.
   b. could learn to drive a stick-shift car if she really wanted to.
   c. would succeed in killing herself the next time.
   d. would soon be feeling happier about living in Okinawa.

9. We can infer that the sergeant
   a. would have continued drinking no matter what activities were available on Okinawa.
   b. would not have been an alcoholic if he had lived anywhere else.
   c. disliked the author and was deliberately refusing to cooperate with him.
   d. was not really an alcoholic.

10. We can infer that the young American woman
   a. had originally wanted to move to Okinawa.
   b. was married to an Okinawan.
   c. did not like the other American wives she was acquainted with.
   d. did not seriously intend to kill herself when she cut her wrist.

Technique Questions

1. Peck writes, "The extent to which people will go psychologically to avoid assuming responsibility for personal problems, while always sad, is sometimes almost ludicrous." What examples does he use to illustrate this point?

   _____

   _____

2. Most of what Peck has to say about the young wife is expressed through dialog. He does, however, tell readers about the woman through a few carefully selected words that are not part of the dialog. What specific details does Peck include in paragraphs 24 and 29, and what do they tell us about the woman?

   _____

   _____

   _____

3. In this excerpt, does Peck give more space to his general points or to his examples? What do you think is his reason for doing so?

_____

_____

Discussion Questions

1. Peck writes that "we must accept responsibility for a problem before we can solve it." What does he mean by that? Do you agree? Use examples from your experience to support your view.

2. Why do you think it's so difficult for people to take responsibility for their problems?

3. Imagine that Peck had written not about the sergeant and the young wife but about two students who refused to take responsibility for their probems in school. What kinds of details might he have included about the students, their problems, and how they sought to blame their problems on others?

Writing Assignments

1. Peck writes, "The extent to which people will go psychologically to avoid assuming responsibility for personal problems, while always sad, is sometimes almost ludicrous." Think of times you have observed people blaming other people or circumstances for their own problems. Then write a paragraph that begins with the following topic sentence:

   Just like M. Scott Peck, I have seen someone refuse to take responsibility for his (or her) own problem.

   Then go on to support that statement with an example. As you develop that example, be sure to explain what the person's problem was, how he had helped create it, and how he blamed other people or circumstances rather than accept responsibility for it.

   As you think of how to develop your paragraph, ask yourself questions such as these:

   • Whom do I know who usually seems to be in one kind of trouble or another?

   • Does that person always seem to blame others for his problems?

   • What are some specific problems that person has in his life?

   • How has he helped to create the problems?

   • Whom or what does the person blame for those problems?

2. Peck explains that the only way to solve a problem is to solve it—in other words, to take responsibility for the problem and find a solution. When did you accept the responsibility for a problem in your own life and figure out a solution for it? Write about what happened. Be sure to answer the following questions:

- How was the problem affecting my life?

- When did I realize that I was at least partially responsible for the problem?

- What solution for the problem did I come up with?

- What happened after I put my solution to work?

In selecting a topic for this assignment, think about various kinds of problems you may have experienced: problems getting along with other people, money problems, marriage problems, problems completing work on time, difficulties holding a job, excessive use of alcohol or other drugs, trouble with the law, and so on. Then ask yourself which of these problems you have accepted responsibility for and solved. Once you have thought of a topic, you might begin with a statement like this:

- This past year, I began to take responsibility for my continuing marriage problems.

- I recently faced the fact that I have a drinking problem and have taken steps to deal with it.

- After years of scraping together just enough money to get from one week to the next, I've acted to deal with my money problems.

This statement could then be supported with one or more examples of the problem, a description of how and when the writer realized the problem, and a detailing of the steps the writer has taken to deal with the problem.

3. Write a paragraph using the same examples that Peck used—except in your paper rewrite those case histories as they might have gone if the sergeant and the young wife had taken responsibility for their problems. Your examples will support the central idea that taking responsibility for one's problems is the first step to solutions.

Do It Better!
Ben Carson, M.D., with Cecil Murphey

Preview

If you suspect that you are now as "smart" as you'll ever be, then read the following selection, taken from the book *Think Big*. It is about Dr. Ben Carson, who was sure he was "the dumbest kid in the class" in school. Carson tells how he turned his life totally around from what was a sure path of failure. Today he is a famous neurosurgeon at Johns Hopkins University Hospital in Baltimore, Maryland.

Words to Watch

inasmuch as (13): since
potential (18): capacity for development and progress
solely (20): alone
rebellious (46): resisting authority
indifferent (58): uninterested
startled (75): surprised

"Benjamin, is this your report card?" my mother asked as she picked up the folded white card from the table. 1

"Uh, yeah," I said, trying to sound casual. Too ashamed to hand it to her, I had dropped it on the table, hoping that she wouldn't notice until after I went to bed. 2

It was the first report card I had received from Higgins Elementary School since we had moved back from Boston to Detroit, only a few months earlier. 3

I had been in the fifth grade not even two weeks before everyone considered me the dumbest kid in the class and frequently made jokes about me. Before long I too began to feel as though I really was the most stupid kid in fifth grade. Despite Mother's frequently saying, "You're smart, Bennie. You can do anything you want to do," I did not believe her. 4

No one else in school thought I was smart, either. 5

Now, as Mother examined my report card, she asked, "What's this grade in reading?" (Her tone of voice told me that I was in trouble.) Although I was embarrassed, I did not think too much about it. Mother knew that I wasn't doing well in math, but she did not know I was doing so poorly in every subject. 6

While she slowly read my report card, reading everything one word at a time, I   7
hurried into my room and started to get ready for bed. A few minutes later, Mother
came into my bedroom.

"Benjamin," she said, "are these your grades?" She held the card in front of me   8
as if I hadn't seen it before.

"Oh, yeah, but you know, it doesn't mean much."   9

"No, that's not true, Bennie. It means a lot."   10

"Just a report card."   11

"But it's more than that."   12

Knowing I was in for it now, I prepared to listen, yet I was not all that   13
interested. I did not like school very much and there was no reason why I should.
Inasmuch as° I was the dumbest kid in the class,
what did I have to look forward to? The others
laughed at me and made jokes about me every
day.

"Education is the only way you're ever
going to escape poverty," she said. "It's the only
way you're ever going to get ahead in life and be
successful. Do you understand that?"

> *"Reading is the way out of ignorance, and the road to achievement. I did not have to be the class dummy anymore."*

"Yes, Mother," I mumbled.

"If you keep on getting these kinds of grades you're going to spend the rest of   16
your life on skid row, or at best sweeping floors in a factory. That's not the kind of
life that I want for you. That's not the kind of life that God wants for you."

I hung my head, genuinely ashamed. My mother had been raising me and my   17
older brother, Curtis, by herself. Having only a third-grade education herself, she
knew the value of what she did not have. Daily she drummed into Curtis and me that
we had to do our best in school.

"You're just not living up to your potential°," she said. "I've got two mighty   18
smart boys and I know they can do better."

I had done my best—at least I had when I first started at Higgins Elementary   19
School. How could I do much when I did not understand anything going on in our
class?

In Boston we had attended a parochial school, but I hadn't learned much   20
because of a teacher who seemed more interested in talking to another female
teacher than in teaching us. Possibly, this teacher was not solely° to blame—perhaps
I wasn't emotionally able to learn much. My parents had separated just before we
went to Boston, when I was eight years old. I loved both my mother and father and
went through considerable trauma over their separating. For months afterward, I
kept thinking that my parents would get back together, that my daddy would come
home again the way he used to, and that we could be the same old family again—but
he never came back. Consequently, we moved to Boston and lived with Aunt Jean
and Uncle William Avery in a tenement building for two years until Mother had
saved enough money to bring us back to Detroit.

Mother kept shaking the report card at me as she sat on the side of my bed.   21
"You have to work harder. You have to use that good brain that God gave you,
Bennie. Do you understand that?"

"Yes, Mother." Each time she paused, I would dutifully say those words.   22

"I work among rich people, people who are educated," she said. "I watch how   23 they act, and I know they can do anything they want to do. And so can you." She put her arm on my shoulder. "Bennie, you can do anything they can do—only you can do it better!"

Mother had said those words before. Often. At the time, they did not mean 24 much to me. Why should they? I really believed that I was the dumbest kid in fifth grade, but of course, I never told her that.

"I just don't know what to do about you boys," she said. "I'm going to talk to 25 God about you and Curtis." She paused, stared into space, then said (more to herself than to me), "I need the Lord's guidance on what to do. You just can't bring in any more report cards like this."

As far as I was concerned, the report card matter was over. 26

The next day was like the previous ones—just another bad day in school, 27 another day of being laughed at because I did not get a single problem right in arithmetic and couldn't get any words right on the spelling test. As soon as I came home from school, I changed into play clothes and ran outside. Most of the boys my age played softball, or the game I liked best, "Tip the Top."

We played Tip the Top by placing a bottle cap on one of the sidewalk cracks. 28 Then taking a ball—any kind that bounced—we'd stand on a line and take turns throwing the ball at the bottle top, trying to flip it over. Whoever succeeded got two points. If anyone actually moved the cap more than a few inches, he won five points. Ten points came if he flipped it into the air and it landed on the other side.

When it grew dark or we got tired, Curtis and I would finally go inside and 29 watch TV. The set stayed on until we went to bed. Because Mother worked long hours, she was never home until just before we went to bed. Sometimes I would awaken when I heard her unlocking the door.

Two evenings after the incident with the report card, Mother came home about 30 an hour before our bedtime. Curtis and I were sprawled out, watching TV. She walked across the room, snapped off the set, and faced both of us. "Boys," she said, "you're wasting too much of your time in front of that television. You don't get an education from staring at television all the time."

Before either of us could make a protest, she told us that she had been praying 31 for wisdom. "The Lord's told me what to do," she said. "So from now on, you will not watch television, except for two preselected programs each week."

"Just *two* programs?" I could hardly believe she would say such a terrible 32 thing. "That's not—"

"And *only* after you've done your homework. Furthermore, you don't play 33 outside after school, either, until you've done all your homework."

"Everybody else plays outside right after school," I said, unable to think of 34 anything except how bad it would be if I couldn't play with my friends. "I won't have any friends if I stay in the house all the time—"

"That may be," Mother said, "but everybody else is not going to be as 35 successful as you are—"

"But, Mother—" 36

"This is what we're going to do. I asked God for wisdom, and this is the 37 answer I got."

I tried to offer several other arguments, but Mother was firm. I glanced at 38 Curtis, expecting him to speak up, but he did not say anything. He lay on the floor, staring at his feet.

"Don't worry about everybody else. The whole world is full of 'everybody else,'   39
you know that? But only a few make a significant achievement."

The loss of TV and play time was bad enough. I got up off the floor, feeling as   40
if everything was against me. Mother wasn't going to let me play with my friends,
and there would be no more television—almost none, anyway. She was stopping me
from having any fun in life.

"And that isn't all," she said. "Come back, Bennie."   41

I turned around, wondering what else there could be.   42

"In addition," she said, "to doing your homework, you have to read two books   43
from the library each week. Every single week."

"Two books? Two?" Even though I was in fifth grade, I had never read a whole   44
book in my life.

"Yes, two. When you finish reading them, you must write me a book report just   45
like you do at school. You're not living up to your potential, so I'm going to see that
you do."

Usually Curtis, who was two years older, was the more rebellious°. But this   46
time he seemed to grasp the wisdom of what Mother said. He did not say one word.

She stared at Curtis. "You understand?"   47

He nodded.   48

"Bennie, is it clear?"   49

"Yes, Mother." I agreed to do what Mother told me—it wouldn't have occurred   50
to me not to obey—but I did not like it. Mother was being unfair and demanding
more of us than other parents did.

The following day was Thursday. After school, Curtis and I walked to the local   51
branch of the library. I did not like it much, but then I had not spent that much time
in any library.

We both wandered around a little in the children's section, not having any idea   52
about how to select books or which books we wanted to check out.

The librarian came over to us and asked if she could help. We explained that   53
both of us wanted to check out two books.

"What kind of books would you like to read?" the librarian asked.   54

"Animals," I said after thinking about it. "Something about animals."   55

"I'm sure we have several that you'd like." She led me over to a section of   56
books. She left me and guided Curtis to another section of the room. I flipped
through the row of books until I found two that looked easy enough for me to read.
One of them, *Chip, the Dam Builder*—about a beaver—was the first one I had ever
checked out. As soon as I got home, I started to read it. It was the first book I ever
read all the way through even though it took me two nights. Reluctantly I admitted
afterward to Mother that I really had liked reading about Chip.

Within a month I could find my way around the children's section like   57
someone who had gone there all his life. By then the library staff knew Curtis and
me and the kind of books we chose. They often made suggestions. "Here's a
delightful book about a squirrel," I remember one of them telling me.

As she told me part of the story, I tried to appear indifferent°, but as soon as she   58
handed it to me, I opened the book and started to read.

Best of all, we became favorites of the librarians. When new books came in that   59
they thought either of us would enjoy, they held them for us. Soon I became fascinated
as I realized that the library had so many books—and about so many different subjects.

After the book about the beaver, I chose others about animals—all types of   60
animals. I read every animal story I could get my hands on. I read books about
wolves, wild dogs, several about squirrels, and a variety of animals that lived in
other countries. Once I had gone through the animal books, I started reading about
plants, then minerals, and finally rocks.

My reading books about rocks was the first time the information ever became   61
practical to me. We lived near the railroad tracks, and when Curtis and I took the
route to school that crossed by the tracks, I began paying attention to the crushed
rock that I noticed between the ties.

As I continued to read more about rocks, I would walk along the tracks,   62
searching for different kinds of stones, and then see if I could identify them.

Often I would take a book with me to make sure that I had labeled each stone   63
correctly.

"Agate," I said as I threw the stone. Curtis got tired of my picking up stones   64
and identifying them, but I did not care because I kept finding new stones all the
time. Soon it became my favorite game to walk along the tracks and identify the
varieties of stones. Although I did not realize it, within a very short period of time, I
was actually becoming an expert on rocks.

Two things happened in the second half of fifth grade that convinced me of the   65
importance of reading books.

First, our teacher, Mrs. Williamson, had a spelling bee every Friday afternoon.   66
We'd go through all the words we'd had so far that year. Sometimes she also called
out words that we were supposed to have learned in fourth grade. Without fail, I
always went down on the first word.

One Friday, though, Bobby Farmer, whom everyone acknowledged as the   67
smartest kid in our class, had to spell "agriculture" as his final word. As soon as the
teacher pronounced his word, I thought, I can spell that word. Just the day before, I
had learned it from reading one of my library books. I spelled it under my breath,
and it was just the way Bobby spelled it.

If I can spell "agriculture," I'll bet I can learn to spell any other word in the   68
world. I'll bet I can learn to spell better than Bobby Farmer.

Just that single word, "agriculture," was enough to give me hope.   69

The following week, a second thing happened that forever changed my life.   70
When Mr. Jaeck, the science teacher, was teaching us about volcanoes, he held up an
object that looked like a piece of black, glass-like rock. "Does anybody know what
this is? What does it have to do with volcanoes?"

Immediately, because of my reading, I recognized the stone. I waited, but none   71
of my classmates raised their hands. I thought, *This is strange. Not even the smart*
kids are raising their hands. I raised my hand.

"Yes, Benjamin," he said.   72

I heard snickers around me. The other kids probably thought it was a joke, or   73
that I was going to say something stupid.

"Obsidian," I said.   74

"That's right!" He tried not to look startled°, but it was obvious he hadn't   75
expected me to give the correct answer.

"That's obsidian," I said, "and it's formed by the supercooling of lava when it   76
hits the water." Once I had their attention and realized I knew information no other
student had learned, I began to tell them everything I knew about the subject of
obsidian, lava, lava flow, supercooling, and compacting of the elements.

When I finally paused, a voice behind me whispered, "Is that Bennie Carson?"   77

"You're absolutely correct," Mr. Jaeck said, and he smiled at me. If he had   78
announced that I'd won a million-dollar lottery, I couldn't have been more pleased
and excited.

"Benjamin, that's absolutely, absolutely right," he repeated with enthusiasm in   79
his voice. He turned to the others and said, "That is wonderful! Class, this is a
tremendous piece of information Benjamin has just given us. I'm very proud to hear
him say this."

For a few moments, I tasted the thrill of achievement. I recall thinking, *Wow,*   80
look at them. They're all looking at me with admiration. Me, the dummy! The one
everybody thinks is stupid. They're looking at me to see if this is really me speaking.

Maybe, though, it was I who was the most astonished one in the class.   81
Although I had been reading two books a week because Mother told me to, I had not
realized how much knowledge I was accumulating. True, I had learned to enjoy
reading, but until then I hadn't realized how it connected with my schoolwork. That
day—for the first time—I realized that Mother had been right. Reading is the way
out of ignorance, and the road to achievement. I did not have to be the class dummy
anymore.

For the next few days, I felt like a hero at school. The jokes about me stopped.   82
The kids started to listen to me. *I'm starting to have fun with this stuff.*

As my grades improved in every subject, I asked myself, "Ben, is there any   83
reason you can't be the smartest kid in the class? If you can learn about obsidian,
you can learn about social studies and geography and math and science and
everything."

That single moment of triumph pushed me to want to read more. From then on,   84
it was as though I could not read enough books. Whenever anyone looked for me
after school, they could usually find me in my bedroom—curled up, reading a
library book—for a long time, the only thing I wanted to do. I had stopped caring
about the TV programs I was missing; I no longer cared about playing Tip the Top
or baseball anymore. I just wanted to read.

In a year and a half—by the middle of sixth grade—I had moved to the top of   85
the class.

Reading Comprehension Questions

1. The word *trauma* in "I loved both my mother and father and went through
considerable trauma over their separating. For months afterward, I kept
thinking that my parents would get back together, . . . but he never came back"
(paragraph 20) means
   a. love.
   b. knowledge.
   c. distance.
   d. suffering.

2. The word *acknowledged* in "One Friday, though, Bobby Farmer, whom everyone acknowledged as the smartest kid in our class, had to spell 'agriculture' as his final word" (paragraph 67) means
   a. denied.
   b. recognized.
   c. forgot.
   d. interrupted.

3. The word *astonished* in "'Obsidian,' I said. 'That's right!' He tried not to look startled, but it was obvious he hadn't expected me to give the correct answer. . . . Maybe, though, it was I who was the most astonished one in class. . . . I had not realized how much knowledge I was accumulating" (paragraphs 74–75, 81) means
   a. loud.
   b. surprised.
   c. mean.
   d. hopeful.

4. Which sentence best expresses the central idea of the selection?
   a. Children who grow up in single-parent homes may spend large amounts of time home alone.
   b. Because of parental guidance that led to a love of reading, the author was able to go from academic failure to success.
   c. Parents should stay committed to their marriages when their children are young.
   d. Today's young people watch too much television day after day.

5. Which sentence best expresses the main idea of paragraph 56?
   a. Bennie's first experience with a library book was positive.
   b. The first book that Bennie ever checked out at a library was about a beaver.
   c. The librarian was very helpful to Bennie and Curtis.
   d. At first, Bennie could not read most of the animal books at the library.

6. Which sentence best expresses the main idea of paragraphs 61–64?
   a. Books about rocks gave the author his first practical benefits from reading.
   b. Curtis took little interest in what his brother had learned about rocks.
   c. The author found a piece of agate by the railroad tracks.
   d. Studying rocks can be a fascinating experience.

7. In Boston, Bennie
   a. had an excellent teacher.
   b. attended a public school.
   c. longed for his parents to get together again.
   d. lived with his father in a tenement building.

8. To get her sons to do better in school, Mrs. Carson insisted they
   a. stop watching TV.
   b. finish their homework before playing.
   c. read one library book every week.
   d. all of the above.

9. We can conclude that Mrs. Carson believed
   a. education leads to success.
   b. her sons needed to be forced to live up to their potential.
   c. socializing was less important to her sons than a good education.
   d. all of the above.

10. We can infer that Bennie Carson believed he was dumb because
    a. in Boston he had gotten behind in school.
    b. other students laughed at him.
    c. he had done his best when he first started at Higgins Elementary School, but still got poor grades.
    d. all of the above.

Technique Questions

1. Instead of pausing to describe Bennie's mother, the authors reveal her character through the specific details of her actions and words. For example, what does paragraph 25 tell us about Mrs. Carson?

   _____

   _____

   _____

2. What is the main order in which the details of this reading are organized—in time order or listing order?   Locate and write down three of the many transitions that are used as part of that time order or listing order.

   _____   _____   _____

3. The author states in paragraph 65, "Two things happened in the second half of fifth grade that convinced me of the importance of reading books." In paragraph 66, the first of those two events is introduced with a listing transition. In paragraph 70, the second event is introduced with another listing transition. Write those two transitions on the lines below.

   _____   _____

Discussion Questions

1. Carson implies that his anxiety over his parents' separation may have been one reason for his inability to learn much. What do you think parents can do to help children through difficult times such as separation and divorce?

2. Part of Mrs. Carson's plan for helping her sons do better in school was limiting them to two television shows a week. How much of a role do you think this limit played in the success of her plan? Do you agree with her that unrestricted television watching can be harmful to children?

3. Carson's mother instructed him, "Education is the only way you're ever going to escape poverty." How true do you think this statement is today? What obstacles do poor students face in getting an education?

Writing Assignments

1. The reading tells about some of Carson's key school experiences, both positive and negative. Write a paragraph about one of your key experiences in school. Use concrete details—actions, comments, reactions, and so on—to help your readers picture what happened. (To see how Carson and Murphey used details to bring classroom scenes to life, look at paragraphs 65–81.)

To select an event to write about, try asking yourself the following questions:

- Which teachers or events in school influenced how I felt about myself?
- What specific incidents stand out in my mind as I think back to elementary school?

Once you know which experience you'll write about, use freewriting to help you remember and record the details. Here is one student's freewriting for this assignment.

> In second grade, Richard L. sat next to me, a really good artist. When he drew something, it looked just like what it was meant to be. He was so good at choosing colors, the use of crayons, water paint. His pictures were always picked by teacher to be shown on bulletin board. I still remember his drawing of a circus, acrobats, animals, clowns. Many colors and details. I felt pretty bad in art, even though I loved it and couldn't wait for art in class. One day the teacher read story about a boy who looked at the mountains far away, wondering what was on the other side, mountains were huge, dark. After reading, it was art time. "Paint something from the story" teacher said. I painted those mountains, big purple brown mountains with watercolor dripping to show uneven slopes and coloring of sunset, a thin crooked slice of very blue sky at top. Next day I sat down in my desk in the morning. Then I saw my picture was on the bulletin board! Later teacher passed by me, bent down, put hand on my shoulder and whispered good job, lovely painting. Made me feel capable, proud. The feeling lasted a long time.

Once the details of the experience are on paper, you will be free to concentrate on a more carefully constructed version of the event. The author of the above freewriting, for instance, needed to think of a topic sentence. So when writing the first draft, she began with this sentence: "A seemingly small experience in elementary school encouraged me greatly." Writing drafts is also the time to add any persuasive details you may have missed at first. When working on her second draft, the author of the above added at the end: "I felt very proud, which gave me confidence to work harder in all my school subjects."

Before writing out your final version, remember to check for grammar, punctuation, and spelling errors.

2. Reading helped Bennie, and it can do a lot for adults too. Most of us, however, don't have someone around to insist that we do a certain amount of personal reading every week. In addition, many of us don't have the amount of free time that Bennie and Curtis had. How can adults find time to read more? Write a paragraph listing several ways adults can add more reading to their lives.

A good prewriting strategy for this assignment is list making. Simply write out as many ways as you can think of. Don't worry about putting them in any special order. You will select and organize the strategies you wish to include in your paper after accumulating as many ideas as you can. Here is an example of a prewriting list for this paper:

Ways adults can increase the amount of time they spend reading

— on the bus to and from work/school

— while eating breakfast

— instead of watching some TV

— choose motivating materials (articles, books about hobbies, problems, etc.)

Feel free to use items from the above list, but add at least one or two of your own points to include in your paper.

3. "Do It Better!" suggests that television can interfere with children's academic progress. Write a paragraph on what you believe is another unfortunate effect of television. You may feel that television includes too much violence, that TV advertising encourages children to want to buy too much, or that TV sitcoms promote poor family values. After deciding what effect you wish to write about, make a list of possible points of support. You may find it helpful to spend a few sessions in front of the TV with a notebook. Following, for instance, is part of a list of notes that can be used to support the point "TV advertising promotes poor nutrition."

During kids' cartoon show:

— A sugary chocolate cereal in which marshmallow ghosts appear once milk is added. Children are pictured enjoying these ghosts appear and loving the cereal.

— Chocolate-dipped cookies are included in boxes of another chocolate cereal. Appealing cartoon characters invite children to look for these boxes.

During talk show:

— Ad for soda (empty calories) shows symbols of Christmas, making the soda seem like a healthy holiday drink.

— An ad for corn chips (high fat) shows happy, healthy faces finishing up a huge bowl of the chips.

Knowledge Is Power
Anna-Maria Petricic

Preview

A schoolgirl in Croatia gazes at a picture of an American comic book hero. The words she reads there create a thirst for knowledge within her. Her pursuit of knowledge eventually carries her thousands of miles from home and through many difficulties. Although Superman may be able to leap tall buildings at a single bound, you may agree that Anna-Maria Petricic's accomplishment is just as admirable.

Words to Watch

proclaimed (1): announced
essence (1): central point
dismayed (4): discouraged
objective (5): unaffected by personal feelings
certified (8): guaranteed as authentic
meager (9): brief and inadequate
terse (9): short and direct
pretentious (10): flashy and egotistical; intended to show off
imprinted (10): fixed; firmly in position
formidable (13): difficult
shrouded (16): covered
resolved (16): firmly decided
earnestly (17): seriously
steadfastly (17): firmly; steadily
civil (18): pleasant; polite
quest (21): pursuit; search
ascended (22): climbed

"Knowledge is real power," proclaimed° the bold letters on a bookmark   1
showing Superman soaring upward from between two blocks of books. As I read this, a wave of energy swept over me. I studied the bookmark, trying to comprehend its exact meaning. It seemed like the essence° of life was revealed on that small piece of red and blue paper. But, as a teenager in high school, I had no idea what it

meant. I only knew that this great excitement I was experiencing had something to do with knowledge. I wanted the power that knowledge brought. For that to happen, I knew I had to attend college. I also knew that this would not be easy.

As a high school student in Sisak, a town near Zagreb, Croatia, all I heard were horror stories about college. "First you sweat preparing for the entrance exams. If you survive that and are lucky enough to be accepted into college, you must deal with your teachers. They will be your enemies for the next four years. The first lesson they teach is that they will do everything they can to crush your confidence, to break your spirit, to make you quit." Such tales were commonly whispered in the high school hallways by students aspiring to go to college.

I was shocked. Surely these stories could not be true. College was supposed to build my confidence in the process of attaining knowledge. Teachers were supposed to encourage me with their wisdom and compassion. They should prepare me for all challenges, not turn me against learning. The more I heard the whispers, the more convinced I became that I must not attend college in my homeland. If I wanted knowledge, I must attend a university in America.

I read all I could about colleges in the U.S. I was dismayed°. The costs were staggering. Then I read about a small, private university in Iowa that was offering work-study scholarships for international students. The school would cover tuition, room, and board in exchange for a twenty-hour-per-week work commitment. In return, students had to show the university that they had sufficient funds in the bank for health insurance and personal expenses. Including airfare from Croatia to America, I calculated that I would need $2,000 per year.

I could hardly contain myself. I dashed into the kitchen that cold winter evening to proudly announce the news to my mother. "I am going to school in America!" My mother looked up at me while still working in the foamy sink full of dirty dishes. "Yes? And who is going to pay for that?" My mother's voice was heavy yet coolly objective°. In my excitement, I overlooked the fact that my mother hardly made enough money to provide for our immediate needs. I brushed that thought aside, not willing to let it spoil my enthusiasm. I wanted my mother's support. Everything else would work out somehow.

I eagerly wrote a letter of inquiry to the American university. Within a couple of weeks, I received a thick envelope. My mother stood beside me while I ripped it open and spread the contents on the table. I picked up the letter on top. It was from the dean of the College of Arts and Sciences. I was blinded with tears as I read the words of encouragement and warm invitation to attend the college. I felt that at this school, my desire for education would be sacredly cherished and respected. My educational heaven was waiting in America. To get there, I knew that I had to be prepared to wage a long, hard battle. And I had to start now.

When she saw how understanding the university was, my mother took a strong stand of support. She vowed to do all she could to help make my dream become reality. She pointed to a row of dictionaries on the bookshelf. I reached for the Croatian-English dictionary and began the first of many long, difficult, and sometimes discouraging steps.

Although my English was quite good, the application forms sent by the college included many words I didn't understand. After a few hours of trying to interpret meanings and of translating, my head was spinning. I needed to take the Test of English as a Foreign Language (TOEFL) and the Scholastic Aptitude Test (SAT). I also needed to send a certified° translation of my high school transcripts. The application deadline was in April. I was not even going to get my high school diploma until June. Suddenly, everything was moving so fast. I couldn't keep up. "Maybe I should postpone this until next year," I thought. We had little money, and I wasn't even sure I could get accepted. I could attend the University of Zagreb for a year, and then transfer the units. My mother suggested that I send a letter to the admissions officer explaining the situation.

After sending the letter, I went to a branch of the University of Zagreb to get 9 information about the entrance exams. I waited for an hour in a small, crowded room thick with cigarette smoke. Two ladies behind the admissions desk provided meager° answers to students' questions. The women were apparently upset that all these students were wasting their precious gossip time. Their sharp, terse° responses offered no help. Instead, they managed to make the students feel guilty for even asking. I gave up in my attempt to find out about the entrance exams.

As I walked toward the exit, I stopped to observe the college students who 10 were in the hallway. They wore torn jeans, and they spoke in pretentious° sentences. Their eyes were dull and they had lifeless smiles imprinted° on pale faces. Burning cigarette butts between their fingers were their only well-defined feature. I did not know whether to feel pity for them or for myself. As I left the building, I was both disappointed and humiliated. I had only been there for an hour, and I wondered how I would feel after four years of classes here. My dream

> *"I refused to expect from life only as much as others thought I should expect. I alone was responsible to make the best of my life."*

had spoiled me. I wanted the luxury of being treated like a human being, and I knew just the place where that would happen.

Shortly, I received a new letter from my admissions officer in Iowa that 11 provided encouragement. He asked me to continue my application process and said that I should not worry about my high school transcripts. They could be mailed as soon as I graduated. What was needed at this time were my test results.

A month later, I took the TOEFL and SAT at the American school in Zagreb. I 12 had studied hard and was satisfied with my performance. The results of both tests were sent directly to the university in America. When the admissions officer received them, he called me to offer congratulations. I had done well. My application was almost complete. Besides my transcripts, which I knew would not be a problem, I needed only one more thing: the money.

My mother joined forces with me in this last, but most formidable°, obstacle. 13 She borrowed money from a friend and deposited it in my account so that I could obtain the bank's confirmation that I had the funds required by the university. However, at the last minute, my mother's friend decided that he needed his money back. I was forced to withdraw the money.

When I returned home from the bank, I found my mother unwrapping our old 14 paintings, works of art by Vladimir Kirin, a famous Croatian artist who was now deceased. Mother had collected his work for as long as I can remember and had planned to open an art gallery in the artist's memory. As I walked across the room, my mother's words stopped me in my tracks. "You have to write an ad for the weekend paper," she said. These paintings meant more than anything to my mother. Yet she was prepared to sell them so that I could live my dream.

The ad was placed. All we had to do was wait for the phone calls. But none   15
came. After two weeks, we ran the ad again, but nothing happened.

I suddenly felt afraid. Even though I could see myself walking around the   16
campus of my new college, even though I could visualize my new classrooms and
teachers, it was all still just a dream. I felt like I was looking at slowly dissolving fog.
The dream world was fading away, leaving the old, gray reality. I was trapped in truth
that I could not accept. I became paralyzed as I imagined myself slowly sinking into
ignorance and despair. I would become one of those lifeless, gray faces that walked
daily to the bus station through the smog-shrouded° streets. I would work with
people who can only afford to think about survival, people who see no values beyond
the crispness of bills in their wallets. The ignorant world threatened to swallow me.
Though scared to death, I resolved° not to yield. I was not just fighting for money; I
was fighting for principle. I would not live a life of deliberate humiliation. I refused
to expect from life only as much as others thought I should expect. I alone was
responsible to make the best of my life. I had to continue my fight.

For the first time in my life, I earnestly° prayed for myself. I went to church in   17
the early afternoon when I knew nobody would be there. My wooden-soled shoes
echoed on the cold floor that led to the main altar. I knelt down and prayed. I prayed
for money. That humiliated me because I have always thought it was selfish to pray
for myself. My prayers had always been devoted to my friends, family, and to those
who suffered. I never prayed for anything for myself because I believed that if God
took care of the world, I would be taken care of. Now, I prayed for the most selfish
thing of all, and I hated myself for it. Full of shame, I prayed, my eyes steadfastly°
on the ground. Finally, I gained enough strength to look up at the crucifix. I
surrendered completely. I forgot all of my thoughts, and my mind began to flow
toward some new space. The pressure dissolved. I felt as if I'd been let out of prison.
I was free. My guilt and shame were gone, and my heart was beating with a new
force. Everything was going to be fine.

In the meantime, my mother continued to search for funds. She called an old   18
friend who owned a jewelry store. He had known me since I was a little girl and
bragged that he would do anything for me. He fell silent when he heard my mother's
request. He was sorry, but he had just invested all of his money in a new project. He
tried to comfort my mother. "I would teach her myself if she were my daughter," he
boasted. "School in America. Who does she think she is? She doesn't need college.
A woman shouldn't be too smart. She can marry either of my two sons. I promise
she will have the freedom to go to church whenever she wants. What more could she
need?" Struggling to remain civil°, my mother thanked him sarcastically and walked
away.

Time was slipping by. I had already obtained a U.S. visa, and I had made my   19
air reservation. The travel agent found a cheap student rate. Despite strict
regulations, she was willing to sell me a one-way ticket. My hopes were raised, but
even the low-cost ticket had to be paid for. And there was precious little time.

That evening, my mother, brother, grandmother, and I gathered in the living   20
room of our small apartment. I stared at the wall. My brother leaned against the
doorway cursing fate. My grandmother tightly held her prayer book, her lips moving
slowly. Gloomy silence threatened to break down the walls. Then, as if by magic,
words I did not think about came from my lips. "Mother, what about a credit card?"
Unlike America, it was not easy to obtain a credit card in Croatia. Yet my mother

knew an influential officer of a local bank. Could he help us? My mother sighed and acknowledged that it was worth a try. Once again my hopes were raised.

I returned home from school the next day to find a sense of calm that our household had not known for weeks. Before I had a chance to ask, my mother smiled and nodded her head. My prayers had been answered. My quest° for knowledge was to become a reality. 21

Later that summer, I was on a flight to America. As the plane ascended° into the clouds, my thoughts turned from the quickly disappearing city I was leaving to the destination I knew so little about. I suddenly realized that I was all alone. I was on my own. Everything that happened from that moment on would be the result of my own actions. I was not afraid. My dream had come true, and I was about to begin living a different reality. 22

That reality turned out to be all that I wanted: loving teachers, a real chance to pursue knowledge, and wonderful friends from all over the world. My life as a college student is better than I ever dreamed. It has not been easy. In my job with the University Food Service, I have had to work very hard. I have also had to deal with some irresponsible and disinterested students who refuse to carry out their assignments or pretend they don't understand simple instructions. I must remind myself that this is the only way to keep my scholarship. But my work has many rewards. I have become assistant director of Food Services. I have also received the first Outstanding Student-Employee Award presented by the university, and my work has been recognized by the Board of Trustees. 23

And I have begun the study of literature. This has opened up a new world for me. Every reading assignment, each class discussion has deepened my understanding of life. I am getting to know myself. I can feel the power growing inside me as I complete each assignment. I am beginning to live the magic of knowledge. In everything I learn, I find the same lesson: I can never know everything, but with what I know, I can accomplish anything. The old Superman bookmark is pasted on my door: "Knowledge is real power." Now I know what it means. 24

Reading Comprehension Questions

1. The word *comprehend* in "I studied the bookmark, trying to comprehend its exact meaning" (paragraph 1) means
   a. remember.
   b. write down.
   c. understand.
   d. pass by.

2. The word *aspiring* in "Such tales were commonly whispered in the high school hallways by students aspiring to go to college" (paragraph 2) means
   a. paying.
   b. hoping.
   c. remembering.
   d. forgetting.

3. The word *attaining* in "Surely these stories could not be true. College was supposed to build my confidence in the process of attaining knowledge" (paragraph 3) means
   a. recognizing.
   b. creating.
   c. pleasing.
   d. gaining.

4. Which sentence best expresses the central idea of the selection?
   a. There are big differences between Croatia and America.
   b. Education is better in the United States than in Croatia.
   c. By not giving up, the author has achieved the college experience she dreamt of.
   d. Colleges and universities should provide more low-cost opportunities for foreign students.

5. A main idea may cover more than one paragraph. Which sentence best expresses the main idea of paragraphs 2 and 3?
   a. In her high school, Petricic heard horror stories about college in Croatia.
   b. Passing the entrance exams for the college in Zagreb is difficult.
   c. Petricic was shocked to hear about Croatian college teachers who wanted to break their students' spirits.
   d. What Petricic heard about college in Croatia made her want to attend an American university.

6. Which sentence best expresses the main idea of paragraph 23?
   a. Even though she has become a successful college student, Petricic is disappointed with life in America.
   b. Despite difficulties, Petricic is happy with how things have turned out in America.
   c. Petricic's hard work in Food Services has paid off with an award and official recognition.
   d. Petricic must work hard to keep her scholarship.

7. According to the author,
   a. one of her mother's friends was able to help her go to college in the United States.
   b. selling precious paintings helped her raise the money she needed.
   c. the University of Zagreb was willing to offer her a scholarship.
   d. she was able to raise the money to begin college in the United States through a credit card.

8. The author implies that
   a. life is constantly changing in Croatia.
   b. credit cards have just been introduced to Croatia.
   c. what Croatian high school students whisper about college in that country is true, at least at the University of Zagreb.
   d. the university in America was one of many that she applied to.

9. From the selection, we can infer that
    a. the author has a loving, supportive family.
    b. because of her job, the author's grades have been only average.
    c. the author's family has moved to America.
    d. all of the above.

10. *True or false?* ____ We can infer that the author is an excellent student employee.

Technique Questions

1. How is the support in the reading mainly organized—by time order or listing order? Locate and write down three transitions that are used as part of that time order or listing order:

    _____   _____   _____

2. One of many examples of Petricic's ability to provide sharp details is in paragraph 17. Instead of saying, "I prayed for help, and I felt my prayers were heard," she presents a series of specific images that allow us to see and experience her prayer. Write down here what is for you the most vivid image in the paragraph:

    _____

    _____

    _____

3. In paragraph 20, Petricic could have merely said, "Mother and I agreed that our last hope seemed to be a credit card. Mother knew an influential officer of a local bank. Could he help us?" Instead, she provides dramatic details to communicate both the facts and feelings of her experience. She makes us feel we are there. What for you is the most vivid image in this paragraph?

    _____

    _____

    _____

Discussion Questions

1. The author writes that when she went to high school, students told horror stories about college. When you were in high school, what was your perception of college? Now that you are in college, has your perception changed? If so, in what ways?

2. Petricic has to keep up a job while going to school. Are you also working while going to college? How do you make time for both activities in your life?

3. At the conclusion of the selection, Petricic writes that she now knows the meaning of the phrase "Knowledge is real power." What does this phrase mean to you?

Writing Activities

1. The author knew that coming to America would not be easy. There were times when she was afraid her dream would not be realized. Write a paragraph telling of something you wanted very badly, but were afraid you would not be able to attain. Describe the struggles you had to overcome to get to your goal. How did you finally reach it? Like Petricic, include some details that communicate how strongly you wanted the goal and how difficult it was to reach. In thinking about a topic for this paper, you may wish to consider the following common goals:

   - A certain job
   - Enough money for college
   - A passing grade
   - Quitting smoking or drugs
   - Overcoming an illness

   Once you've decided on the goal you wish to write about, use it to write a topic sentence, such as any of the following:

   - After several false starts, I finally quit smoking.
   - It took me a year of saving and seeking financial assistance to get enough money to attend college.
   - After two years of medical treatment and support, I feel I have learned to live with my illness.
   - Following a careful budget, I was finally able to afford to . . .

   To develop supporting material for your topic sentence, trying freewriting. For example, here is part of one person's freewriting about the struggle to quit smoking:

   > The first time I tried to quit, it lasted a short time. Only a month or less. I made the mistake of not getting rid of all the cigarettes in the house, I kept a few here and there for emergencies. But there should be no emergencies when you quit. Once I took a few puffs on a cigarette I found in the silverware drawer. It was all over—I ran out that day to buy a pack. I told myself I would smoke only one or two cigarettes a day until I was ready to really quit. That type of promise is always a lie because I can't really control myself once I start smoking. It's either all or nothing, and for me, even a puff or two isn't nothing. It wasn't long before I started

thinking about quitting again. I was coughing a lot and several news stories were about people with lung cancer and the father of someone in my apartment building died of lung cancer. Also I read in a magazine that smoking causes wrinkles. Finally, about a year ago . . .

2. Petricic would not have been able to come to America without the support of her mother. Who has helped you the most in your quest for an education? Write a paper explaining who this person is and how he or she has helped you. Here are some possible topic sentences for this paper:

   • My best friend has helped me with my college education in several ways.

   • If it weren't for my father, I wouldn't be in college today.

   • It was my aunt who impressed upon me the importance of a college education.

   To develop support for this paper, try listing the problems you faced and the ways this person has helped you deal with each problem. Alternatively, you could do some freewriting about the person you're writing about.

3. Petricic's desire to go to college in America became a family effort. What has your family worked on together? Perhaps several members of your family put on a wedding or took turns caring for a sick relative. Write a paper about a joint family effort of some sort. Remember to begin with a general point such as the following:

   • It took weeks of family planning and cooperation to make my father's surprise fiftieth birthday party successful.

   • Two years of family therapy have helped to improve my relationship with my parents.

   • Thanks to help from my family, my wedding party was a great success.

   To help your readers "experience" what happened, dramatize one or more key scenes, as Petricic has done. Below are some examples of colorful details from her essay.

   • "I am going to school in America!" My mother looked up at me while still working in the foamy sink full of dirty dishes. (Paragraph 5)

     (The quotation shows Petricic's enthusiasm and determination. By describing her mother's activity, Petricic helps us envision the exact scene. She also provides an everyday setting for the practical question her mother asks: "Yes! And who is going to pay for that?")

   • As I walked toward the exit, I stopped to observe the college students who were in the hallway. They wore torn jeans, and they spoke in pretentious sentences. Their eyes were dull and they had lifeless smiles imprinted on pale faces. (Paragraph 10)

     (Instead of stating that the students were not the type of classmates she sought, Petricic uses descriptions to communicate her point.)

- My wooden-soled shoes echoed on the cold floor that led to the main altar. I knelt down and prayed. I prayed for money. That humiliated me. . . . (Paragraph 17)

(This scene helps readers see Petricic's experience in church. It emphasizes how badly she wanted to study in America.)

A Journey Into Light
Daisy Russell

Preview

The horror of an abusive father, the shame of illiteracy, the fear of ridicule: these are forces that shaped Daisy Russell's childhood. But there were also a loving and courageous mother, a quick and hungry mind, and a core of inner strength that even Daisy barely knew she had. In this essay, Daisy describes her journey from a frightened, beaten child to a strong woman, determined that her experience will benefit others.

Words to Watch

shun (9): keep away from
devour (22): to take in greedily
Laubach (24): a learning-to-read program named after its founder, Frank Laubach
banter (24): playful conversation

I'm 45 and in college; it has been a long and hard trip. I have had to overcome many obstacles to get here, but the trip was worth it. 1

I would like to give you a small glimpse into my childhood and try to tell why it has taken me nearly thirty years to get my education. I would like to explain how as a child I survived the horrors of child abuse: physical abuse by my father, sexual abuse by an uncle, and the most damaging: psychological abuse. Some of my scars show, but the most damaging scars don't: the scars of the soul. 2

My troubles started the day I was born, and by God's will was born a "good-for-nothing girl." My father wanted a son, and I was all he got; as far as he was concerned, girls were good for two things: having babies and keeping house, and you didn't need an education for either. 3

My father's regard for me did not grow any higher as I got older. In fact, when I was about a year old, he tried to get rid of me permanently. He did not try to kill me. Instead, his plan was to give me away to a couple who couldn't have children. 4

Mother was at work that day. My father was supposed to be taking care of me. By the grace of God Mother happened to get off work a little early. As she walked up to the front door of the house where we lived, the door opened and out walked a strange man and woman; I will call them the Smiths. Mrs. Smith was holding me in her arms. 5

In shock, Mother asked Mrs. Smith, "What are you doing with my baby?" Equally shocked, Mrs. Smith answered, "What do you mean, your baby?" Mother replied, "That's my baby you have in your arms and her name is Daisy. Give her to me." With tears in her eyes, Mrs. Smith handed me over to Mother. Her dreams of having a baby were shattered once again.

The Smiths and my mother turned to my father. "Floyd, what's going on here? What were these people doing with our baby?" Mother asked. My father remained silent. It was Mr. Smith who told Mother what my father had done. He had told the Smiths that my mother had died and that he couldn't take care of me. The Smiths hadn't cared if I was a boy or a girl; they just wanted a baby to love. I can't imagine what my father was planning to tell my mother when she got home and found me gone, but you can bet it was a well-rehearsed lie. My father was concerned only with himself. He didn't care whom he hurt or how miserable he made my life or my mother's, just so long as he was happy.

In search of that happiness, he moved us all over the country looking for the pot of gold at the end of the rainbow. I don't think he ever found it. The moving wasn't so bad until I started school; then with each move I got further and further behind in school. I never knew from one day to the next when I left the house in the morning whether I would return there in the evening. It was nothing for me to walk out of school at the end of the day and see my parents sitting there in the car with everything we owned packed in the back. I would take off my shoes and crawl over the front seat into the back where Mother had made a bed for me on top of everything. Sometimes we only moved across the state; other times it would be halfway across the country. I was in seventeen schools between the first grade and the sixth, and some of those schools I was in more than once. When Mother would tell Dad we needed to stay in one place so I could catch up in school, he would simply laugh and ask, "Why?" and then say, "Girls don't need an education."

> "I would like to explain how as a child I survived the horrors of child abuse: physical abuse by my father, sexual abuse by an uncle, and the most damaging psychological abuse."

This kind of nomadic life was exceedingly hard on me; I had no roots, no place to call home. I learned not to make long-term plans. Psychologically this kind of life could have had different effects on me. It could have made me a very outgoing child who grabs for everything that comes her way, but what it did to me was make me a very frightened, shy, withdrawn, lonely, and illiterate child. I was too shy and frightened to tell the teacher that I didn't understand what she wanted me to do, that I couldn't read for fear that everyone in the class would find out and laugh at me. I got so hopelessly behind in school that it became a place to fear, to dread, to shun° at all costs. I feared and dreaded school so much that I would lie in bed and take a beating rather then get up and go to school. Physical pain was easier for me to bear than the emotional pain of ridicule, humiliation, and loneliness I faced each day at school. At the age of sixteen I dropped out of school. I was in the eighth grade and still doing third-grade work because I couldn't read beyond that level. I just got tired of beating my head against a brick wall; by this time I was totally convinced that I was the most worthless and stupidest kid on the face of the earth.

Had I had the love and support of both my parents, I think I would have done 10 better in school, even with all the moving. As I said earlier, my father wanted a son and I was all he got; I know in my heart that some of the beatings he gave me were because I was not the son he so desperately wanted. When I talk of beatings, I'm talking about him using his fist on my face to the point people couldn't tell what I looked like. I'm talking about busted lips, black eyes, and being kicked in the ribs with heavy work boots. My mother tried to protect me as best as she could, but she was no match for my father. The physical pain was sometimes easier to handle than the knowledge that my father didn't want me, not because I was bad, but just because I was a stupid, useless girl.

The beatings and the moves blur together in my memory, but there is still one 11 place and time I can't seem to forget, even after almost thirty-seven years of trying. I can still close my eyes and see and feel the violence that took place there.

We were living in Decatur, Illinois. The year is 1957, I think. Mother had 12 rented an apartment in this big old gray and white house. There were four apartments: two upstairs and two downstairs. We lived in one of the downstairs apartments. We had a living room, a kitchen, and one bedroom, and we shared a bathroom with the apartment next to us. I slept on the couch in the living room. Sleeping on the couch wasn't always bad. When Mom and Dad were fighting about his drinking, which was most nights, I would lie on my side and press my back just as tight as I could into the back of the couch. I'd pull the blankets up as far as I could under my chin, close my eyes, and escape into a world of make-believe, where there was no fighting, no hurting, and no ugly words.

How I dreaded Friday nights. Dad got paid on Friday, and by the time he got 13 home he was usually drunk. Then the fighting would start. Dad got very mean when he started drinking. One particular Friday night the fighting was worse than ever. All Mother was trying to do was get money from Dad so she could pay the rent and buy groceries. This made Dad very angry. He kept screaming, "This is my money. I worked for it, not you, so why should I give any to you." I heard Mother keep trying to explain that she needed to pay the rent. He screamed, "Shut up!" and I heard Mother cry out in pain, then begin to cry. Dad had hit her in the face.

I was way too little to help her. All I could do was lie there and cry for my 14 mother as I prayed to God for help. How I hated and feared this man—this man who was my father!

That night the fighting went on much longer than normal. I had to go to the 15 bathroom desperately. I lay there in my cocoon of blankets until I almost wet my bed. Finally I got up and tried to sneak to the bathroom, which was on the other side of the kitchen. When I walked into the kitchen, Mother and Dad were sitting at the table there. My mother's cheek was already starting to swell. After Dad saw me, he told me to come and sit on his lap. I would have if he had given me a chance.

But when I said, "I have to go to the bathroom," he jumped out of his chair and 16 slammed his big fist into my mouth. Blood went everywhere. My mother screamed at him, "Floyd, she's just a child. In the name of God don't hit her again. You could kill her," as she somehow put her body between me and him. He kept reaching around Mother trying to get to me. I was trapped. The kitchen wall was at my back. There were kitchen cabinets on my left and the stove to my right. There was no place to run, no place to hide from this drunken madman. The only thing that stood between me and his blows was my loving and courageous mother. Mom took a lot of the beating that was meant for me. He did manage to make contact with me once again, his big fist slamming into my left eye. This seemed to satisfy him, because he stopped hitting Mom and me.

My mother turned around and looked at me with such sad and frightened eyes. 17
Her face looked as bad as mine did. I stood there trembling with fear and pain, crying, blood running out of my mouth, my eye starting to swell shut. I was so frightened, so bewildered. What had I said or done to make him so mad at me? Why did he seem to take such delight in hurting me?

The next day, Mother and I were not too pretty to look at. My eye had swollen 18
shut and was already starting to turn black. My bottom lip was so sore and swollen I couldn't eat anything solid or drink anything hot. I lived on water, juice, and liquid Jello. Mother's body was bruised and battered from her efforts to protect me.

When I went to school on Monday I told the teacher I had fallen running up the 19
basement steps and hit my face on one of the steps. I was too embarrassed and frightened to tell her the truth. I think she believed me, for all she said was, "You poor thing; don't you know better than to run up steps?" I never stayed in one school long enough for the teachers to suspect child abuse. Even if they had, schools then didn't get involved in abuse cases like they do today.

As if the physical and psychological abuse by my father weren't enough to 20
bear, I had an uncle that sexually abused me from the age of about two to the age of six or seven. I didn't like what he was doing to me, and I tried to stay away from him as much as I could. I always came away from these encounters in a mild state of shock. It never came to actual intercourse, but there are ways of having sex with a child without intercourse. Parents didn't talk to their children then like they do today about sex or what to do if someone touches them in a way they don't like. All of this happened to me before I was ten years old.

When I was ten, the physical abuse by my father got so bad that Mother left 21
him. Actually, Mother and I ran away from home; if we hadn't, I think he would have killed us sooner or later. My father had become an extremely abusive alcoholic; he would do things when he was drinking that he wouldn't remember later when he sobered up. It has taken me nearly thirty years to overcome the psychological damage my father did to me, but I have done it. I'm no longer the shy, withdrawn, and lonely child I once was. I still get frightened when I try new things; the old uncertainties sometimes come back; but, unlike when I was a child, I have friends and family that love and believe in me.

After quitting school, it took me nearly twenty years to teach myself to read. 22
But I did it with the aid of a dictionary, stubborn determination, and driving my mother crazy with "Mom, what word is this?" I now read anything and everything I can get my hands on. I've been told I don't read a book, I devour° it. To me, reading a book is like sitting a starving man down to a ten-course meal; he can't eat fast enough. I'm always looking, always searching for the knowledge that was locked away from me for so many years. Being able to read is like being released from a dark, cold, and lonely prison, and at last being able to walk in the warmth and the light of the sun.

On December 5, 1979, I went to work for Bendix (now Allied Signal) 23
Aerospace, Kansas City division, the most important move of my life. If I could have looked into the future on that day and seen how over the next fourteen years

my life was going to change, I think I would have said, "No way, this is not for me" and turned and ran as hard as I could back home. The first ten years working for Allied Signal were quite uneventful; then, in the fall of 1989, I enrolled in the reading program at work. This was not an easy thing to do, to tell another adult that I had a reading problem. It took all the courage I could muster up to walk back to department seventeen and talk to Verna Cooper, the lady in charge of the reading center at that time. I could sight read quite well, but if it was a word I hadn't seen or heard before, I had no way of figuring it out. By being moved around in school as much as I was, I had no background in phonics at all. I needed the phonics program not only for reading, but for spelling. Spelling has always been a nightmare for me; if I can't read the word, how can I study the word to know how to spell it?

Verna teamed me up with Earl Riggs, a Laubach° reading tutor. Over the next 24 year and a half, Earl helped me with more than just phonics. He helped me to improve my self-respect, self-worth, and self-image. Earl never laughed at me, even when he was trying to teach me to spell the word "far." I could hear the "F" and the "R," but not the "A," so I would leave it out. Earl would say, "There's an 'A' in the word *far*" and I would say, "If you say so"; then he would come back with "Trust me, there is." This kind of banter° went on all the time. Earl was more than a tutor; he became a friend. I still see Earl from time to time, to let him know what his student has been up to.

The reading program was the means to a newer and brighter future for me. The 25 program helped me to build self-confidence in my ability to do anything that I set my mind to do. I felt so good about myself and what I had accomplished that when Allied Signal opened up the in-house math program to all employees, I jumped at the chance.

I found my true love—math; I found out that I liked working with numbers. I 26 was enjoying the math program so much that, when Allied Signal offered on-site college courses through Longview College in the fall of 1991, I thought I would try an algebra class. This is what you call putting the cart before the horse; I'm a grade-school dropout and I'm thinking of taking a college class. Well, I don't know whether it was my own ability or the fact that I had a fantastic teacher, but for the first time in school I got an "A" in something. My self-image and self-confidence reached a new high the day I received my grade report; I realized that I could do anything that I was willing to work hard at.

In the spring of 1992, Allied Signal started an in-house G.E.D. program at 27 work. I didn't think twice about it; I joined immediately, despite the fact that I had already signed up for another math class at Longview College. Over the next eight months, it seemed I was either going to school or doing homework. Between my math class and the G.E.D. class, I always had a ton of homework to do each week. Without the love and support of my husband, Don, I don't think I could have made it. I finished the math class in April of 1992, but it took me three more months before Art Wortman, our G.E.D. teacher, told me I was ready to take the G.E.D. test. At first I was unsure I was ready, but I should have known better than to doubt Art, because the fourteen students he said were ready passed with flying colors. I sent off to Jefferson City, Missouri to get permission to take the test. I took the test in August, and was told I wouldn't find out until sometime in September whether I passed or not, . . . talk about a long month.

When I got home from work the night of September 6, 1992, I found an   28
envelope from Jefferson City in my mailbox. I took the envelope to my bedroom so
I could be alone if I had failed. I slowly opened the envelope and took out three
pieces of paper: one was my grade test results, one was a try-again form, and the last
was my diploma; I had passed. I dropped all three pieces of paper on the bed,
covered my face with my hands, and started to cry. My husband gently opened the
bedroom door and came in. All I could do was point at the bed and cry; all he said
was, "I knew you could do it," as he took me in his arms.

I have many things to be proud of—learning to read, getting my G.E.D., finally   29
realizing my dream of going to college—but the thing I am proudest of is becoming
a Laubach reading tutor. I've come full circle from being illiterate to helping others
to find their way out of the darkness of illiteracy. I now have a student, and I try to
have as much patience with her as Earl had with me. I also work with the reading
board here at work; I talk to them freely about what it was like not being able to read
and write, so they might understand a little better what our students face each day of
their lives. I'm also working towards becoming a Laubach tutor trainer; I still have a
long way to go before I accomplish this, but I'll get there.

I talk freely and openly about being a new reader, whether it's here at work, at   30
the mall, the beauty shop, just anywhere where there is someone who will listen to
me. I tell them that if they or someone they know has trouble with reading or
writing, there is help. I go on to tell them that they have nothing to be ashamed of,
that the people who need to hang their heads in shame are the adults who had control
over their lives as children. I remind them that it was the adult's responsibility to see
that the children got a proper education. If this person is an employee of Allied
Signal, I tell them the phone number to call here at work and gently encourage them
to call. If they happen to be a stranger, I hand them the phone numbers for the local
Laubach reading centers in and around Kansas City. My voice alone is but a mere
whisper in the dark, but added to thousands of voices, it becomes a mighty roar.

I will continue my education until I hit a wall that I can't figure out a way to   31
either go over, around, through, or under. If this should happen, I'll just take two
steps back and see if I can't blast it into little pieces. I will not give up. I'll never
stop learning; when I stop learning, I stagnate and the world just passes me by and
leaves me stumbling in the dark of the past instead of walking in the light of the
future.

Reading Comprehension Questions

1. The word *nomadic* in "I was in seventeen schools between the first grade and
   the sixth. . . . This kind of nomadic life was exceedingly hard on me; I had no
   roots, no place to call home" (paragraphs 8–9) means
   a. stable.
   b. interesting.
   c. wandering.
   d. abusive.

2. The word *stagnate* in "I'll never stop learning; when I stop learning, I stagnate and the world just passes me by" (paragraph 31) means
   a. fail to grow.
   b. become aggressive.
   c. develop rapidly.
   d. advance socially.

3. Which statement best expresses the central idea of the selection?
   a. Daisy Russell plans to work toward becoming a Laubach tutor trainer.
   b. Daisy Russell's parents should have tried harder to provide her with a quality education.
   c. Learning to read helped Daisy Russell finally overcome a childhood of abuse and despair.
   d. There are numerous community organizations which help adults get their G.E.D's.

4. Which statement best expresses the main idea of paragraphs 29–30?
   a. Russell works with the reading program at Allied Signal.
   b. Getting her G.E.D. was a proud moment in Russell's life.
   c. Since discovering the joy of reading, Russell has worked to help others become readers.
   d. There are reading centers in Kansas City and most other American cities.

5. As a result of her family's frequent moves during her childhood, Russell became
   a. a quick and eager learner.
   b. an outgoing child who made friends easily.
   c. a shy child with learning difficulties.
   d. an angry child who frequently got into fights.

6. Russell's abuse by her father stopped when
   a. Russell and her mother ran away from home.
   b. Russell's father was killed in a fight.
   c. Russell's father was jailed for abusing her.
   d. Russell's father realized the harm he was doing his daughter.

7. The first college class Russell took at Allied Signal was a course in
   a. reading.
   b. algebra.
   c. sign language.
   d. creative writing.

8. Daisy Russell has probably become a Laubach reading tutor because she
   a. can get promotions at work if she is a tutor.
   b. is bored and needs something to do in her spare time.
   c. wants to share the power of reading.
   d. was asked to do so by Earl Riggs, her former tutor.

9. From paragraph 9 we can infer that
   a. Russell's teachers were not very good ones.
   b. emotional pain can be worse than physical pain.
   c. Russell was asked to leave school at age 16.
   d. students who do not do well in school should drop out.

10. Russell says, "I've been told I don't read a book, I devour it" (paragraph 22). From this statement, what can we infer about Russell?
    a. Russell is not proud of her love of reading.
    b. Reading satisfies a need deep inside her.
    c. She is not very enthusiastic about reading.
    d. Russell rarely reads where others can see her.

Technique Questions

1. "A Journey Into Light" is organized, in general, according to time and so contains many time transitions. For instance, look at paragraph 15. Pick out three time transitions used there, and write them here:

   _____   _____   _____

2. Instead of just telling us that she was happy to earn her G.E.D., Russell dramatizes the scene for us. In what paragraph does she do so? What is the most vivid and effective detail in the paragraph for you?

   _____

   _____

   _____

3. In "A Journey Into Light," Russell compares learning to read to "being released from a dark, cold, and lonely prison, and at last being able to walk in the warmth and light of the sun" (paragraph 22). At what other point in the essay does she effectively use images of darkness and light? Write that part below.

   _____

   _____

   _____

   _____

   _____

   _____

Discussion Questions

1. Russell writes that although she suffered awful physical blows, the most damaging scars she has are "scars of the soul." What does she mean by "scars of the soul"? Why might these scars be the most damaging?

2. Russell was able to survive and do well despite the most difficult of upbringings. Describe how someone you know has reacted to a very hard childhood. What did he or she have to contend with when growing up? Has that person been able to rise above it, or is he or she still struggling?

3. Russell writes that she believes she would have more easily learned to read had she had the love and support of both her parents. What was the attitude toward reading in your household when you were growing up? How do you think parents can encourage their children to read?

Writing Assignments

1. In paragraph 28, Russell dramatizes a joyous moment in her life. Write a paragraph about a moment in your life when you experienced a certain emotion. The emotion might be fear, pride, sadness, relief, disappointment, anger, happiness, or some other feeling. You should focus on a specific incident that happened in a relatively short period of time. Your paragraph will come alive if you directly quote some of the words that you or others said.

   You might begin by thinking of an incident in your life where you felt a certain emotion strongly. Then spend about ten minutes freewriting about the experience. Don't worry about spelling or grammar or the like; instead, just get down all the details that you can that seem related to the experience.

   Such prewriting should help you decide whether your topic is promising enough to develop further. If it is not, freewrite about another incident. If it is, then see if you can write a topic sentence that names the emotion you will focus on. For example:

   • Seeing my baby daughter for the first time was one of the happiest moments of my life.

   • I never felt angrier than when I was unjustly accused of copying an assignment.

   Next, go on to make up a list of all the details involved in the experience. Then go through your list, arranging the details in time order, and adding any other details that occur to you. Use the list as a guide to prepare a rough draft of your paper. Add time signals such as *first, next, then, after, while,* and *finally* to help connect details as you move through your narrative.

   After the first draft is finished, try to set it aside for a while before going back to work on a second draft. And before turning in the final draft to your instructor, don't forget to proofread your paper carefully for grammar and punctuation and spelling mistakes.

2. In paragraph 9 of her essay, Russell writes that she would often take a beating rather than go to school and deal with the ridicule and embarrassment she experienced there. Write a paragraph about how the fear of looking foolish affected your behavior in grade school or high school. Choose an example of a time you acted in a particular way because you were afraid of being ridiculed. Describe how you behaved, and be sure to explain just what kind of embarrassment you were trying to avoid.

   Your paragraph might begin with a topic sentence like one of the following:

   • Not wanting other students to turn on me, I joined them in making fun of a high school classmate who was very overweight.

   • My mother's idea of how I should dress caused me a great deal of embarrassment in school.

   • Because I didn't want to admit that I needed glasses, I had a lot of problems in fifth grade.

3. Using the example of the word "far," Russell describes how she and her tutor worked together so she could learn to spell and read words. Have you faced the problem of learning a new skill or performing a task that, at first, seemed almost impossibly difficult? Write a paragraph in which you discuss the steps you went through to finally learn this skill or accomplish this task.

   Here are some sample opening sentences:

   • Despite my early fears, I am now almost as comfortable with English as I am with Spanish.

   • At the age of 37, I finally learned to cook for myself, but not without some ugly disasters.

   • Adding a regular exercise routine to my life seemed impossible last year, but I have actually done it.

   • Although it wasn't long ago that computers seemed beyond me, I have finally joined the computer generation.

Half a Pound of Ham
Bernadete Piassa

Preview

Imagine yourself as a foreign-born person waiting in line for service at an American deli counter. You worry about whether your hesitant, accented English will be understood. You feel a wall of loneliness that cuts you off from the people that surround you. Bernadete Piassa, who grew up in Brazil, describes her anxious thoughts as she waits her turn to place an order. As you read her essay, ask yourself how you would react if you were one of the shoppers listening to her broken English.

Words to Watch

cordial (10): friendly
authoritarian (10: like a dictator
vulnerable (12): open to criticism
flee (12): run away from

"Half a pound of Virginia baked ham, please." No, wait. The voice is not 1
clear enough. Let me try again. "Half a pound of Virginia baked ham, please." Good. That sounds better. I just hope I don't fail this time. I just hope I don't stutter. I just hope my voice doesn't come out very low and the saleswoman doesn't have to say. "Excuse me?" Oh, how I hate these words!

I am at Richboro's Shop & Save grocery story standing in line, waiting for my 2
turn to be helped. All I want is ham—just half a pound of Virginia baked ham. However, I need all my strength to remain in line. Part of me wants to run away and just grab a ham off the shelf, the kind that comes already packed and is not so good, of course, but at least one doesn't need to ask for it from the salesperson. The other part of me wants to get the freshly sliced ham that tastes delicious, smells delicious, but is tucked away safely behind the counter, where the saleswoman is the only one able to reach it.

I am a coward, or at least sometimes I behave like one. But I don't like to admit 3
this, so I am standing in line. I am getting the freshly sliced ham even if this costs me all my energy. Even if I have to get sweaty and anxious, I will ask for it.

I bet you are laughing at me. I bet you are wondering how come I am not able   4
to order something so simple. But I am not American like you. My English is
broken. That's why although I want to ask only for half a pound of ham, I need to
rehearse.

If you were in line, you could smile at the saleswoman. You could chat with   5
other customers while you waited your turn. You could ask for ham and even change
your mind afterwards. You would be relaxed, just performing one of the small duties
that you execute in your daily life without even thinking about it. Probably, after
getting what you had asked for, you would simply go on with your shopping, just
forgetting about the ham until you had to pay for it.

But for me, the ham is serious business. If I don't buy it, I will be a coward. If I   6
buy it, the ham will be my trophy, and when I get home and try it, it will have a
special taste—the taste of victory, of accom-
plishment. You see, I can't fail. I really have to
rehearse.

I need to confess to you that this is not the
first time I have asked for ham. I had bought it
before, several times in fact. And every time I
had seen the saleswoman and the other
customers looks. I had seen them stare at me and
place a stamp on my face: foreigner!

Foreigner! That's what they know instantly
about me. They have no idea that I am a
journalist, that I am a mother of three children,
that I live right there, just two blocks away from the grocery. But they do know that
I am a foreigner, an outsider, an alien, a stranger. And they look at me in a different
way: suspicious, curious, wondering.

> "I bet you are laughing at
> me. I bet you are
> wondering how come I am
> not able to order
> something so simple. But I
> am not American like you.
> My English is broken."

There are a thousand questions floating in their eyes. I can almost feel them.   9
However, I just smile, for I don't want to give any explanation. I am so tired of
explanations, so tired of having to prove that I came from a good family and yes,
your kids can play with mine without getting harmed, no, I am not going to eat you,
yes, I speak three languages, I am not an illiterate, no, I don't intend to destroy
America's values, yes, I would like to see your country in better shape, no, I am not
going to steal Americans' jobs.

The endless explanations, the questions in the air, the look on someone's face . . .   10
all this makes me long for my own country. Over there I could be myself without
having to live always tense, trying to prove that I am a good person. I could be
cordial° and chat with other customers in the line because I knew the jokes and the
small talk they were used to. I could even be authoritarian°, if I wished, and the
saleswoman would feel that I was more important than she and wouldn't mind my
impoliteness. But here I just don't know the right jokes, the right words. I can't stand
tall, proud, and demand what I want. Here I am small, quiet, and talk only in whispers.
That's why I need to rehearse, when I want to buy half a pound of Virginia baked ham.

It is almost my turn now, and once more I ask myself if I won't fail again, if the   11
saleswoman won't say "Excuse me?" making me feel even more ashamed of myself,
of my English that will always come out with a foreign accent.

"Why do I feel so vulnerable° here?" I ask myself, without waiting for an   12
answer. The world of foreigners is a world of questions not answered, of

misunderstanding, of tears not always shed. A lonely world of people who don't belong in their home country anymore, but still don't belong in their new one. People who during the day struggle to live in the place they chose to stay, while at night go back, in their dreams, to the place they decided to flee°. The world of foreigners is a world of soaring souls, floating in space looking for a home, for a meaning.

"May I help you?"   13

Lost in my thoughts, I had almost forgotten about the ham, and the person   14
behind the counter scares me. Putting together all my strengths, I say, in a firm voice, "Half a pound of Virginia baked ham, please."

"Excuse me?" she asks, a voice of someone used to hearing the right words, the   15
right accent, at the right place.

"Half a pound of Virginia baked ham, please," I repeat loudly. And this time   16
she hears me. She turns her back to slice the ham, weighs it, gives it to me, I pay for it, and, at home, I try it. As I thought, the ham has a very sweet taste. At the very end, however, it has the same bitterness of thoughts that remain for a long time in our minds until they become sour.

Reading Comprehension Questions

1. The word *chat* in "If you were in line, you could smile at the saleswoman. You could chat with other customers while you waited your turn" (paragraph 5) means
    a. wait.
    b. look.
    c. talk.
    d. argue.

2. The word *execute* in "If you were in line, you could smile at the saleswoman. . . . You would be relaxed, just performing one of the small duties that you execute in your daily life without even thinking about it" (paragraph 5) means
    a. carry out.
    b. sign.
    c. avoid.
    d. work hard at.

3. Which of the following sentences best expresses the central idea of the essay?
    a. There are several ways in which foreigners can adjust to a new country.
    b. Piassa faces many everyday challenges in adjusting to life in the U.S.
    c. There are good reasons for Piassa to return to her native country.
    d. Piassa took the trouble to order Virginia baked ham because she feels that it is the sign of a true American.

4. Which sentence best expresses the main idea of paragraph 5?
    a. An American would find it easy to buy ham at an American deli counter.
    b. If you were in line at a deli counter, you could smile at the saleswoman.
    c. If you were in line at a deli counter, you could ask for ham and then change your mind.
    d. Waiting at a deli counter should be a pleasant social experience.

5. Which sentence best expresses the main idea of paragraph 10?
    a. In her native country, Piassa did not have to prove she was good.
    b. Piassa needs to rehearse to buy half a pound of Virginia baked ham.
    c. The difficulties of being a foreigner make Piassa long for the ease of living in her native country.
    d. In her native country, Piassa could be impolite if she wished, ordering ham as if she were more important than the saleslady.

6. The author feels that if she avoided asking for the freshly sliced ham, she would be
    a. wise.
    b. a coward.
    c. less of a foreigner.
    d. a better mother.

7. Piassa calls the ham she will bring home
    a. unimportant.
    b. foreign.
    c. a trophy.
    d. too expensive.

8. Piassa
    a. is a journalist.
    b. has three children.
    c. speaks three languages.
    d. all of the above.

9. Piassa implies that Americans
    a. have poor values.
    b. are suspicious of foreigners.
    c. are cowardly.
    d. are dangerous to foreigners.

10. We might conclude from the reading that Piassa
    a. will soon move back to her native land.
    b. has always hated standing in line.
    c. has no sense of humor.
    d. does not feel at home now in either her native country or in America.

Technique Questions

1. Piassa could have written in a general way about the many discouraging challenges that foreigners face. Why do you think she chose to write in a very specific way about one small everyday challenge?

    _____

    _____

    _____

2. Piassa writes, "There are a thousand questions floating in their eyes." This is a pretty general statement. What details does she use to tell the reader specifically what some of those questions are?

_____

_____

_____

3. How does Piassa organize the material in her essay? Does she use a *listing order* to detail the difficulties she faced as a foreigner, or does she use a *time order* to describe her purchase of the ham—or does she use a combination of both?

_____

Discussion Questions

1. Piassa writes, "I am so tired of explanations" (paragraph 9). What does she feel the need to explain? Why does she feel this need?

2. How might you react if a person ahead of you in line was speaking with a hard-to-understand accent? Would you be impatient or hostile? Why do you think some people react like this?

3. What kind of person is Piassa? What are some of her personal qualities that reveal themselves as you read her essay?

Writing Assignments

1. Piassa feels "ashamed" when a salesperson has trouble understanding her. In a paragraph, tell about a time you felt ashamed or embarrassed. Provide details that show clearly what happened. Explain what you and the other people involved said and did. Also, explain how you felt and why you were so uncomfortable.

   For example, the paragraph might begin with a sentence like this:

   • I was deeply ashamed when I was caught cheating on a spelling test in fifth grade.

   The paragraph could continue by telling how the writer cheated and how he was caught; how the teacher and other students looked, spoke, and acted; what the writer did when he was caught; and what emotions and thoughts the writer experienced throughout the incident.

   Below are some other topic sentence possibilities. Develop one of them or a variation on one of them. Feel free as well to come up with and write about an entirely different idea.

   • My first formal date was the occasion of an embarrassing moment in my life.

- To this day, I wince when I think of an incident that happened to me at a family party .

- I can still remember the shame I felt in my teenage body when I had to use the shower room at school.

- An event that occurred in high school makes my cheeks glow hot and red even today.

2. Piassa feels out of place at the supermarket because she is a foreigner. Write about a time that you felt out of place, as though you didn't belong. Maybe you, like Piassa, were in a foreign country. Or maybe you were in a new school, a new neighborhood, a new job, or a new group of people. To think about how to develop this paper, ask yourself questions like these:

- What brought me into the situation?

- What about the situation made me feel like an outsider?

- What did the people around me do or say?

- What did I imagine other people were thinking about me?

- What thoughts and emotions were running through me?

- How did my feeling like an outsider affect the way I acted?

As you write this assignment, be sure to include plenty of concrete details to help the reader understand your experience. Tell exactly where the incident took place, who else was there, what you and others did and said, and what thoughts and feelings you were experiencing.

3. Piassa needed courage in order to order a half a pound of ham. Write about a time that you had to have courage. Think of an action that frightened you, but that you felt you needed to take anyway. Perhaps you were afraid to ask someone out on a date, or to say "no" when someone asked you to do something you felt was wrong, or to perform a dangerous activity. In your paper, describe the frightening situation that faced you and how you made the decision to act with courage. Then tell what happened—the actions that you took, the responses of those around you, significant things people said, and how things turned out.

For example, you might begin with a statement like this:

- When I was in junior high, it required courage for me to resist the temptation to shoplift with my favorite cousin.

That passage would then continue with a description of what the cousins did and said, how the writer found the courage to say "no" to the idea, how the shoplifting cousin reacted, and how the writer felt throughout the whole process.

As you describe the incident, use time transition words to make the sequence of events clear, such as "*At first* I didn't think I could do it. *Later*, however, I had an idea." (Information about time transitions appears on pages 9–10.)

Learning Survival Strategies
Jean Coleman

Preview

"Experience is the best teacher." It's an old saying, and a true one. Jean Coleman, a former community college student, is rich in experience. She has passionate opinions about what students really need to know as they begin their college careers. In this essay, she invites others to benefit from what she and her fellow students have learned about college survival.

Words to Watch

vocational (5): work-related
paralegal assistant (7): a person trained to assist a lawyer
persist (10): continue on
endured (13): carried on despite hardship
dismayed (14): discouraged
developmental (17): meant to improve skills in a subject
grim (24): gloomy
projected (25): gave the impression of
destinies (31): futures

For four years I was a student at a community college. I went to night school as a part-time student for three years, and I was able to be a full-time student for one year. My first course was a basic writing course because I needed a review of grammar and the basics of writing. I did well in that course and that set the tone for everything that followed.

It is now eleven years since I started college, and I have a good job with a Philadelphia accounting firm. When I was invited to write this article, the questions put to me were, "What would you want to say to students who are just starting out in college? What advice would you give? What experiences would it help to share?" I thought a lot about what it took for me to be a successful student. Here, then, are my secrets for survival in college and, really, for survival in life as well.

"Be Realistic."

The first advice that I'd give to beginning students is: "Be realistic about how   3
college will help you get a job." Some students believe that once they have college
degrees the world will be waiting on their doorsteps, ready to give them wonderful
jobs. But the chances are that unless they've planned, there will be *nobody* on their
doorsteps.

I remember the way my teacher in a study skills course dramatized this point in   4
class. He played a student who had just been handed a college degree. He opened up
an imaginary door, stepped through, and peered around in both directions outside.
There was nobody to be seen. I understood the point he was making immediately. A
college degree in itself isn't enough. We've got to prepare while we're in college to
make sure our degree is a marketable one.

At that time I began to think seriously about (1) what I wanted to do in life and   5
(2) whether there were jobs out there for what I wanted to do. I went to the
counseling center and said, "I want to learn where
the best job opportunities will be in the next ten
years." The counselor referred me to a copy of the
Occupational Outlook Handbook published by
the United States government. The *Handbook* has
good information on what kinds of jobs are
available now and which career fields will need
workers in the future. In the front of the book is a
helpful section on job hunting. The counselor also
gave me a vocational° interest test to see where my skills and interests lay.

> *"To not be open to growth is to die a little each day. Grow or die— it's as simple as that."*

The result of my personal career planning was that I eventually graduated from   6
community college with a degree in accounting. I then got a job almost immediately,
for I had chosen an excellent employment area. The firm that I work for paid my
tuition as I went on to get my bachelor's degree. It is now paying for my work toward
certification as a certified public accountant, and my salary increases regularly.

By way of contrast, I know a woman named Sheila who earned a bachelor's   7
degree with honors in French. After graduation, she spent several unsuccessful
months trying to find a job using her French degree. Sheila eventually wound up
going to a specialized school where she trained for six months as a paralegal
assistant°. She then got a job on the strength of that training—but her years of
studying French were of no practical value in her career at all.

I'm not saying that college should serve only as a training ground for a job.   8
People should take some courses just for the sake of learning and for expanding their
minds in different directions. At the same time, unless they have an unlimited
amount of money (and few of us are so lucky), they must be ready at some point to
take career-oriented courses so that they can survive in the harsh world outside.

In my own case, I started college at the age of twenty-seven. I was divorced,   9
had a six-year-old son to care for, and was working full time as a hotel night clerk. If
I had had my preference, I would have taken a straight liberal arts curriculum. As it
was, I did take some general-interest courses—in art, for example. But mainly I was
getting ready for the solid job I desperately needed. I am saying, then, that students
must be realistic. If they will need a job soon after graduation, they should be sure to
study in an area where jobs are available.

"Persist."

The older I get, the more I see that life lays on us some hard experiences. There are times for each of us when simple survival becomes a deadly serious matter. We must then learn to persist°—to struggle through each day and wait for better times to come—as they always do.   10

I think of one of my closest friends, Neil. After graduating from high school with me, Neil spent two years working as a stock boy at a local department store in order to save money for college tuition. He then went to the guidance office at the small college in our town. Incredibly, the counselor there told him, "Your IQ is not high enough to do college work." Thankfully, Neil decided to go anyway and earned his degree in five years—with a year out to care for his father, who had had a stroke one day at work.   11

Neil then got a job as a manager of a regional beauty supply firm. He met a woman who owned a salon, got married, and soon had two children. Three years later he found out that his wife was having an affair. I'll never forget the day Neil came over and sat at my kitchen table and told me what he had learned. He always seemed so much in control, but that morning he lowered his head into his hands and cried. "What's the point?" he kept saying in a low voice over and over to himself.   12

But Neil has endured°. He divorced his wife, won custody of his children, and learned how to be a single parent. Recently, Neil and I got letters informing us of the twentieth reunion of our high school graduating class. Included was a short questionnaire for us to fill out that ended with this item: "What has been your outstanding accomplishment since graduation?" Neil wrote, "My outstanding accomplishment is that I have survived." I have a feeling that many of our high school classmates, twenty years out in the world, would have no trouble understanding the truth of his statement.   13

I can think of people who started college with me who had not yet learned, like Neil, the basic skill of endurance. Life hit some of them with unexpected low punches and knocked them to the floor. Stunned and dismayed°, they didn't fight back and eventually dropped out of school. I remember Yvonne, still a teenager, whose parents involved her in their ugly divorce battle. Yvonne started missing classes and gave up at midsemester. There was Alan, whose girlfriend broke off their relationship. Alan stopped coming to class, and by the end of the semester he was failing most of his courses. I also recall Nelson, whose old car kept breaking down. After Nelson put his last $200 into it, the breaks failed and needed to be replaced. Overwhelmed by his continuing car troubles, Nelson dropped out of school. And there was Rita, discouraged by her luck of the draw with teachers and courses. In sociology, she had a teacher who wasn't able to express ideas clearly. She also had a mathematics teacher who talked too fast and seemed not to care at all about whether his students learned. To top it off, Rita's adviser had enrolled her in an economics course that put her to sleep. Rita told me she had expected college to be an exciting place, but instead she was getting busywork assignments and trying to cope with hostile or boring teachers. Rita decided to drop her mathematics course, and that must have set something in motion in her head, for she soon dropped her other courses as well.   14

In my experience, younger students seem more likely to drop out than do older students. I think some younger students are still in the process of learning that life   15 slams people around without warning. I'm sure they feel that being knocked about is especially unfair because the work of college is hard enough without having to cope with other hardships.

In some situations, withdrawing from college may be the best response. But there are going to be times in college when students—young or old—must simply determine, "I am going to persist." They should remember that no matter how hard their lives may be, there are many other people out there who are quietly having great difficulties also. I think of Dennis, a boy in my introductory psychology class who lived mostly on peanut butter and discount store loaves of white bread for almost a semester in his freshman year. And I remember Estelle, who came to school because she needed a job to support her sons when her husband, who was dying of leukemia, would no longer be present. These are especially dramatic examples of the faith and hope that are sometimes necessary for us to persist.

"Be Positive."

A lot of people are their own worst enemies. They regard themselves as unlikely to succeed in college and often feel that there have been no accomplishments in their lives. In my first year of college especially, I saw people get down on themselves all too quickly. There were two students in my developmental° mathematics class who failed the first quiz and seemed to give up immediately. From that day on, they walked into the classroom carrying defeat on their shoulders the way other students carried textbooks under their arms. I'd look at them slouching in their seats, not even taking notes, and think, "What terrible things have gone on in their lives that they have quit already? They have so little faith in their ability to learn that they're not even trying." Both students hung on until about midsemester. When they disappeared for good, no one took much notice, for they had already disappeared in spirit after that first test.

They are not the only people in whom I have seen the poison of self-doubt do its ugly work. I have seen others with surrender in their eyes and have wanted to shake them by the shoulders and say, "You are not dead. Be proud and pleased that you have brought yourself here to college. Many people would not have gotten so far. Be someone. Breathe. Hope. Act." Such people should refuse to use self-doubts as an excuse for not trying. They should roll up their sleeves and get to work. They should start taking notes in class and trying to learn. They should get a tutor, go to the learning center, see a counselor. If they honestly and fully try and still can't handle a course, only then should they drop it. Above all, they should not lapse into being "zombie students"—ones who have given up in their heads but persist in hanging on for months, going through hollow motions of trying.

Nothing but a little time is lost through being positive and giving school your best shot. On the other hand, people who let self-doubts limit their efforts may lose the opportunity to test their abilities to the fullest.

"Grow."

I don't think that people really have much choice about whether to grow in their lives. To not be open to growth is to die a little each day. Grow or die—it's as simple as that.

I have a friend, Jackie, who, when she's not working, can almost always be 21
found at home or at her mother's. Jackie eats too much and watches TV too much. I
sometimes think that when she swings open her apartment door in response to my
knock, I'll be greeted by her familiar chubby body with an eight-inch-screen
television set occupying the place where her head used to be.

Jackie seems quietly desperate. There is no growth or plan for growth in her 22
life. I've said to her, "Go to school and study for a job you'll be excited about." She
says, "It'll take me forever." Once Jackie said to me, "The favorite time of my life
was when I was a teenager. I would lie on my bed listening to music and I would
dream. I felt I had enormous power, and there seemed no way that life would stop
me from realizing my biggest dreams. Now that power doesn't seem possible to me
anymore."

I feel that Jackie must open some new windows in her life. If she does not, her 23
spirit is going to die. There are many ways to open new windows, and college is one
of them. For this reason, I think people who are already in school should stay long
enough to give it a chance. No one should turn down lightly such an opportunity for
growth.

"Enjoy."

I hope I'm not making the college experience sound too grim°. It's true that 24
there are some hard, cold realities in life, and I think people need to plan for those
realities. But I want to describe also a very important fact—that college is often a
wonderful experience. There were some tough times when it would have been easy
to just give up and quit, like the week when my son's babysitter broke her arm and
my car's radiator blew up. If school had not been something I really enjoyed, I
would not have made it.

To begin with, I realized soon after starting college that almost no one there 25
knew me. That might seem like a depressing thought, but that's not how it felt. I
knew that people at college had not made up their minds about what kind of person
Jean Coleman was. I imagined myself as shy, clumsy, and average. But in this new
environment, I was free to present myself in any way I chose. I decided from my first
week in school that my college classmates and instructors were going to see the new,
improved Jean. I projected° a confidence I didn't always feel. I sat near the front in
every class. I participated, even took the lead, in discussions. Instead of slipping away
after class, I made a point to chat with my teachers and invite other students to have
coffee with me. Soon I realized that my "act" had worked. People regarded me as a
confident, outgoing woman. I liked a lot this new image of myself as a successful
college student.

Another of the pleasures of college was the excitement of walking into a class 26
for the first time. At that point, the course was still just a name in a catalog. The
possibilities for it seemed endless. Maybe the course would be a magic one
sweeping me off my feet. Maybe the instructor would be really gifted in opening
students' minds to new thoughts. Maybe through this course I would discover
potential in myself I never knew existed. I went into a new class ready to do
everything I could—through my listening, participation, and preparation—to make it
a success. And while some courses were more memorable than others, I rarely found
one that didn't have some real rewards to offer me.

I even enjoyed the physical preparation for a new class. I loved going to the 27 bookstore and finding the textbooks I'd need. I liked to sit down with them, crack open their binding and smell their new-book scent. It was fun to leaf through a textbook and see what seemed like difficult, unfamiliar material, realizing that in a few weeks I'd have a better grasp of what I was seeing there. I made a habit of buying a new spiral-bound notebook for each of my classes, even if I had others that are only partially used. Writing the new course's name on the notebook cover and seeing those fresh, blank sheets waiting inside helped me feel organized and ready to tackle a new challenge. I was surprised how many other students I saw scribbling their class notes on anything handy. I always wondered how they organized them to review later.

Surely one of the best parts of returning to school was the people I've met. 28 Some of them became friends I hope I'll keep forever; others were passing acquaintances, but all of them have made my life richer. One of the best friends I made is a woman named Charlotte. She was my age, and she, like me, came back to school after her marriage broke up. I first met Charlotte in a basic accounting class, and she was scared to death. She was convinced that she could never keep up with the younger students and was sure she had made a big mistake returning to college. Since I often felt that way myself, Charlotte and I decided to become study partners. I'll never forget one day about three weeks into the term when I found her standing in the hallway after class, staring as if into space. "Charlotte?" I said, and she turned to me and broke into a silly grin. "Jean, I get it!" she exclaimed, giving me a quick hug. "I just realized I was sitting there in class keeping up as well as anyone else. I can do this!" Seeing Charlotte's growing confidence helped me believe in my own ability to succeed.

I found that I was looked to as an "older, wiser woman" by many of my 29 classmates. And while I didn't pretend to have all of the answers, I enjoyed listening to their concerns and helping them think about solutions. My advice to them probably wasn't much different from what other adults might have said—take college seriously, don't throw away the opportunities you have, don't assume that finding "the right person" is going to solve all the problems of life, start planning for a career now. But somehow they seemed to find listening to such advice easier when it came from me, a fellow student.

Getting to know my instructors was a pleasure, as well. I remember how I used 30 to think about my high school teachers—that they existed only between nine and three o'clock and that their lives involved nothing but teaching us chemistry or social studies. But I got to know many of my college instructors as real people and even as friends. I came to think of my instructors as my partners, working together with me to achieve my goals. They weren't perfect or all-knowing—they were just people, with their own sets of problems and shortcomings. But almost all were people who really cared about helping me get where I wanted to go.

In Conclusion

Maybe I can put all I've said into a larger picture by describing briefly what my 31 life is like now. I have many inner resources that I did not have when I was just divorced. I have a secure future with the accounting firm where I work. My son is doing OK in school. I have friends. I am successful and proud and happy. I have my fears and my loneliness and my problems and my pains, but essentially I know that I have made it. I have survived and done more than survive. I am tough, not fragile, and I can rebound if hard blows land. I feel passionately that all of us can control our own destinies°. I urge every beginning student to use well the chances that college provides. Students should plan for a realistic career, get themselves organized, learn to persist, be positive, and open themselves to growth. In such ways, they can help themselves find happiness and success in this dangerous but wonderful world of ours.

Reading Comprehension Questions

1. The word *peered* in "He opened up an imaginary door, stepped through, and peered around in both directions outside. There was nobody to be seen" (paragraph 4) means
   a. twirled.
   b. looked.
   c. joked.
   d. hid.

2. The word *overwhelmed* in "Overwhelmed by his continuing car troubles, Nelson dropped out of school" (paragraph 14) means
   a. questioned.
   b. strengthened.
   c. defeated.
   d. unconcerned.

3. Which sentence best expresses the central idea of the selection?
   a. All people experience great problems in the course of their lives.
   b. Following certain guidelines will help you succeed in school and in life.
   c. Divorce can be the beginning of a new and better life.
   d. Certain survival skills can help you become a successful accountant.

4. Which sentence best expresses the main idea of paragraphs 3–8?
   a. Students should make sure that college prepares them for a career they will enjoy and for which jobs are available.
   b. The author discovered in the Occupational Outlook Handbook which kinds of jobs are available now and which will be available in the future.
   c. A bachelor's degree in French is not likely to land a college graduate a good job.
   d. The author is now working as an accountant and also toward becoming a certified public accountant.

5. Which sentence best expresses the main idea of paragraph 30?
   a. The author realized that her college instructors had private lives of their own.
   b. The author enjoyed getting to know and working with her college instructors.
   c. In high school, the author thought her teachers had no private lives.
   d. The author realized that most of her college instructors weren't perfect.

6. The author feels that people who drop out of school
    a. usually have a good reason.
    b. never have a good reason.
    c. often give up too quickly.
    d. always have bigger problems than those who stay in school.

7. The author suggests in paragraph 18 that successful students
    a. do not have self-doubts.
    b. are sometimes "zombie students."
    c. keep trying despite self-doubts.
    d. concentrate on listening instead of taking notes.

8. The author implies that successful people
    a. don't need to struggle in school.
    b. manage to avoid problems.
    c. welcome opportunities to grow.
    d. are unusually lucky.

9. From paragraph 25, we can conclude that in college the author
    a. became depressed.
    b. met many of her fellow students from high school.
    c. had no self-doubts.
    d. changed herself significantly.

10. The author suggests that
    a. older college students are very lonely.
    b. older college students have to work harder at their studies than other students.
    c. younger students welcome the company of older students.
    d. after a certain age, people should not return to college.

Technique Questions

1. Coleman uses many transition words to move her reader from one idea to the next. List five transition words that appear in the essay.

   _____   _____   _____

   _____   _____

2. Instead of presenting her advice in a dry, general way, Coleman provides many specific examples of people she knows to support and dramatize her points. What detail in particular about Coleman's friend Neil (paragraphs 11–13) helps him come vividly alive for you?

   _____

   _____

   _____

3. Coleman also supports her points by providing specific details about her own experience. What details about herself did you find most memorable?

_____

_____

_____

Discussion Questions

1. Coleman suggests that students should find out what jobs will be available in the future and then get a degree in a related field. What type of career do you think you'd be interested in, and why? What degree will help you enter that field?

2. Coleman ends her introduction (paragraphs 1 and 2) by stating, "Here, then, are my secrets for survival in college and really, for survival in life as well." Which of her points—"Be Realistic," "Persist," "Be Positive," "Grow," and "Enjoy"— do you feel are most important for you to remember?

3. What does Coleman mean in paragraph 17 when she states, "A lot of people are their own worst enemies"? Have you found that self-doubts sometime keep you or people you know from trying harder? How can self-doubts be dealt with?

Writing Assignments

1. What career plans have you made so far? Write a paragraph about how you expect college to prepare you for a specific job. If you haven't decided quite yet, write about the possibilities. In your paragraph, tell readers about your interests and their relationship to the career or careers you have in mind. Also discuss your evaluation of job opportunities in your career. Your topic sentence will be a general statement about your career goals, such as any of these:

   • I am aiming for a nursing career, which I believe is a realistic goal.

   • Because of my artistic talent and the opportunities for designers, I've decided to major in graphic arts.

   • I am aiming for a double degree, in business and in cooking, because I hope one day to have my own restaurant—a business that is always needed.

2. "A lot of people are their own worst enemies," writes Coleman. We all know people who hurt themselves. Write a paragraph describing someone you know who is his or her own worst enemy. In your paper, introduce the person and explain his or her hurtful behaviors. You may wish to conclude your paragraph with suggestions for that person. A useful way to gather ideas for this paper is to combine two prewriting techniques—outlining and listing. Begin with an outline of the general areas you expect to cover. Here's an outline that may work:

— Introduce the person

— Describe the hurtful behavior(s)

— Suggest changes

Once you have a workable outline, then use list making to produce specific details for each outline point. For example, here are one person's lists for the the first two points above:

Person

— Vanessa

— Just graduated high school

— Works at a department store

— Wants to go to college, but needs money

Hurtful behaviors

— Just moved into own apartment, which takes much of monthly income—could have stayed at home

— Spends a lot of money on clothing

— Makes no effort to find financial aid for school

Changes

— Stop spending so much and start saving

— Get information from school financial aid offices

3. Coleman writes, "There are times for each of us when simple survival becomes a deadly serious matter. We must then learn to persist—to struggle through each day." What has been your worst struggle? Write a paper describing the problem, what you had to do to deal with it, and how things worked out. You may also wish to comment on how you'd handle the problem today if you had to do it again.

As you work on the drafts for this paper, consider including the following to add interest and clarity:

• Exact quotations of what people said

(Note Coleman's use of quotations in paragraphs 22 and 28. See pages 223–228 for information on how to use quotation marks.)

• Descriptions of revealing behavior, actions, and physical characteristics

(See Coleman's description of behavior in paragraph 21 and of actions in paragraphs 27 and 28.)

• Time transitions to clarify relationships between events

(Note Coleman's use of time transitions in, for example, paragraph 6. See page 9 for a list of time transitions.)

Limited Answer Key

An Important Note: To strengthen your grammar, punctuation, and usage skills, you must do more than simply find out which of your answers are right and which are wrong. You also need to figure out (with the help of this book, the teacher, or other students) why you missed the items you did. By using each of your wrong answers as a learning opportunity, you will strengthen your understanding of the skills. You will also prepare yourself for the chapter tests, for which answers are not given here.

ANSWERS TO THE PRACTICES IN PART TWO

Basic Punctuation and Paper Form

Practice 1, page 57

1. My car has trouble starting on cold mornings.
2. How many courses are you taking this semester?
3. That helicopter is going to crash!
4. Please fill out an application and then take a seat.
5. Look out—he's got a gun!
6. Iced tea was first served at the 1904 World's Fair.
7. Can I use your computer?
8. I asked my brother if I could use his computer.

Practice 2, page 59

1. The title should be centered.
2. The word *meetings* in the title should be capitalized.
3. A line should be skipped after the title.
4. The paragraph's first line should be indented.
5. There should be a margin on the right side.

Parts of Speech

Practice 1, page 66

Answers will vary. Here are some possibilities:

1. jacket
2. Randall
3. paper
4. rock
5. job

Practice 2, page 67

1. bats, head, children
2. artist, paint, sleeve
3. dog, fleas, leg
4. Gwen, homework, ink
5. farmers, seeds, moonlight

Practice 3, page 68

1. He, it
2. They, her
3. They, their
4. He [*or* She], them
5. she, it

Practice 4, page 69

Answers will vary. Here are some possibilities:

1. cut
2. sleep
3. asked
4. mows
5. lost

Practice 5, page 69

1. am
2. were
3. look
4. is
5. feel

Practice 6, page 70

1. should
2. could
3. must
4. has been
5. does

Practice 7, page 71

1. with
2. in
3. Without
4. of
5. by

Practice 8, page 72

Answers will vary. Here are some possibilities:

1. large, hungry
2. old, worn
3. dark, lonely
4. wilted, overripe
5. slight, sore

Practice 9, page 73

Answers will vary. Here are some possibilities:

1. quickly
2. carefully, slowly
3. softly
4. happily
5. rarely, very

Practice 10, page 74

1. or
2. but
3. so
4. and
5. nor

Practice 11, page 75

1. because
2. When
3. Even though
4. Before
5. until

Subjects and Verbs

Practice 1, pages 82–83

Answers will vary. Here are some possibilities:

1. burglar
2. oranges
3. lizard
4. chain
5. sister
6. puppies
7. Julie
8. English
9. cat
10. She

Practice 2, page 84

1. <u>blueberries</u> ~~in this pie~~
2. <u>crowd</u> . . . ~~around the injured boy~~
3. <u>woman</u> ~~with a pierced nose~~
4. <u>Leaves</u> ~~from our neighbor's tree~~
5. ~~During the school play,~~ <u>Betsy</u>
6. <u>flyer</u> . . . ~~in our mailbox door~~
7. <u>dust</u> ~~under your bed~~
8. <u>Some</u> ~~of our roof shingles~~
9. <u>shows</u> . . . ~~on late-night TV~~
10. <u>One</u> ~~of my best friends~~

Practice 3, pages 85–86

Answers will vary. Here are some possibilities:

1. hovered
2. swim
3. hit
4. grazed
5. complained
6. bounced
7. draws
8. listened
9. laughs
10. ran

Practice 4, page 87

1. was
2. smells
3. are
4. feels
5. taste
6. am
7. look
8. seems
9. is
10. were

Practice 5, pages 88–89

1. *Helping verb:* was   *Main verb:* complaining
2. *Helping verb:* will   *Main verb:* decorate
3. *Helping verb:* should   *Main verb:* take
4. *Helping verb:* should have   *Main verb:* washed
5. *Helping verb:* has   *Main verb:* planted
6. *Helping verb:* should be   *Main verb:* eaten
7. *Helping verb:* will   *Main verb:* accept
8. *Helping verb:* could have been   *Main verb:* killed
9. *Helping verb:* must have   *Main verb:* forgotten
10. *Helping verb:* might have   *Main verb:* injured

Practice 6, pages 89–90

1. is not wearing
2. hurried
3. is waiting
4. should ride
5. will love
6. has promised
7. should be boiled
8. is sipping
9. should have been washed
10. have been trying

Verb Tenses

Practice 1, page 98

1. drills
2. practices
3. ring
4. makes
5. dig
6. trim
7. cleans
8. tells
9. discovers
10. remember

Practice 2, page 99

1. seemed
2. sailed
3. wondered
4. knocked
5. named
6. jumped
7. talked
8. checked
9. wiped
10. played

Practice 3, page 100

1. will play
2. will plant
3. will iron
4. will attend
5. will circle

Practice 4, pages 100–101

2. has lived
3. have checked
4. has boiled
5. have mixed

Practice 5, page 101

2. had struggled
3. had asked
4. had intended
5. had invited

Practice 6, page 102

2. will have attended
3. will have finished
4. will have hired
5. will have designed

Practice 7, pages 102–103

2. is beeping
3. are blooming
4. am practicing
5. are pacing

Practice 8, page 103

2. was beeping
3. were blooming
4. was practicing
5. were pacing

Practice 9, page 104

2. will be beeping
3. will be blooming
4. will be practicing
5. will be pacing

Practice 10, page 104

1. is
2. were
3. was
4. are
5. were

Practice 11, pages 105–106

1. ~~crashes~~ crashed
2. ~~heated~~ heat
3. ~~picks~~ picked
4. ~~cross~~ crossed
5. ~~appeared~~ appear
6. ~~promise~~ promised
7. ~~delivered~~ delivers
8. ~~surges~~ surged
9. ~~work~~ are working
10. ~~disappears~~ disappeared

Irregular Verbs

Practice 1, pages 114–115

2. a. drove; b. driven
3. a. drew; b. drawn
4. a. spoke; b. spoken
5. a. took; b. taken
6. a. became; b. become
7. a. rode; b. ridden
8. a. brought; b. brought
9. a. made; b. made
10. a. knew; b. known

Practice 2, pages 115–116

1. written
2. sold
3. worn
4. eaten
5. lost
6. fallen
7. broke
8. spent
9. begun
10. hid
11. gone
12. stole
13. risen
14. taught
15. slept
16. chosen
17. shook
18. threw
19. become
20. drunk

Practice 3, pages 117–118

1. has
2. are
3. does
4. was
5. do
6. are
7. have
8. were
9. did
10. was
11. is
12. have
13. was
14. has
15. am
16. has
17. do
18. did
19. was
20. were

Subject-Verb Agreement

Practice 1, pages 124–125

1. sorts
2. sort
3. listens
4. listen
5. wriggles
6. wriggle
7. whistles
8. whistle
9. argues
10. argue

Practice 2, page 125

1. The dogs growl softly.
2. Your sneakers need tying.

3. The pigs chew on corn cobs.
4. My nieces blow soap bubbles.
5. The porkchops sizzle on the grill.
6. Their sons play football.
7. Guards block the door.
8. The shadows get longer and longer.
9. Our neighbors complain about everything.
10. The instructors read the school newspaper.

Practice 3, page 126

1. flakes ~~in this cereal~~ taste
2. woman ~~with the dark sunglasses~~ is
3. people ~~in Europe~~ speak
4. boy ~~by the swings~~ is
5. person ~~in my classes~~ sleeps

Practice 4, page 127

1. are . . . messages
2. is . . . box
3. stands . . . fence
4. grow . . . herbs
5. were . . . clouds

Practice 5, page 128

1. Everybody . . . is
2. Neither . . . feels
3. Nobody . . . knows
4. Each . . . needs
5. Something . . . sounds

Sentence Types

Practice 1, pages 134–135

Answers will vary. Here are some possibilities:

1. Purple
2. hit
3. waiter
4. threw
5. Papers . . . leaves
6. Liver . . . cabbage
7. fell . . . rolled
8. eat . . . watch
9. Alice . . . shop
10. Nick . . . Fran . . . ate

Practice 2, pages 136–137

Answers will vary. Here are some possibilities:

1. we decided to go out for coffee.
2. her coat was muddy.
3. it tasted like dishwater.
4. she did all her grocery shopping.
5. he had to take them to the cleaners.
6. did I pass the course.
7. nobody answered it.
8. the host ran out of food in an hour.
9. she didn't arrive until 11:15.
10. you could take a summer school course.

Practice 3, page 137

Answers may vary.

1. The city workers are on strike, so the streets are lined with garbage bags.
2. The television was on, but no one was watching it.
3. The room is painted yellow, and it has big, sunny windows.
4. A storm was approaching quickly, so the campers found shelter in a cave.

5. Dean likes whole-wheat toast for breakfast, but Chris prefers sugar-coated cereal.

Practice 4, page 139

Answers will vary. Here are some possibilities:

1. <u>when</u> her boyfriend asked her to marry him.
2. <u>Although</u> I was offered a free ticket to the game
3. <u>after</u> she worked out at the gym.
4. <u>Because</u> I wanted to do some last-minute studying
5. <u>even though</u> I worked only three days.
6. <u>Until</u> he was fourteen
7. <u>If</u> you go to the convenience store
8. <u>Since</u> I want to buy a car
9. <u>before</u> he began writing his draft.
10. <u>Because</u> the tickets cost twenty-five dollars

Practice 5, pages 140–141

Answers may vary.

1. The travelers slept in their station wagon because all the motels in the area were full.
2. While the campers slept, raccoons tore apart their backpacks.
3. The band finally began to play after we had sat through an hour of recorded music.
4. When there is a playoff game in the city, traffic is jammed for miles.
5. Since his wife died, Mr. Albertson has been lonely.
6. While a fan just moves the air, an air conditioner cools it.
7. Although my father and mother are separated, they do not plan to divorce.
8. After the test was over, we decided to get something to eat.
9. When Julie asked Leonard out on a date, her legs were trembling.
10. Because we're trying not to waste paper, we usually use cloth napkins.

Sentence Fragments

Practice 1, page 149

Answers will vary. Here are some possibilities:

1. I heard laughter coming from inside the house.
2. she had to call a locksmith.
3. Everyone sang along
4. you'll have to see a doctor.
5. I turn the thermostat down
6. I got an extension until next week.
7. start saving for it now.
8. Fred went back to sleep
9. the driver left the package with a neighbor.
10. I tripped and dropped my books.

Practice 2, page 150

1. <u>After he bought a cup of coffee,</u> Eric hurried to the office.
2. The batter argued with the umpire <u>while the crowd booed.</u>
3. All the food will spoil <u>unless the refrigerator is fixed soon.</u>
4. <u>Because the movie was so poor,</u> many people left the theater.
5. Everything was peaceful <u>before Martha stormed into the room.</u>
6. <u>When two guests began to argue,</u> the hostess moved the party outside.
7. <u>Although the car accident was a bad one,</u> the passengers were unharmed.
8. <u>Since we forgot to buy a battery,</u> our son can't play with his new toy today.
9. Our leaves blew into the neighbor's yard <u>before I found time to rake them.</u>
10. The police believed the witness <u>until he picked the wrong person out of a lineup.</u>

Practice 3, page 151

1. I bought an expensive coat <u>which was made of soft leather.</u>
2. The police visited the high school <u>that has a big drug problem.</u>
3. The dog growled at the toddler <u>who was screaming loudly.</u>
4. The pilot refused to fly the jet <u>that had ice on its wings.</u>
5. My neighbor is a quiet man <u>whose working day begins at midnight.</u>

Practice 4, pages 152–153

Answers may vary. Here are some possibilities:

1. The owner has opened a take-out window. She wants <u>to attract more customers to the diner.</u>
2. <u>Rising high into the sky,</u> the blue hot-air balloon could be seen for miles.
3. <u>To get off the horse,</u> the circus rider did a forward flip.
4. <u>Eating the spinach,</u> I felt bits of sand in my mouth.
5. The dog sat quietly near the baby's high chair. He was <u>waiting for crumbs to fall.</u>
6. The hikers broke branches. They wanted <u>to mark the trail for their return trip.</u>
7. The family saves plastic bags and bottles. They like <u>to take</u> them <u>to the recycling center.</u>
8. The man jumped into the firefighters' net, <u>praying loudly all the while.</u>
9. <u>Glancing out the window,</u> Rudy spotted someone taking tomatoes from his garden.
10. <u>To enter the contest,</u> my sister wrote a jingle for her favorite potato chips.

Practice 5, pages 154–155

Answers may vary. Here are some possibilities:

1. Everybody enjoyed Thanksgiving dinner <u>except the turkey</u>.
2. Citrus fruits are full of nutrients, <u>especially vitamin C</u>.
3. We had to read several novels for class, <u>including *Lord of the Flies*</u>.
4. Gary is a rude person at times. <u>For instance,</u> he interrupts <u>an instructor during a lecture</u>.
5. With braces I cannot eat certain foods, <u>such as popcorn and apples</u>.
6. Andy had to work all summer in a stuffy warehouse <u>without air conditioning</u>.
7. Don't touch anything in the science lab, <u>especially the bubbling tubes on the table</u>.
8. The dentist said the procedure wouldn't hurt, <u>except for the shot to numb my gums and teeth</u>.
9. There are healthier ways to prepare chicken than frying. <u>For example,</u> there is <u>broiling</u>.
10. The detective searched the room for clues, <u>such as old letters, receipts, and ticket stubs</u>.

Practice 6, pages 156–157

Answers may vary. Here are some possibilities:

1. The landlord unclogged the drain <u>and found a dishcloth stuck in the pipe</u>.
2. The dealer shuffled the cards <u>and asked the man to choose one</u>.
3. The cries for help grew more and more faint. <u>Then</u> they <u>stopped completely</u>.
4. The wallet has room for paper money and credit cards <u>but has no pocket for coins</u>.
5. The dog lifted its head to bark at the mailman <u>and then went back to sleep</u>.
6. The movie had a catchy soundtrack and popular actors. <u>Yet</u> it <u>made little money at the box office</u>.
7. Each morning, the secretary checks the answering machine for messages. <u>Then</u> he <u>opens the mail</u>.
8. The wide receiver made a terrific run down the field <u>but then fumbled the football</u>.
9. Roz skipped her afternoon classes. <u>And</u> she <u>worked on a paper due the next morning</u>.
10. Someone stole a rare bird from the zoo <u>but soon returned it with a note of apology</u>.

Run-Ons and Comma Splices

Practice 1, page 164

1. RO knit / his
2. CS rang / the
3. CS basement / it
4. RO gym / the
5. RO doctor / he
6. RO lucky / she
7. CS vacation / we
8. RO children / they
9. CS married / she
10. RO toe / she

Practice 2, pages 165–166

1. Hamsters are small. They are also very cute.
2. Grape juice spilled on the carpet. It made permanent stains.
3. Kareem's brownies are great. He adds nuts and chocolate chips.
4. My sister is raising triplets. All three of them have red hair.
5. "Weeds" can be attractive. Some are even good to eat.
6. The police officer was puzzled by the crime. He found no fingerprints.
7. There was an accident on the bridge this morning. Traffic was stopped for an hour.
8. Coupons help shoppers save money. They also help stores to sell products.
9. The television show was canceled after six episodes. It was not very funny.
10. Chipmunks have dug many holes in our yard. Now it looks like a miniature golf course.

Practice 3, page 167

1. , but
2. , and
3. , so
4. , and
5. , but
6. , so
7. , but
8. , and
9. , but
10. , so

Practice 4, page 168

1. The garden is overgrown, and the fence is falling down.
2. I called Robin three times last night, but she never answered.
3. The motorcycle wouldn't start, so the man called a taxi.
4. The alarm clock fell on the floor, and then it started to ring.
5. I was out of jelly and butter, so I spread yogurt on my toast.
6. The flowers in that yard look wonderful, but the grass needs cutting.
7. Gina is allergic to animals, so she can't have a pet.
8. A window was broken, and the jewels had been taken.
9. Mr. Dobbs is friendly with his customers, but he is rude to his workers.
10. My back itched in a hard-to-reach place, so I scratched it on the doorpost.

Practice 5, pages 170–171

Answers may vary.

1. Because I care for my elderly parents, I have very little free time.
2. After the water began to boil, I added the ears of corn.
3. Our neighbor is watering his lawn although the forecast is for heavy rain.

4. We will have to leave in exactly ten minutes if we want to see the kickoff.
5. While the children swam in the bay, their parents sunned on the beach.
6. After I finished my written report, I spent the rest of the night studying.
7. Although the movie was filmed in black and white, it is being shown on TV tonight in color.
8. Since Lauren is going to Spain next summer, she is studying Spanish this year.
9. I take the train to my downtown job since finding a space to park can be very difficult.
10. James ordered two scoops of vanilla ice cream although there were thirty-two flavors available.

Practice 6, page 171

1. My Human Behavior final exam is next week. I am very worried about passing it.
2. For the past month I've been working full-time, so it's hard to find time to study.
3. Although I will ask the teacher for extra help, it may be too late.

Pronouns

Practice 1, page 181

1. photographer
2. cat
3. Kate and Barry
4. coffee . . . Martin
5. Nora . . . Nora and her brother

Practice 2, pages 181–182

1. it . . . movie
2. her . . . Marlene
3. his . . . horse
4. he . . . man
5. they . . . Carla and Vicki

Practice 3, pages 182–183

1. its . . . everything
2. his . . . neither
3. it . . . anything
4. her . . . each
5. he or she is . . . nobody

Practice 4, page 184

1. they
2. you
3. me
4. we
5. I
6. I
7. we
8. I
9. they
10. they

Capital Letters

Practice 1, page 191

1. My
2. The, No
3. Anna, Puerto, Rico
4. If, I'm, Detective, Harrison
5. Mrs., Domino's, Pizza
6. Rockefeller, Center, Manhattan
7. Asian, Chinese, Fifth, Avenue

8. Mexican, Baptist, Italian, Catholic
9. Dr., Findley
10. American, Medical, Association, Hawaii

Practice 2, page 193

1. August
2. Fritos
3. Introduction, Biology
4. *Beauty, Beast*
5. Log, Cabin, Eggo
6. An, Embarrassing, Moment
7. New, Year's, Day, Dad
8. *Love, First, Bite*
9. *Newsweek*, Sunday, *Watchers*
10. Grandpa, Snickers, *Wheel, Fortune*

Commas

Practice 1, page 200

1. architect, inventor,
2. waiter, . . . walker,
3. sign, . . . road,
4. traps, . . . mail,
5. lions, . . . horses,

Practice 2, page 201

Answers will vary. Here are some possibilities:
1. marbles, chewing gum, and rubber bands.
2. grandmother, my older sister, and my boss.
3. Working out, watching sports on TV, and reading

Practice 3, page 201

1. day,
2. horserace,
3. flowers,
4. book,
5. room,

Practice 4, pages 201–202

Answers will vary. Here are some possibilities:
1. studying, he went for a walk.
2. bed, I could see three pairs of shoes.
3. sounded, everyone hurried for the exits.

Practice 5, page 202

1. wings, . . . thick,
2. Arthur, . . . legend,
3. boss, . . . rumored,
4. Ross, . . . belief,
5. hometown, . . . stations,

Practice 6, page 203

Answers will vary. Here are some possibilities:
1. Lisa, who is my best friend, just had major surgery.
2. Frozen yogurt, which is my favorite snack, is low in calories.
3. Dolores, wearing an all-white outfit, posed at the top of the stairs.

Practice 7, page 204

1. buzzing,
2. ready,
3. forecast,
4. badly,
5. Florida,

Practice 8, page 204

Answers will vary.

Practice 9, page 205

1. eight,"
2. shirt," . . . husband,
3. care,"
4. said,
5. pay," . . . man,

Practice 10, page 205

Answers will vary.

Apostrophes

Practice 1, page 212

1. we're
2. you'll
3. couldn't
4. what's
5. I'd
6. they'll
7. didn't
8. you're
9. can't
10. who's

Practice 2, page 213

1. wasn't . . . didn't
2. isn't . . . don't
3. He'd . . . it's
4. wouldn't . . . shouldn't
5. I'd . . . haven't

Practice 3, page 213

Answers will vary.

Practice 4, page 214

2. cat — cat's purr
3. father — father's hobby
4. neighbor — neighbor's temper
5. Cindy — Cindy's sunglasses
6. story — story's ending
7. bee — bee's stinger
8. day — day's news
9. museum — museum's mummy
10. Michael Jackson — Michael Jackson's best song

Practice 5, page 215

2. my mother's white rug
3. The athlete's knee
4. Vietnam's climate
5. Gail's house
6. A gorilla's diet
7. Diane's nickname
8. Noah's ark
9. The photographer's camera
10. The bride's wedding dress

Practice 6, pages 216–217

1. prince's, meaning "belonging to the prince"
   dragons: plural, meaning "more than one dragon"
2. country's, meaning "belonging to that country"
   stripes: plural, meaning "more than one stripe"
3. hunters: plural, meaning "more than one hunter"
   seal's: meaning "belonging to a seal"
4. doodles: plural, meaning "more than one doodle"
   Jack's: meaning "belonging to Jack"
5. grasshopper's, meaning "belonging to the grasshopper"
   legs: plural, meaning "more than one leg"
   times: plural, meaning "more than one time"
6. chocolates: plural, meaning "more than one chocolate"
   mother's: meaning "belonging to my mother"
7. minutes: plural, meaning "more than one minute"
   sun's: meaning "belonging to the sun"
8. train's, meaning "belonging to the train"
   cars: plural, meaning "more than one car"
   tons: plural, meaning "more than one ton"
9. curtains: plural, meaning "more than one curtain"
   lilacs: plural, meaning "more than one lilac"
   room's, meaning "belonging to the room"
10. hypnotist's, meaning "belonging to the hypnotist"
    tools: plural, meaning "more than one tool"
    ticks: plural, meaning "more than one tick"

Practice 7, page 217

Answers will vary.

Quotation Marks

Practice 1, pages 224–225

1. "That . . . violence,"
2. "Please . . . call."
3. "Do . . . break,"
4. "Row . . . stream."
5. "I'm . . . walls."

Practice 2, page 225

Answers will vary.

Practice 3, page 226

1. "It . . . nice," . . . "to . . . salt."
2. "I . . . sweater," . . . "but . . . bed."
3. "I'm . . . writing."
4. "Our . . . unfair," . . . "He . . . do?"
5. "Why . . . store," . . . "and . . . tonight."

Practice 4, page 227

2. My sister said, "I'll help you with your math homework if I can wear your new blouse."
3. The bookstore manager grumbled, "I can't accept books that have writing in them."
4. Our gym teacher announced, "You will have to run one lap for each minute you are late to class."
5. The artist joked, "I began painting landscapes when the local art supply store had a sale on green paint."

Homonyms

Practice 1, page 235

1. It's . . . its
2. You're . . . your
3. There . . . their . . . They're
4. to . . . two . . . too

Practice 2, page 235

Answers will vary.

Other Commonly Confused Words, pages 236–241

brake / break
1. break 4. brake
2. break 5. break
3. brake

right / write
1. write 4. write
2. right 5. right
3. right

hear / here
1. Here 4. hear
2. hear 5. here
3. here

than / then
1. then 4. then
2. than 5. than
3. then

hole / whole
1. whole 4. whole
2. hole 5. hole
3. whole

threw / through
1. threw 4. threw
2. through 5. through
3. through

knew / new
1. new 4. knew
2. knew 5. new
3. new

wear / where
1. Where 4. wear
2. wear 5. where
3. where

know / no
1. know 4. No
2. no 5. know
3. know

weather / whether
1. whether 4. weather
2. weather 5. whether
3. whether

passed / past
1. passed 4. passed
2. past 5. past
3. passed

whose / who's
1. Who's 4. who's
2. Who's 5. whose
3. Whose

peace / piece
1. piece 4. piece
2. peace 5. peace
3. piece

Proofreading

Practice 1, pages 249–250

Answers may vary.

1. That bookcase is too heavy on top, and it could fall over.
2. He announced that he had solved the mystery and would soon reveal the name of the murderer.
3. It belonged to my great-grandfather. He brought it to the United States from Norway.
4. Before you leave the house, please close all the windows in case it rains.
5. It is on a lake in the mountains. We can swim, fish, and sunbathe there.

6. Whales are always sighted there at a certain time of the year.
7. Hsia is from Taiwan. She uses the English name Shirley.
8. Rosalie went to the beauty parlor on Friday intending to get her long hair trimmed just a little.
9. Every smudge of dirt or spill of food shows on the white surface and is nearly impossible to get rid of.
10. Although that waiter is quick and hard-working, he is not friendly with customers.

Practice 2, page 251

1. ~~swimmed~~ swam
2. ~~wears~~ wear
3. ~~does~~ did
4. ~~growed~~ grew
5. ~~are~~ is
6. ~~answers~~ answered
7. ~~is~~ are
8. ~~sleeped~~ slept
9. ~~are~~ is
10. ~~claimed~~ claims

Practice 3, page 252

1. sauce,
2. Bob's
3. yelled,
4. Chicago
5. "Please . . . Tom,"
6. summer
7. doesn't
8. character,
9. watermelons
10. question," . . . "I

Practice 4, page 253

1. telephones
2. looks
3. jokes
4. barns
5. makes
6. speaks
7. closes
8. grows
9. cans
10. freckles

Practice 5, page 254

1. pieces **of** this
2. forgot **to** buy
3. Some **of** the
4. great **with** the
5. won **a** prize
6. piano **and** the
7. up **the** steep
8. surprised **by** Helen
9. coffee **with** cream
10. hard **to** pay

Practice 6, pages 254–255

1. **too** many flies
2. It's **your** own fault
3. **whose** sweatshirt
4. If **you're** hungry
5. on **its** collar
6. **they're** coming here
7. **two** practical reasons
8. on **their** covers
9. Although **it's** tempting
10. time **passed** slowly

Practice 7, page 255

1. English course**s**
2. Donna**'s** dog. **It**
3. cans, . . . on **the** deserted beach.
4. takes . . . college, **where**
5. tip, police . . . house. **They**

Dictionary Use

Spelling and Syllables, page 262

2. 3
3. 5
4. 4

Pronunciation Symbols, page 263

1. a
2. b
3. b
4. a

2. sŏl′ĭ-tĕr′ē
3. ĭk-străv′ə-gənt
4. yo͞o-năn′ə-məs

Accent Marks, page 264

1. a. 3 b. first
2. a. 5 b. third
3. a. 3 b. second
4. a. 4 b. third

Practice A, pages 265–266

1. first
2. 3
3. 1
4. short
5. difficult to alleviate or cure

Practice B, page 266

1. 4
2. first
3. short
4. single; sole
5. happening or done alone

Spelling Hints

Practice A, page 269

1. varieties
2. relied
3. tripped
4. deceive
5. believe

Practice B, page 270

1. holiness
2. growled
3. abusing
4. brief
5. freight

Nonstandard Verbs

Practice A, page 272

1. decided
2. added
3. makes
4. laughed
5. wishes

Practice B, page 272

1. plays
2. attends
3. watered
4. pulls
5. pounded

Misplaced Modifiers

Methods of correction may vary.

Practice A, page 274

1. I'm returning the shirt that is too small to the store.
2. The customer rudely demanded that the waiter take her order.
3. We watched with helpless anger as our house burned to the ground.
4. By the end of the war, almost twenty countries were involved in the fighting.
5. The bracelet made of gold links on Roberta's arm belongs to her mother.

Practice B, page 274

1. The man bought a tie with yellow and blue stripes at the department store.
2. The plants with small purple blossoms by the lamp are violets.
3. Carrie has nearly sixty freckles on her face.
4. The woman that is waving in that boat is trying to tell us something.
5. The child with fuzzy orange hair playing on the jungle gym is my nephew.

Dangling Modifiers

Methods of correction may vary.

Practice A, page 276

1. While jogging, Anton thought of a good topic for his English paper.
2. Because I was touched by the movie, tears came to my eyes.
3. Bored by the lecture, Jed began to think about dinner.
4. After the carpet was shampooed, Trish was surprised by its new look.
5. As Earth is moving around the sun, its speed is more than 66,000 miles per hour.

Practice B, page 276

1. Since he was born on the Fourth of July, Rob's birthday cake was always red, white, and blue.
2. Because I was out of money, my only choice was to borrow from a friend.
3. While Peg was waiting for an important call, her phone began making weird noises.
4. Loudly booing and cursing, the fans made their disapproval of the call clear.
5. After Stella ate one too many corn dogs, her stomach rebelled.

Parallelism

Practice A, page 278

1. feeding the dog
2. complain a lot
3. stale peanut-butter crackers
4. a second-grade teacher
5. reading books

Practice B, page 279

1. lifting hand weights
2. scuffed shoes
3. taking notes carefully
4. jeans from a thrift shop
5. pumpkin pie

Pronoun Types

Practice A, page 285

1. I
2. themselves
3. him
4. Whose
5. these

Practice B, page 285

1. who
2. her
3. that
4. its
5. Those

Word Choice

Answers may vary. Here are some possibilities:

Practice A, pages 287–288

1. Today
2. Because
3. understand
4. carefree
5. decided

Practice B, page 288

1. Because
2. in trouble
3. now
4. very light
5. disgusted

Punctuation Marks

Practice A, page 294

1. socks.
2. socks?
3. us!
4. wouldn't
5. seen,

Practice B, page 295

1. (1)
2. twenty-eight
3. nurse;
4. brother—
5. items:
6. "You . . . dollars."

Adjectives and Adverbs

Practice A, page 298

1. ~~more full~~ fuller
2. ~~slow~~ slowly
3. ~~importantest~~ important
4. ~~baddest~~ worst
5. ~~good~~ well

Practice B, page 298

1. ~~quick~~ quickly
2. ~~quiet~~ quietly
3. ~~more~~ most
4. ~~badder~~ worse
5. ~~good~~ well

Numbers and Abbreviations

Practice A, page 301

1. ~~102~~ One hundred and two
2. ~~3~~ three
3. ~~univ.~~ university
4. ~~thirteen~~ 13
5. ~~hosp.~~ hospital

Practice B, page 301

1. ~~5~~ five
2. ~~Amer.~~ America
3. ~~30~~ thirty
4. ~~ref.~~ reference
5. ~~eighty~~ 80

Index